Law and Socie

Volume 3

The Law's Flaws

Rethinking Trials and Errors?

Volume 1
Criminological Theory. Just the Basics
Robert Heiner

Volume 2
Is Legal Reasoning Irrational? An Introduction to the Epistemology of Law
John Woods

Volume 3
The Law's Flaws. Rethinking Trials and Errors?
Larry Laudan

Law and Society Series Editors
Robert L. Heiner   rheiner@plymouth.edu
John Woods   john.woods@ubc.ca

The Law's Flaws
Rethinking Trials and Errors?

Larry Laudan

© Individual author and College Publications 2016
All rights reserved.

ISBN 978-1-84890-199-5

College Publications
Scientific Director: Dov Gabbay
Managing Director: Jane Spurr

http://www.collegepublications.co.uk

Original cover design by Laraine Welch
Printed by Lightning Source, Milton Keynes, UK

TABLE OF CONTENTS

Tables and Figures

Acknowledgements

I have several friends and colleagues to thank for helping me put together this effort at identifying (and trying to remedy) some of the numerous sources of error in the criminal justice system. They include Ronald Allen, Michael Risinger, Alex Stein, Robert Bone, Alec Walen, and Stephen Clark. Without them, the book could scarcely have been put together. I also owe a mighty debt to the statisticians who labor earnestly at the Bureau of Justice Statistics in Washington, D.C. Fully nine-tenths of the data on which I have drawn were assiduously collected and organized by dozens of analysts there.

In readying this book for publication, I have leaned heavily on my faculty assistant, Vicky Killgore, and my library consultant, Stephen Wolfson, in the Law School at the University of Texas at Austin. They have helped enormously in putting the text into a publishable format.

Finally, I want to express my fondness for my dear wife, Rachel, who has both strongly encouraged this project and shown extraordinary patience and interest as I have regaled her over the last five years, upon discovering some of the astounding statistics that fill this book.

Prologue

A TRIGGER WARNING?

Sensitive readers should take note of the fact that, in various respects, this book will challenge many beliefs about the criminal law held dear by much of the press and the general population. Among other myths this book will attempt to dispel, it will argue that we should seriously doubt:

1). The belief that the two-century old standard of proof ('proof beyond a reasonable doubt') must not be changed because it is required by the Constitution and because it alone protects the innocent. Both claims are patently false. The U.S. Constitution fails to specify a standard of proof and, more importantly as this book will show, that standard is not a very good protector of the innocent. Making matters worse is the stubborn refusal of the Supreme Court to either define what is meant by 'proof beyond a reasonable doubt' or to explore whether that standard is serving the ends of justice. This vague standard, combined with the deliberate ignorance within the legal system about the frequency with which it produces erroneous convictions and acquittals, tell us that the legal system desperately lacks the information it needs either to earn the confidence of its citizens or to reduce the frequency of the many egregious mistakes that occur.

2). The near-universal belief that we are incarcerating far too many criminals—a familiar cliché of modern American life. While that may be true where misdemeanors and drug crimes are concerned, it most certainly does *not* apply to violent crimes. On average, we are convicting only about 17% of those who commit violent crimes. Five-of-every six violent felons get away with it scot-free. Ironically, while the felony conviction rate nearly doubled between 1980 and 2006, the violent felon conviction rate has remained largely unchanged.[1] We have a duty to our citizens to find and convict more of those violent trouble-makers.

3). The widely-held conviction that we are locking serious criminals away in prison for unreasonably long stays. As the data cited below in chapter 8 will show, the average time served by someone convicted of aggravated assault is 17 months; for armed robbery, 17 months; for rape, 4 years; and for murder, 13 years.

Do any of these figures strike you as giving those felons more than their 'just deserts'? Add to that the information that probation with *no* jail time whatever is offered to 26% of those convicted of aggravated assault, to 17% of convicted armed robbers, to 10% of convicted rapists and to 4% of convicted murderers and it becomes clear that many violent felons, even if convicted, are getting off lightly.

4). Legislators and appellate courts over the years have made it increasingly difficult to identify guilty defendants by a). putting in place many rules of procedure that exclude highly relevant evidence; b). giving defendants significant control over what evidence can and can't be used against them; c). requiring judges to instruct jurors to avoid giving any weight to certain types of evidence that are arguably highly relevant; and d). remaining wedded to an ancient, thirteenth-century Anglo-Saxon idea (double jeopardy) to the effect that under no circumstances could an acquittal be appealed nor could new inculpatory evidence be adduced as a basis for retrying an acquitted but very probably guilty defendant.[2] Several English-speaking countries (most prominently England but including Canada and Australia as well) have recently seen the error of their ways and allowed re-trial after an acquittal, provided evidence of a defendant's guilt emerges after his first trial. The U.S. is not among them.

My approach to making out the case for these and other claims will involve a combination of conceptual analysis and empirical data. In any event, wary readers have been forewarned that they may encounter some dismaying surprises.

This is chiefly a book about the criminal law, more specifically, about the principles and rules of procedure that drive the legal adjudication of *violent* crime cases. It aims to take an approach to those issues that is simultaneously data-based and conceptually grounded, two features currently lacking in much of the literature about the subject. In the process, we will see that many of the everyday clichés about crime and its handling by the state turn out to be ill-founded, both empirically and philosophically.

To elaborate on a previous example, one constantly hears the refrain that we are incarcerating too many felons convicted of violent crimes (often cited is the US jail and prison count of some 2m behind bars, roughly half of whom were convicted of a crime of violence). As already noted, barely 20% of those who commit such crimes wind up in a cell at all. Then there is the frequently-voiced worry that we are falsely convicting too many innocent defendants. At the most, some 3% of convictions for violent crimes are convictions of the innocent. By contrast, as we shall see, some 40% of those acquitted committed the crime. That disparity, as I will show in detail, is wholly at odds with any viable account of how the state is supposed to protect its citizens.

Another very common trope—especially fashionable among those in the defense bar and the press—is that the rules of procedure for determining guilt or innocence create a 'tilted playing field' that works strikingly in the prosecution's favor. To the contrary, as I will show, the actual skewing of the balance scale via a very heavy thumb is overwhelmingly to the advantage of the defendant, whether he is guilty or innocent.

Lastly, in this brief preview, I shall mention a politically correct piece of conventional wisdom to the effect that we have resorted to overly and unconscionably long sentences, especially for those convicted of violent crimes. (Everyone seems to think that California's famous 'three-strikes-and-you're-out' rule is somehow typical. It is not.) The fact is that the average felon convicted of a violent crime serves far less time behind bars than his sentence would suggest. In the case of murder, the average sentence imposed by the court is 20.3 years; the average *time served* before release is 12.4 years. A convicted rapist will be sentenced to about 8.8 years, usually serving only 4 years. A convicted armed robber, while normally sentenced to some 7.2 years in prison, will on average serve 1.4 years in prison. Finally, a defendant convicted of aggravated assault is apt to get a sentence of 5.2 years but, like the armed robber, will be held in custody for less than a year and a half. Failure to take sentences seriously inflicts a risk of egregious harms on all of us since many of those receiving these sentences and then an early release are serial felons, often with a stunning record of recidivism. Once they have returned prematurely to the streets, a great many revert to a criminal career, inflicting harm that would have been prevented had they been imprisoned for the time specified as their just punishment.

But this is not just a book about pertinent data. It will describe a broad framework in which we can reason objectively and systematically about the age-old dilemmas of 'crime and punishment'. For instance, we now have in place a standard of proof ('proof beyond a reasonable doubt') that the highest courts in the land refuse to define, leaving jurors free to define the idea however they like. We need to be asking how demanding the criminal standard of proof should be and why and then define it more clearly for jurors. We also need to explore the numerous exclusionary rules that impact the outcomes of trials and pleas and to figure out whether their continuance is desirable.

The book itself is the outgrowth of an article I published a few years ago in Vol. 1 of the *Oxford Studies in Law and Philosophy*.[3] In this much-expanded version, the key claims of that analysis are tested by vastly more data than I had access to then and the arguments themselves are (I trust) both more subtle and fine-grained than I had room for in that journal.

I begin by noting the obvious: criminal proceedings can be, should be, and often are incredibly awesome affairs, governed by elaborate rules, characterized by dramatic moments and leading to a conclusion that can have stunning repercussions, both for the accused, the victim, and for the rest of society. At least in theory, a trial is a search for the truth about a purported crime: Did it actually occur? If so, is it highly likely that the defendant perpetrated it? These are obviously *empirical* questions about a past event.

It hardly needs saying that there are many other forms of empirical inquiry besides the law: science (natural and social), engineering, medicine, and opinion polling, to name only the more familiar. Curiously, one of the principal features that mark off legal inquiry from most other forms of empirical research is that the participants in legal proceedings—including the judges, the lawyers and the jurors—are massively ignorant about whether the methods of investigation they use are up to snuff. That is, to put it mildly, rather strange since anyone doing serious empirical research is expected to know how reliable their methods are and how often they lead to error. An obstetrician, reporting a positive pregnancy test result to a patient, is expected to be able to answer the obvious question: "What is the rate of false positives?" An engineer who has designed a new ignition switch for an automobile is expected to be able to tell his employers how often, and under what circumstances, it is apt to fail. A pollster is expected to be able to tell us the margin of error associated with the results he reports.

But if we pose comparable questions to those involved in legal inquiry, such answers are not only rarely forthcoming but the questions about accuracy typically elicit a look of surprised consternation on the faces of judges and lawyers. For instance, most actors in the legal system are unsure how often the truly innocent are convicted. They generally concede that it would be interesting, even useful, to know that; but they would rather leave it to others (such as Innocence Projects) to figure that out. When asked about how often false negatives (that is, acquittals of the guilty) occur, they not only concede that they haven't any idea but they find it strange that one might even pose the question. To the best of my knowledge, *no* legal system in the world has initiated or funded serious research to find out how often it makes one or the other of these errors, let alone both of them. Such ignorance speaks not only to an intellectual and moral laxness but also to the abandonment of the cardinal rule of any self-respecting system of empirical inquiry, to wit, devising and then utilizing methods to figure out how often its results are reliable. Even worse than the fact that virtually all judges are ignorant of the error rates in criminal trials is the revelation that in a study by Gatowski it was found that a measly 4% of a sample of 364 state judges could say correctly what the phrase 'error rate' means![4]

This ignorance of, and indifference to, error rates is especially bizarre given that more often hangs on the outcomes of criminal trials than on many other forms of empirical inquiry. Sending someone to prison (or worse) for 10-15 years exacts an extraordinary price if he is innocent. Turning a violent, serial felon loose by acquitting him of a crime that he committed (and when the state believes it is likely that he committed the crime, but not likely enough to satisfy the prevailing standard of proof) likewise has egregious repercussions. If we expect doctors to know the error rates of the tests they rely on and pollsters to report the margins of error in the results they announce, is it really asking too much to insist that the criminal justice system needs to acquire, and to communicate to the public, information about how often it produces true and false results? Indeed, how can judges and the other actors in the justice system expect the general public to put confidence in their verdicts if the justice system itself does not bother to collect (or at least point to) data on the successes and failures of their inquiries? Black robes and white wigs may command respect but not if those wearing them are clueless about how often and why the system over which they preside fails.

It is more than a little ironic that ever since a famous case in the early 1990s, *Daubert v. Merrell Dow Pharmaceutical*,[5] the Supreme Court has (quite properly) insisted that any expert witness called to testify be able to give information about the error rates of the methods that he used in reaching his conclusions. For similar reasons, the aim of this book is to insist that the justice system cannot lay claim to expertise and reliability in the solution and prosecution of crimes nor can it command our confidence until and unless it can tell us how often trials err (and why).

You might think that this problem could be remedied by reminding ourselves that convictions can be appealed and overturned (even if pertinent, this would still leave us completely in the dark about the success/failure rates of acquittals, which are immune from appeal). But even where convictions are concerned, the appellate process rarely delves deeply into the question whether the convicted defendant is factually innocent. Almost invariably, the question an American appellate court faces when confronted by an appealed conviction is whether the trial was conducted according to the existing rules of evidence and procedure. If serious procedural errors occurred, the appellate court will typically overturn the verdict, allowing for a retrial of the accused. The problem is, as we shall see below in detail in chapter 6, that the rules of trial are not all designed to find the truth; worse still, many rules undermine that quest. The principal motive of many of them is to protect the rights of the accused and a host of them are truth-thwarting rather than truth-conducive. Protecting the defendant's rights is no small matter but neither is it one that enables us to draw any conclusions whatever about the *reliability* of ensuing verdicts.

Appellate courts can tell us whether a verdict of guilty was fairly arrived at (where 'fairness' means compliance with the existing rules of procedure) but little or nothing about whether it was factually correct. It is crucial to recognize –as this book will argue repeatedly—that procedural integrity most certainly does *not* imply empirical accuracy precisely because many of the rules in play have little or nothing to do with accuracy and more than a few of them actually work so as to increase the frequency of factually wrong verdicts. Indeed, it is arguable that trials would be more likely to result in true verdicts if some of the existing procedural rules now in place were violated rather than complied with.[6] The key point here, however, is that we cannot look to the rulings of appellate courts as reliable indicators of the truth or falsity of legal verdicts.

This is more than mildly surprising. In any legitimate system of inquiry, one is trying to find out the truth about the matters under scrutiny. Higher courts in the US are constantly reminding us, as they should do, that the aim of a trial is to get at that truth. As Attorney General Janet Reno put it in 1996: "our system of criminal justice is best described as a search for the truth."[7] Circuit Court and Supreme Court rulings echo repeatedly the same aim. For instance: "From the time an accused is first suspected to the time the decision on guilt or innocence is made, our criminal justice system is designed to enable the trier of fact to discover the truth according to law."[8] And: "It should always be borne in mind that, while the prosecution of a criminal case is properly to be conducted with vigor, as is also its defense, a trial is neither a game nor a battle, but is a search for the truth in respect of the issues of fact involved."[9] I am, therefore, not inventing things when I claim (as some legal scholars might deny), that the principal aim of a criminal trial is to find out the truth. A trial is thus, unquestionably, designed as a form of empirical inquiry and should be evaluated as such.

As we shall see in detail in later chapters, American criminal trials not only often fail to find out what the truth is but they are laden with many rules of procedure which are universally acknowledged to be serious obstacles to getting at the truth. Half a century ago, England's most distinguished jurist, Lord Devlin, on a visit to Chicago, noted pointedly that: "Trial by jury is not an instrument of getting at the truth; it is a process designed to make it as sure as possible that no innocent man is convicted."[10] Put differently, American criminal law aims to make as sure as it can that those it convicts are truly guilty but is wholly indifferent to how often it falsely acquits the guilty. That feature is a serious symptom of a warped version of inquiry and the 'search for the truth'.

Our problem of trying to get a grasp on the errors made in criminal trials is further confounded by the fact that several key legal concepts run awry of the ordinary epistemic meanings of those same terms, frequently creating considerable confusion in both the legal literature and the press. Most notorious among them is the 'not guilty' verdict. The press, the courts and lay citizens are often inclined to think that if a defendant has been found 'not guilty' that means that his jurors concluded that he did not commit the crime. In the law, however, 'not guilty' means nothing of the sort. What it means there is that defendant's guilt was not established beyond a reasonable doubt. That patently does not entail that it is reasonable to believe he did not commit the crime. Acquittals are often described in press headlines as 'exonerations', as if pointing to defendant's factual innocence, when they usually mean nothing of the sort. Likewise confusing is the common use of the term 'wrongful conviction'. That is often construed to mean that the convicted defendant did not commit the crime, that it was a false conviction. But, again, that is not what it means. The courts will often overturn a conviction on purely procedural grounds, which usually tells us nothing about the factual guilt or innocence of the defendant. Courts will also exonerate a defendant (thereby overthrowing a 'wrongful conviction') if new evidence emerges of his innocence post-trial. You might think that shows that the defendant did not commit the crime but it generally does not, since a defendant-favorable result in an exoneration hearing represents a judgment that the new evidence raises a reasonable doubt about defendant's guilt. That is certainly a good legal reason for setting aside his prior conviction. But, standing alone, it is not a definitive indicator of the defendant's factual innocence, since the existence of a 'reasonable doubt' about guilt is not necessarily powerful evidence of factual innocence.

Accordingly, a key aim of this book is to make a stab at doing some of the work that courts should have been undertaking themselves or at least sponsoring others to undertake. Our analysis will focus on one important family of crimes and trials: those involving violent offenses. It will attempt to estimate roughly the current rates of both false positives and of false negatives for such crimes. Once we can identify what errors are occurring, we can begin to ask why. Specifically, we can see that, if some of the existing rules of trial are responsible for many of the errors, then we can turn our minds to the question of how to reduce those errors by revising the rules that led to them.

But getting a rough idea of the frequency of legal errors and revising the rules that produced them is only a first step. We also need to ask ourselves another question which the legal system virtually never asks of itself: to wit, is the error profile, which the existing rules and procedures lead to, producing error rates that are acceptable? (By the 'error profile' I mean specifically the ratio of the errors that are produced, usually described as the ratio of false acquittals (or false negatives) to false convictions (false positives).

In sum, it is urgent to demand both:

1). that a) the legal system find out how often it gets its acquittals and convictions wrong, b) if those error rates turn out to be unacceptably high, then c).measures need to be taken to reduce errors or to distribute them differently than it now does; and

2). that the legal system insure that the harms produced by the two errors are acceptably low, by insuring that the ratio of the two errors reflects their respective harms.

This combined project of finding out approximately how many errors we commit (and identifying the sources of those errors and the remedies for them) along with adjusting the relative frequencies of the two errors until it is acceptably low, is what this book is about.

In due course we shall see (note especially the data in Table 5 in chapter 3) that the criminal justice system is rife with errors, both of omission and of commission. In 2008, for instance, there were some 1.7 million violent crimes (meaning murder, rape, armed robbery or aggravated assault) in the United States. Forty-seven percent of them went unreported to the police. Of those that were reported, 30% led to no arrest. Among those producing an arrest, 39% led to an acquittal or dropping of charges. Overall, therefore, less than a quarter (23%) of those violent crimes led to convictions (and some 3% of those were erroneous). This obviously means that some 1.3 million violent felons receive a get-out-of-jail-free card every year. As the next four chapters will document, hundreds of thousands of unarrested and unconvicted felons moved on to commit additional violent crimes during the time when they should have been convicted and imprisoned. Even among those arrested, many were acquitted, including (as we shall see in chapter 3) some 88,000 probably guilty felons who were acquitted, chiefly because the law demands a very high standard of proof before it will convict anyone. Failures occurred right down the line, from a refusal of many citizens to report their victimhood to a failure of police to solve hundreds of thousands of reported crimes and to a failure of the judicial system to convict many of those for whom there was good reason to believe them guilty. This book will focus especially on the third sort of failure, that is, failures of the judicial system to convict many guilty defendants then in custody and thought likely to be guilty.

Of course, many of those arrested by the police turned out to be genuinely innocent and should have been acquitted. But, as we shall see, a sizeable chunk of those dismissed, discharged or acquitted arrestees were factually guilty. What is more troubling is that errors of this sort were generally not chance events or the result of prosecutorial incompetence but a consequence of the fact that the legal system is *deliberately* engineered to acquit a great many guilty persons. The fine points of that engineering are not as widely understood or known as they should be. A key ambition of this book is to document the magnitude of such errors, to explore the reasons why citizens are rarely aware of the frequency of such errors and why the actors in the judicial system (especially the judiciary and the defense bar) go to great pains to avoid doing anything either to publicize or to reduce such errors.

Put differently, this book will grapple with a plethora of intriguing puzzles about the criminal law and how the justice system impacts all of us in one way or another. Some of those impacts are for the good; the law often—but not often enough— manages to protect us from the 'bad guys' by incapacitating them and deterring some of those tempted to follow in their footsteps. In other cases, however, the law is basically the bad guy itself, occasionally convicting the innocent and frequently letting the guilty go scot-free to continue their predations on the rest of us, even when there is substantial evidence of their guilt.

While the chief errors that will interest us here are those resulting from mistaken verdicts of guilty or not-guilty, there are several other (often erroneous) decisions of the justice system that will also command our attention. For instance, courts routinely grant bail to most of those awaiting trial for a violent crime; some of those bailees will rape and murder and commit other violent crimes while free on bail. Others will become fugitives, dropping from sight altogether and escape prosecution indefinitely. Further along the track, a *convicted*, violent offender (even if he was convicted of murder or rape) may get a sentence as mild as probation –euphemistically known as 'community supervision'— despite the potential dangers such a person poses to the rest of us. (I repeat: those convicted of murder or rapes are sometimes sentenced to nothing more than probation.) Finally, parole boards routinely shorten the sentences of convicted, violent felons, and many of these parolees are rearrested for new violent crimes within months of their release on parole, crimes they obviously could not have committed had they been denied parole.

Sometimes, the error points in the other direction. The state may incarcerate a serial offender with a lifetime sentence, when the crime for which he has just been convicted is a relatively mild felony (often exemplified in what are called 'three strikes and you're out' sentences). We are also prone to criminalize many activities (especially drug-related crimes) that are probably best dealt with by means other than incarceration; drug addicts arguably need treatment —when it can be efficacious—more than they need prisons. (Speaking of the three-strikes rule, which is often cited as being chiefly responsible for prison overcrowding, it is worth noting that in California —the second state to adopt such a policy— a 2015 report reveals that no more than one-half of one percent of that state's prison population are 'three-strikers'.[11]

Another glaring weak point in the American legal system is its relative indifference to the victims of crimes, whether past or future ones. Victims of crimes have remarkably little say in how the sentence-reduction decisions are meted out in plea-bargaining and scarcely nothing to say about what crimes a defendant is eventually charged with if he goes to trial. In comparison with several other developed countries, America's claim that it 'respects the rights of victims' is true only if we take a very truncated view of what those rights should entail. (In Germany, for instance, a violent crime victim typically has a lawyer representing her during the trial. That advocate can introduce evidence, cross-examine witnesses, and even initiate the appeal of a verdict of not guilty.)

This essay will examine these and several other ways in which the justice system is ill-designed and rests on very shaky conceptual foundations. Consider a few of the instances:

- As chapter 5 will show, literally no one (least of all the Supreme Court) understands exactly what a 'reasonable doubt' is. The Court deliberately will not define it, nor (in many jurisdictions) is the judge allowed to respond to jurors' requests for an explanation or clarification of its meaning. That ought to be more than mildly troubling since the reasonable doubt standard is what determines whether a defendant is convicted or acquitted.

- Many in the legal community have been spouting the line for the better part of three centuries that falsely convicting an innocent person is ten times worse than acquitting a guilty one, even though no one has ever plausibly explained why the costs of a false conviction are an order of magnitude greater than the costs of freeing the guilty.

- Then there's the familiar trope—especially popular among defense attorneys—that the criminal defendant, especially a poor one, faces an adversary in court (the state) with vastly more resources and more access to the evidence than the defendant himself enjoys. Accordingly, many argue (wrongly, as we shall see in this book) that the playing field in a criminal trial is hopelessly tilted in the state's favor and therefore, that we should alter the rules of trial in the defendant's favor so as 'to level the playing field'.

This book sets out to offer more than just a catalogue of the more egregious errors associated with current criminal law practices. More importantly, it will try to describe a conceptual framework within which we can attempt to understand many of the mechanisms that lead to errors and by means of which we can hope to remedy some of them, thereby making the world less risky and more fair for all of us. The key focus in that framework will be on the *risks* of harm imposed on ordinary citizens by a legal system that works with vague concepts and rules that often make little sense and have only the flimsiest of rationales.

Obviously, any serious discussion of these issues must exhibit two traits often absent from the legal literature: a). the analysis of empirical data about criminal trials and punishments; and b). a commitment to abandon a style of discussion filled with tired clichés and grounded on dubious ideologies. In short, we need solid data and robust arguments. That inevitably means that portions of the book may prove to be mildly tough sledding, requiring the integration of both unfamiliar data and fresh lines of argument. The payoff comes (I hope) in grasping the link between the arguments for a fresh perspective on errors in the law and the data that test those arguments.

Part I Identifying and Weighing the Errors in the Prosecution of Crimes

> [The] function of the legal process is to minimize the risk of erroneous decisions.—Chief Justice Berger (1974)[12]
>
> There is no gainsaying that arriving at the truth is a fundamental goal of our legal system.— Justice White (1980)[13]

The four chapters in this section will explore three core questions: What are the principal errors that occur in the handling of a criminal case? How frequent are those errors? And what harms and risks of harm result from them?

Chapter 1 Posing the Problem: A Brief Primer on Violent Crimes, their Perpetrators and their Victims

> Miscarriages of justice harm those wrongfully arrested and convicted. They [also] harm victims. They harm us all ... and undermine the legitimacy of our system of justice. Brian Forst[14]

Some 800 years ago, the famous Jewish philosopher, Moses Maimonides, insisted that when it comes to criminal proceedings, we must design things in such a way that convicting the innocent virtually never occurs. Since he grasped that it was impossible to avoid such errors altogether (except by never convicting anyone), he qualified it by arguing that, even though we occasionally if inadvertently convict the guilty, we must make sure that such an error occurs vastly less often than its counterpart error, the acquittal of the guilty.[15] He went so far as to specify that we should design trials so that we have at least 1,000 false acquittals for every false conviction. Specifically, he insisted "It is better... to acquit a thousand guilty persons than to put a single innocent man to death." (Recall that in those days, virtually all serious crimes were treated as capital offenses.) Sad to say, he gave no argument whatever for picking that ratio (and no proposal for a standard of proof that would yield it).

Almost 600 years later, one of England's greatest jurists, Lord William Blackstone, came along and suggested that we should be aiming rather lower than Maimonides had in mind; specifically, Blackstone insisted that the target should be at least 10 false acquittals for every false conviction. Like Maimonides, he gave *no* justification whatsoever for fixing on that ratio. A few thinkers of the day demurred. Voltaire opined that we should aim at something like 2 false acquittals for every false conviction.[16] Benjamin Franklin, finding himself somewhere between Maimonides and Blackstone, thought the ratio should be 100-to-1.[17] Curiously, not one of these thinkers gave the slightest argument for their hat trick of producing a pair of numbers without even a flimsy justification for their proposed ratios of errors, save to say that 'a false conviction is worse than a false acquittal', which does nothing to resolve the huge gulf between Voltaire's 2-to-1 and Maimonides' 1,000-to-1.

When the idea of the standard that we now know as 'proof beyond a reasonable doubt' emerged at the end of the eighteenth century, there quickly developed a general consensus that this new standard came very close to capturing Blackstone's version of the desired ratio, 10-to-1. That remains the hopeful consensus among most of today's jurists and legal scholars, even though none of them has come up with a justification for fixing on the 10-to-1 ratio or a technique for figuring out whether 'proof beyond a reasonable doubt' yields such a result.[18]

This is clearly disconcerting. It means that the most important rule governing the conduct of criminal trials is ill-defined and, making matters worse, no one has shown that it generates and distributes errors as we think they should be, even though we currently have few if any reasons for believing that one distribution is superior to another. In short, we have invented a decision rule for settling questions of guilt or innocence ("acquit unless there is no reasonable doubt about defendant's guilt") without knowing whether our current standard will indeed produce something like 10 false acquittals for every false conviction and without having developed a solid rationale for believing that a false conviction really is ten times (or any other multiplier that you like) worse than a false acquittal.

It's obviously long overdue that we set that situation right once and for all, after almost a millennium of unclear standards of proof and arbitrary stipulations of the respective harms of the two principal errors that can occur at trial. This book aims to do precisely that (among other things). I shall draw heavily on a rising tide of empirical data that allow us to compute (approximately) a). the costs/harms of both false acquittals and false convictions and b). the frequencies of those two errors in contemporary criminal trials. Once we grasp the approximate values of those two variables, we can then examine the crucial question whether our criminal justice system does or does not manage to produce false acquittals and false convictions in a way that mirrors their respective costs. Such a project is obviously ambitious but its realization is no longer beyond our reach. This book aims to show

how to do empirically what centuries of *a priori* legal theorists (who thought mere stipulation was enough) have dismally failed at.

More generally, this is a book about the criminal law and, more specifically, about the management (and sometimes deplorable mismanagement) of the handling of cases of *violent* crimes. Its primary focus will be on the adjudication of cases dealing with such crimes. It will show that we are all put at risk by the numerous ways in which the current justice system judges and then punishes—or, more frequently, fails to punish—the perpetrators of such deeds.

Before we turn our attention to diagnosing the mistakes and haphazard measures taken to deal with violent felons, it might be useful to make some rudimentary descriptive points about how the criminal justice system functions in dealing with the most serious of crimes. Here is a brief profile of the violent crime situation in the U.S. in 2008, which will serve as the exemplar year for much of the analysis in this book.

In that year, there were approximately 1.7m violent crimes in the United States, meaning homicides, rapes, armed robberies and aggravated assaults.[19] There were another 1m unsuccessful attempts at those crimes (attempted murder, attempted robbery, and so on). Our focus will be exclusively on the completed crimes and their prosecution. In response, police arrested some 595k suspects. Charges were dropped by prosecutors or dismissed by judges against some 217k arrestees. The remaining pool led to 333k plea bargains, leaving a bare 45k defendants who actually went to trial. Of those, 30k were convicted and 15k were acquitted. Altogether, 363k felons were convicted (either by plea or trial) and the other 232k arrestees went free. Even of those who were convicted, the 'sentence' imposed (if it can be called that) for many of these violent felons was probation, meaning that they were still on the streets, able to carry out whatever harmful mischief they were minded to.

In sum, some 1.3m violent offenders got away with it in 2008. While no two years exhibit an identical profile, it is fair to say that, since the turn of the century, this has been the general picture: roughly 70-75% of those who commit violent crimes escape justice (in the sense of a conviction) and another 10%

5

(despite being convicted) escape time in prison. Whatever theory of punishment you favor, such numbers are disconcerting. Whether you think we must punish the guilty because they deserve it (and we have the duty to give them their 'just deserts') or that we must incarcerate them to protect the rest of us from their predations, it is almost impossible to say that the state is doing the job we expect of it in terms of protecting its innocent citizens from violent harm.

Needless to say, not all violent crimes are of equal concern nor do they occur with anything like equal frequency. In 2008, there were 22k arrests for murder, 36k for rape, 288k for aggravated assault and 158k for armed robbery. Neither are they equivalent in terms of the harm done. Murder and rape are unquestionably the most egregious, although it is important to remember that significant numbers of the victims of violent robbery and assault suffer not only significant psychological trauma from the event itself but, in many cases, egregious injuries (206k robbery victims and 253k assault victims were injured during the crime[20]), the results of which some victims carry with them for the rest of their days. I lump these four crimes into the same bundle largely because that is the way that the major data-collecting and -reporting agencies (the FBI, the Bureau of Justice Statistics [hereafter: BJS] and other federal and state agencies) usually do it.

A few words are in order about the profiles of both the perpetrators and the victims. Begin with the latter: A male is 1.2 times more likely to be a violent crime victim than a female.[21] A person aged between 14 and 24 is 2,800% more likely to be a violent crime victim than one aged 65 or older.[22] Even though 'young adults' (aged 14-24) constituted only 16.4% of the US population in 2008, they were victims of 49% of homicides.[23] A black person is 2.7 times more likely to be violently victimized than their white counterpart.[24] An adult (defined as 'over 15') is 1.4 times more likely to be the victim of a violent crime committed by an acquaintance or family member than by a stranger.[25] Black victims of violent crimes report the crime to the police in 59% of the cases; white victims report the crime in only 46% of them.[26] An instance of 'strength in numbers': a divorced, separated or never-married person is 6.2 times more likely to be the victim of a violent crime than a married person is.[27] On the other hand, a father is twice as likely to be murdered by his children as a mother is.[28] One final curiosity: men convicted of violent crimes spend about 50% more time in prison (average: 29 months) than women do for the *same* crimes (20 months).[29]

On the whole, violent criminals are strikingly ill-educated in comparison with the rest of the population. Some 37% of those in prison for violent crimes never finished high school (compared with 18% of the general population who do not). Some 11% of violent offenders attended college (2% of them graduating), while 48% of the general population attended college (22% graduating).[30] Among the incarcerated jail and prison population, 58% of the prisoners have mental health problems, 69% were drug users before imprisonment, and 65% were heavy alcohol consumers.[31] A final interesting point that bears squarely on one of the issues to be debated in this book is that when the victims who reported crimes to the police were asked why they did so, 10.5% responded that they wanted to 'see the offender punished' while 22.6% reported the crime because they wanted to 'prevent further crimes by the offender'.[32] (Crime prevention evidently looms larger than retribution among crime victims, at least among those who report crimes.)

As for the perpetrators: it is widely known that criminal acts are much more likely to be perpetrated by men than by women. Violent crimes are no exception (81% v. 17%; 2% gender unknown).[33] The most striking difference between the sexes among perpetrators is homicide, where 9-of-10 murderers are men.[34] Three out of every four violent crimes are committed by single offenders.[35] Surprisingly, the offender in a violent crime uses a firearm in only 9.8% of the cases; a knife is used in another 5.4%.[36] (So much for the theory that America has so many violent crimes *because* the country has some 300m guns.[37] By these figures, roughly 1 in every 2,000 firearms will be used in violent crimes in a given year.) Studies of the linkage between intoxication and crime indicate that "36% of those convicted of a violent crime had been drinking alcohol when they committed their conviction offense."[38] In a 2004 BJS study, it was found that ~10% of those serving prison time for a violent crime committed the crime to obtain money for drug purchases.[39] On college campuses, by contrast, "41% of violent crimes committed against college students ... were committed by an offender perceived to be using drugs."[40] (It would seem that the perpetrator of a violent crime is much more likely to be drunk or addicted to drugs than carrying a firearm.)

Violent crimes in the US are highly *intra*-racial; 68% of such crimes against whites are committed by whites while 67% of such crimes against blacks are committed by blacks.[41]

When these violent crimes occur, and if they are reported to the police, investigation obviously ensues. If the police are lucky and 'get their man', an arrest occurs. Our concerns in this book will begin at the point of arrest. The following diagram represents the usual subsequent stages in that process (although there are some variations between the states):

Arrest→ initial screening→ preliminary hearing→ arraignment→ bail granting or denial→ (trial or plea bargain)→ sentencing (if convicted)→ possible appeal (perhaps leading to reversal or retrial) → possible exoneration

Decisions—important decisions—must be made at each point of this complex process by (among others) police officers, prosecutors, grand jurors, trial judges, defense counsel, trial jurors and appellate judges. All manner of ambiguous and ill-defined criteria or decision rules guide them along this track. For instance: Is there 'probable suspicion' to warrant an arrest? Is there 'probable cause' to charge the defendant? Is there 'clear and convincing evidence' to show that defendant is 'dangerous' and should be denied bail? Has the prosecutor produced proof of defendant's guilt 'beyond a reasonable doubt'? If the defendant claims an affirmative defense (such as self-defense), can he show that to be true by a 'preponderance of the evidence'? If a convicted defendant produces new evidence of his innocence after trial, can he persuade a judge that there is 'clear and convincing evidence' that there are reasonable doubts about his guilt?

It will be the aim of this book to show that at *every* one of these decision points, there is not merely the possibility of error but, in many cases, a relatively high probability of error. Such errors, as we will see in detail in later chapters, come with a very high price tag. If an arrestee is granted bail and commits a violent crime while awaiting trial, our wisdom in hindsight shows that the judge miscalculated the dangerousness of the defendant. A prosecutor may decide to drop charges against the defendant, not because he appears to be innocent but because the prosecutor's budget and personnel resources are stretched beyond existing limits.[42] At the trial, the jury may convict a truly innocent defendant and send him to jail for years, serving time for a crime he didn't commit. Alternatively, the jury may decide that, while there is impressive evidence of defendant's guilt, it is not quite strong enough to convict him beyond a reasonable doubt, thereby freeing someone who is probably guilty and who, when back on the streets, is highly likely to recidivate, claiming still other innocent victims.

Speaking of trials, it is important to stress that nowadays, they are relatively rare. Table 1 shows that pleas are overwhelmingly the dominant mechanism for disposing of cases that are not dropped by prosecutors.

Table 1. The Shrunken Role of Trials by Jury: the Sources of Convictions for Violent Crimes[43]			
Crime	Jury Trial	Bench Trial	Plea Bargain
Murder	36%	2%	62%
Rape	10%	2%	88%
Robbery	9%	2%	89%
Assault	5%	3%	92%
TOTAL	8%	2%	90%

Our principal aim here will be a). to assess the frequency of these various errors in both trials and pleas; b). to make a stab at calculating the harms done by these errors, and c). to analyze which rules of procedure are principally responsible for causing them. Once we have a plausible ballpark estimate of those figures, we will be in a strong position to recommend ways of changing the rules of the system so as to reduce those errors, thereby curtailing the harms that currently ensue from the handling of cases of violent crimes.

THE MYOPIC APPROACH TO ERRORS

Curiously, the first of our two principal errors, the false conviction, has garnered virtually all the attention, whether we are talking about the consciousness of the average citizen, the writings of legal scholars or the opinions of judges and legislators. Each of us can recall times when the front page of local newspapers—almost always above the fold—carried bold headlines of the sort: "Man convicted six years ago of rape is exonerated and freed." By contrast, ask yourself when you last read a story reporting that someone acquitted of a violent crime was, it turns out, unequivocally guilty. Even in legal circles, this second sort of error goes largely unnoticed and, on those rare occasions when it does arise in academic discussions, it usually elicits a shrug of indifference.

Lest you doubt the near total obscurity of the problem of false acquittals, ponder the fact that on the 'lawyer's internet encyclopedia' (LexisNexis), which includes virtually all important criminal cases, law review articles, and pieces of US legislation, there are 6,332 articles, statutes or cases that discuss false (or, as they are often called, 'wrongful') convictions and only 144 cases, statutes or articles that refer to false or wrongful acquittals. In short, the first error garners 4,400% more attention than the second.[44] A search for the same terms in Google books published prior to 2009 indicates that false (or wrongful) convictions are 4,600% more likely to be written about in books than are false (or wrongful) acquittals.[45]

Courts and the media have both become preoccupied with false convictions to the exclusion of false acquittals for a very simple reason. An erroneous acquittal will almost always escape detection, not because it would be especially difficult to identify false acquittals if we earnestly looked for them but because almost no one gives a damn about their occurrence. Exacerbating matters further still, the doctrine of double jeopardy prevents taking any decisive action against an acquitted defendant, even if an egregious error in his favor occurred in his trial. We don't see headlines about how many people are victimized by the falsely acquitted because the structure of the justice system virtually precludes their discovery. Few countries in the world take the American perspective that false negatives are of little note. In most of them, it is as routine to appeal and reverse acquittals as convictions. And such countries have no constitutional obstacle to sending back for trial a previously acquitted defendant, if new and inculpatory evidence emerges. We Americans labor under the illusion that false negatives are unworthy of attention because a). we have in place no official machinery for determining when or whether they happened and b). the legal system would refuse to do anything to rectify the mistake, no matter how obvious the guilt of the once-acquitted defendant might be.

Aside from the failure of our legal system to look for false acquittals, might there be good reasons why false convictions monopolize the attention of those writing about legal errors? Yes and no. It is generally believed, and I fully concur, that a single instance of a false conviction is a more egregious error than a single instance of a false acquittal. But, as the next three chapters will show, the fact that we cannot undo an already settled false acquittal is no reason to ignore or to downplay the importance of this type of error. For one thing, almost everyone associated with the legal system agrees that we are *deliberately* producing far more false acquittals than false convictions. As we have noted, the conventional (Gladstonian) wisdom is that we are and that we should be producing some ten false acquittals for every false conviction.[46] However, the fact that a single false conviction is worse than a single false acquittal patently does *not* mean that the aggregate harms produced by a system yielding 10 false acquittals for every false conviction are principally attributable to the false convictions. Indeed, in chapter 4, I will show that, overall, the false acquittals currently produced by our legal system are doing vastly *more* harm to innocent citizens than are the false convictions it produces.

Moreover, as chapters 5 and 6 will argue, we could —by making a few judicious changes in the rules of the justice system— drastically reduce the frequency of false acquittals and thereby the total number of innocent victims of that system. While existing false acquittals cannot be undone (thanks to double jeopardy), we can nonetheless fairly easily reduce the frequency of such errors in the future. As I will show in detail, we already know how to reduce the frequency of false acquittals. Our willingness to do so depends on understanding just how harmful an abundance of false acquittals can be and what are the factors that produce (often deliberately) this bountiful harvest of guilty arrestees who go scot-free. What we can do, and what this book will propose doing, is to tinker with the trial system so that it will produce fewer false acquittals in future than it now does and, in the process, drastically reduce the aggregate harm to innocent victims produced by that system.

Before moving on to those themes, however, I need to lay out briefly some of the terminology we will be using in the rest of the book. Rather than speaking of false or wrongful convictions, hereafter I shall generally refer to 'false positives', meaning specifically one of two things: a). a formal finding of guilt by a jury or judge imposed on an innocent defendant; or b). a plea bargain agreement in which an innocent defendant confesses guilty of a crime he did not commit. And, in lieu of speaking of false or wrongful acquittals, I will mean by a 'false negative' one of two things: a). a formal finding of 'not guilty' by a jury or judge of a truly guilty defendant; or b). a decision by a prosecutor or judge to drop or dismiss charges against an arrestee in custody who actually committed the crime with which he was charged.

One other remark is in order about the self-imposed limits on this analysis:

I shall have nothing to say about capital punishment–save for this paragraph. While such punishments are extremely rare, they should be abolished altogether in my view.[47] My chief reason for proposing their abolition is that the harshness and irreversibility of an execution (combined with the inevitability that from time to time the legal system will convict and execute an innocent person), creates a moral conundrum whose very existence, rare as it is, warps the entire public discussion of criminal justice. The abolition of capital punishment would enormously facilitate a hardheaded and dispassionate discussion of crime and punishment. I urge the reader to consider the analysis offered here as if we lived in a society that did not occasionally resort to the deliberate killing of a very small subset of those found guilty of heinous crimes.

It is vitally important to understand the subtle ways in which our two errors arise and how they interact with one another. As for false positives, we have quite a store of data pointing to their causes, in large measure thanks to the work of the various Innocence Projects in the United States, devoted to trying to win exonerations for the innocent who have been convicted (especially if sent to death row). Careful scrutiny of such exonerations reveals many places where judgments of guilt can go wrong. Eyewitness testimony, which sometimes counts as the most telling evidence in a trial, is less reliable than one might suppose, especially when the witness and the defendant are strangers and of different ethnicities.[48] Similarly, as we shall see in later chapters, expert testimony is not always reliable. Sometimes fingerprint experts misidentify a set of prints as matching the defendant's when they do not or vice versa.[49] Handwriting expertise is even dicier. Occasionally, an innocent defendant will confess to a crime he didn't commit, perhaps because he wants to shield the real perpetrator or because, although he has an alibi, he doesn't wish to bring the alibi witness forward for fear that doing so would bring harm to her. On other occasions, an accomplice will falsely finger the defendant as the guilty party in order to avoid prosecution himself. In short, flawed evidence is the error-producing agent in many of the false positives that have been studied.

Quite a different explanation lies behind the huge number of false negatives. Sometimes, obviously, an arrested guilty felon escapes conviction because the evidence the police have been able to assemble is either weak or otherwise subject to rebuttal; other times, however, highly relevant incriminating evidence is kept out of the trial by virtue of the multitude of exclusionary rules that stand between the jury and the pertinent evidence. Still, the overwhelming reason for most false negatives is not a flawed case made by the prosecutor nor a lack of strong inculpatory evidence but the fact that, to convict someone of a crime, our system generally requires that the jury must be unanimously persuaded of his guilt to a degree of near certainty (proof beyond a reasonable doubt).

Suppose, for the sake of discussion, we assume that this standard is roughly equivalent to a level of confidence of 90% or greater. Doubtless, many trial juries are persuaded that an actually guilty defendant probably committed the crime in question. (Think of the public reaction to the verdict in the universally-followed case of O.J. Simpson and the post-trial reports of the jurors in that trial themselves.) It takes only a 50+% probability of guilt to be persuaded of that. Before the jury convicts him, however, it will have been instructed, sternly and repeatedly, that all its members must be almost sure of his guilt. Hence, no juror who thinks it 60%, 70% or 80% likely that the defendant committed the crime may declare him guilty. Even if the evidence presented satisfies what the legal system calls 'clear and convincing evidence' of defendant's guilt, he must be acquitted unless there remains no remnant of a reasonable doubt. Because the evidence profiles of many truly guilty defendants fail to meet the exacting threshold of proof beyond a reasonable doubt, such persons will receive a verdict of not-guilty (better expressed as 'guilt not proven') even when most or even all of the jurors strongly believe them to be the culprit.

Often, indeed very often, a plausible case for guilt will not even get to a jury or a plea bargain because the prosecutor will drop the charges filed by the police. Why, you might ask, would a prosecutor do that? There are three principal answers: a). the typical prosecutor, having limited personnel and financial resources, can scarcely afford to take to trial all those charged with crimes; b). if he is an elected official, as most chief prosecutors at the state level are, he will be reluctant to bring to trial cases that he thinks it likely that he might lose, not because he thinks the defendants in question are innocent but because these probably guilty defendants have an evidence profile that is perhaps not strong enough to virtually guarantee a guilty verdict and he does not want a lousy record of lost cases to accompany him to the next election; and c). because evidence has newly emerged that the defendant is actually innocent.

It is a rudimentary theorem of logic that the higher the standard of proof is, the more likely it is that the typical, truly guilty defendant will be acquitted if tried and perhaps he will not even be brought to trial. It is likewise provable that the higher the standard of proof, the less likely it will be that an innocent defendant will be found guilty. It is this pair of relations that explains the tensions between these two errors that will dog us throughout the rest of this study. If we say to ourselves (as many jurists and legal scholars do) that we must take new and additional measures to minimize the likelihood of a false positive, then we are apt to try to modify the legal system by a variety of additional rules that make it even harder than it now is for the prosecutor to establish the guilt of a defendant. (Indeed, that is a quick thumbnail summary of the history of Supreme Court jurisprudence about criminal law in the last half century.) Such steps clearly raise the prosecutor's burden of proof even higher that it is set by the 'proof beyond a reasonable doubt' standard. Those new defendant-friendly rules and procedures doubtless reduce the frequency of false positives, which was often their original intent. The generally unforeseen or hugely discounted consequence of this policy is a dramatic leap in the frequency of false negatives much greater than the resulting reductions in false positives. As we shall see further along, a convicted defendant is 3,000% more likely to be truly guilty than truly innocent. By contrast, an acquitted defendant is less than twice as likely to be innocent as guilty.

Reducing the likelihood of a false positive obviously would have the result that the risk of an innocent person going to prison is lower than it would otherwise be using a lower standard. But the same action significantly increases the risk that an innocent citizen will soon be victimized by an arrested and guilty serial felon who, instead of being convicted for the violent crime he committed, is released on the grounds that his guilt, while much more probable than not, was not proven to a moral certainty. If the state is properly to discharge its dual commitments a). to protect the innocent from false convictions and b). to protect its citizens from the malicious acts of truly guilty felons who, having been in the hands of the state and strongly suspected of having committed a violent crime, were nonetheless given their liberty, then we drastically need to re-think how willing we should be to acquit or drop the charges against those who, on the available evidence, appear to be genuinely guilty. Spelling out that linkage will be our task in the next chapter.

THE SERIOUSNESS OF SERIALITY

Before getting down to the main business before us, there is one more issue that needs to be brought front and center, since it will be a key part of much that follows: the obscenely high rate of recidivism among violent offenders. The issue impinges on everything ranging from decisions to grant bail, and setting the severity of a convicted felon's sentence, to later decisions about the use of probation and parole as ways of tempering a sentence. Recidivism is difficult to measure with any precision since most crimes go unreported to the police and many of those reported never lead to an arrest, let alone to a conviction. Accordingly, looking at John Doe's arrest record or his conviction history is apt to understate drastically how often he has committed felonies. What we learn, however, from Doe's arrest and conviction history sets a kind of minimal threshold of his criminality. His actual criminality, it is universally agreed, is almost certainly higher than what we can learn from his arrest/conviction record. If two-thirds of violent crimes go unsolved, we have little hard data about how many, if any, of those unsolved crimes Doe committed. Even though official recidivism figures probably vastly understate the criminal activities of the ill-intentioned, they still drive home how seriously we must take the repeat or habitual offender and the steps we should take to reduce the future harms he is apt to perpetrate. The review of a few numbers here should show how serious the recidivism problem is. Ponder these facts:

—36% of those arrested for violent crimes committed those violent acts while they were on probation, bail or parole for a different crime; in short, the latter three acts of generosity on the part of the state enabled more than one-third of the solved violent crimes that occur every year.[50]

—70% of those arrested for a violent crime have prior arrests; 56% have prior arrests for serious felonies.[51]

—21% of those released from prison (under age 25) were charged for a new violent crime within 5 years of their release.[52]

—of the 404k prisoners released from prison in 2005, this cohort were arrested for 1.17m crimes by 2010 (roughly 2.9 crimes each). Within 6 months of their release, 25% had been re-arrested for a new crime.[53]

In sum, serial felons pose an on-going threat to the rest of the population. That threat is exacerbated a). when serial felons are falsely acquitted for a crime that they actually committed, b). when their prior seriality is ignored and they are placed on probation (with no prison time) after being convicted of a violent crime, c). when sentencing judges ignore their prior records, or parole officers grant early release in spite of a lengthy record of multiple crimes and d). when serial felons awaiting trial are granted bail. This seriality is also downplayed by the tendency of trial judges, during the trial of a violent felon, to block the admissibility of evidence of his prior crimes and prior convictions. (Specifically, in trials where the defendant chooses not to testify, the trial judge will exclude the admission of prior crimes evidence in about 90% of the cases involving serial felons.[54]) This information is excluded not because it is deemed irrelevant but because it is, in the language of the Federal Rules of Evidence, likely to be 'unfairly prejudicial'.

Chapter 2 The Social Contract: Managing Crime and Protecting the Innocent from False Conviction

> The end of punishment, therefore, is no other than to prevent the criminal from doing further injury to society, and to prevent others from committing the like offence.—Cesare Beccaria[55]

Before we turn to look at the pertinent data in the next few chapters, I want to sketch out a conceptual framework within which this discussion will take place. Since the seventeenth century, there has been a tendency to think of crime and punishment in the context of a hypothetical social contract between a state and its citizens. A typical scenario goes something like this: Living in a state of nature and without the rule of law, a person can do whatever he can get away with. Unless one happens to be the toughest and the most powerful in the neighborhood, that means that one's life, liberty and possessions are constantly at risk from the self-serving actions of more powerful neighbors and predators. A state with the rule of law poses an alternative to this bloody Hobbesian nightmare. Promising to protect its citizens from the illegal predations of the stronger and more powerful, the state demands only that citizens obey the law and agree to yield a monopoly on the use of force to the (presumably) benevolent state.[56]

Even while the state promises to reduce vastly the risks to its citizens posed by the mal-intentioned, the contract acknowledges that the state is also imposing a risk of its own making. Since the state intends to use courts and the law to adjudicate charges of law-breaking, it is inevitable that occasionally an innocent citizen will be falsely arrested, condemned and punished for a crime that he didn't commit.[57] Accordingly, so the theory goes, the contract between the state and the citizen must not only include a clause protecting him from the risk of being a crime victim but likewise a clause protecting him from being falsely convicted and punished by the state. The social contract is attractive just in so far as the state is able to deliver on these two undertakings.

First proposed along these lines by Cesare Beccaria almost three centuries ago, this pair of commitments—reduction and management of crime and protection from false conviction—have been lynchpins in many theories of crime and punishment in the last two centuries.[58] Neither clause of this version of the social contract is easy to fulfill (Indeed, some scholars would deny that this was a genuine 'social contract' as usually understood.) Eliminating crime altogether is clearly impossible; even reducing it to acceptable levels can be inordinately difficult. Likewise, decisions about who the law-breakers are often prove fraught and, inevitably, are sometimes mistaken. The attractiveness or repellence of any state (and especially its criminal justice system) to its citizens will depend to a large degree on how effectively it resolves these two fiendishly interconnected problems.

It will prove instructive to ask ourselves at the outset how well the modern state is discharging its dual obligations. You might imagine that a state will have fulfilled its contractual obligations to its citizens so long as the dual risks of being a crime victim or being falsely convicted are lower under the rule of law than they were (hypothetically) in the state of nature. After all, what we know of the hunter-gatherers, who perhaps make a convenient surrogate for the state of nature, makes it clear that life was then very cheap. Lawrence Keeley has calculated that inter-tribal warfare—including raids, skirmishes and the like—meant that 20-25% of all adult males died from homicide.[59] If this homicide rate were laid down as the baseline for deciding whether modern states were a success, the latter would clearly get the nod.

Still, adopting this benchmark as the measure for contractual success is patently too undemanding. Upon joining the state, individuals agree to give up vast amounts of their freedom of action —their liberty—in return for the protections offered by the state. Almost every law on the statute books represents one further, liberty-infringing prohibition. Accordingly, determining whether a state meets its part of the bargain involves not only comparing the risks to life and limb in the state of nature and under the rule of law respectively but also involves asking whether the liberty losses associated with citizenship are more than compensated for by the heightened protection afforded by that citizenship. On this model, states that take away more liberties from their citizens than others do must deliver more security than can be reasonably expected in the latter.[60]

As we will see in detail below, the scorecard is decidedly mixed in virtually every modern state but in a singularly skewed fashion. While failures of both crime reduction and false conviction occur in every society, there is virtually no Western society in which the state does not do a far better job of limiting the risk of false conviction than it does of limiting the risk of being the victim of a serious crime. As we will see in detail farther on, it is statistically unusual for an innocent person to be convicted of a serious felony. (This is not to say that false convictions do not happen tens of thousands of times every year. It *is* to say that the ordinary citizen's risk of being in this unhappy and unjust situation is mercifully very low.) This is in marked contrast to the ordinary citizen's chances of becoming the victim of a serious crime, a risk that varies from high to very high, depending on the state and the crime in question.

Consider some concrete data.[61] In the US, the annual risk that an average citizen ran of being the victim of a violent crime (during the period 1973-1995)—meaning assault, homicide, armed robbery, or rape—was about 5 percent. At that rate, his *lifetime* risk of being so victimized was 5 in 6.[62] Fortunately, violent crime rates have fallen significantly in the last generation. The comparable figure now would be an annual risk of 2.5% that someone will attempt a violent crime on you.[63]

In short, it is likely that any randomly selected American will at some time in his life be raped, robbed at gun- or knife-point, or violently assaulted. (These numbers leave homicide out of the picture.) Focusing on that worst outcome, the annual chance of being murdered in the US (in 2008) was about 0.006%, producing a lifetime risk of about 0.4%.[64] (The lifetime risk that an American male will be murdered is about one per cent.) The annual risk of rape for a woman in the US in 2003 was about 0.1%. If these prospective numbers strike you as higher than plausible, it is well to stress that they are in line with other data. For instance, in a retrospective study (that examined actual as opposed to attempted victimizations) published in 2000 by the National Institute of

Justice, it is reported that 17.6% of women in the US and 3% of the men have already been rape victims. The same study found that every year there are physical assaults—simple or aggravated—against 8.5 in every 100 males and assaults annually against 5.9 in every 100 females.[65] While the risk of being murdered or raped or assaulted in the hypothetical state of nature would almost certainly have been higher than these numbers, it remains clear that the state—at least the American state—is still tolerating what any reasonable person would regard as an unacceptably high degree of grave risk to life and limb for its citizens.

While some of the serious crime numbers are lower than this in several other developed countries, few of them can give much comfort to social contract buffs. In England and Wales, for instance, although the annual risk of being murdered is about 1 in 100,000, a woman's annual risk of being raped is an unseemly 1:300 and her risk of her being violently assaulted is 1:500.[66] Overall, the annual risk of being the victim of a violent crime in the UK is about 3 percent.[67] Roughly similar figures apply across most of the developed world. Whatever the underlying causes may be, the level of protection from serious felonies offered by the modern state raises genuine doubts about whether those states are complying with their crime-control obligations under the social contract.

It's not just that crime rates are high. Apprehension and punishment rates remain abysmally low. Table 2 shows the percentages of various crimes in the US and in England and Wales that eventually lead to a conviction and (usually) imprisonment. The only mildly encouraging numbers here—those for rape—are grossly exaggerated since they deal only with rapes reported to the police. If we factor in that report rates of rape in England hover around 12% (and in the US a bit higher than that), it is clear that the police and courts are convicting rapists between one and two percent of the time.[68] Even where other serious, violent crimes are concerned, the picture is likewise grim. In 1994, there were 4.2 million violent crimes (including attempts) in the US. In that same year, some 95,000 felons were sent to prison for such crimes, producing a ratio of about one person imprisoned for every 45 serious crimes.[69] The situation has improved dramatically since then but not enough; of 1.7m completed violent crimes in 2008, barely 20% of them led to a conviction.

Table 2. Percent of serious crimes leading to conviction[70]		
Crime	US (1994)	England & Wales (1995)
Rape	20%	10%
Robbery	2%	<1%
Assault	2%	1%
Burglary	2%	<1%
Car Theft	2%	1%

While the crimes rates in the US have dropped dramatically since the 1990s, the conviction rates remain very low (with the exception of homicide). Rape conviction rates have also improved significantly since the 1980s and 1990s. Now, contrast these statistics with the risk of being falsely convicted and the discrepancies become stunning. While the lifetime risk of an American being the victim of a serious crime is, as we saw, about 1-in-2, his chances of going to prison at some point in his life, convicted of a serious crime that he did not commit, is, at the most, 0.25% and probably *much* less.[71] That is, he is at least 20,000% more likely to be a victim of a serious crime than to be falsely convicted of one. While his lifetime risk of being murdered is about 1:250 (0.4%), the lifetime risk that an innocent American will be convicted of homicide is, erring on the side of the generous, about 0.007%. (Murder cases are much more likely to lead to apprehension and conviction than any of the other violent crimes.) Hence, the average American is some 57 times more likely to be murdered than to be falsely convicted of murder. Similarly large discrepancies between the risk of false conviction, on the one hand, and the risk of being a violent crime victim, on the other, show up in virtually every modern society, and with respect to virtually every category of serious crime.[72]

Such numbers make clear that it massively understates the case to say that modern states are doing a much better job of protecting the innocent from conviction than they are at protecting the innocent from violent felons. If these two obligations were wholly distinct from one another, this would be little more than an idle curiosity, akin to saying: "Look how much better the state is at (say) delivering clean drinking water than it is at controlling bankruptcies." But, of course, these obligations are *not* independent. We know full well that the greater the pains a state takes to protect its innocent citizens from false conviction, the more difficult it is for the state to control crime, since measures adopted to achieve the former end will typically make it more difficult to convict the guilty, which in turn—as we shall see shortly—make controlling crime much more difficult. Contrariwise, if a state decides to cut the crime rate by making it easier to convict felons, it will foreseeably increase the percentage of innocent persons falsely convicted of crimes they did not commit. Since there are indisputably many trade-offs between the commitments themselves, it would thus be folly to suppose that these two problems can or should be treated independently.

Yet that is precisely the approach that many nation-states, and most theorists of the state, have taken. Specifically, they argue (as we will see in detail in later sections) that our decisions about how to structure a criminal trial should be driven principally if not entirely by the desire to reduce false convictions, above all else. Further, courts and legislators, aided and abetted by various prominent theorists of the criminal law (from Kant to Dworkin), have insisted that decisions about the protections to be put in place so as to avoid false convictions must be made with little or no regard to the problems of crime management and control.[73] Taking this advice to heart, states behave as if one of the two clauses of the social contract—the need to minimize false convictions—is both more urgent and more fundamental than the other clause—protecting the innocent from crime. This is mildly strange since there is nothing in the social contract that would motivate such a prioritizing, so we will eventually have to look elsewhere for an explanation of this asymmetry.

The preference of states for safeguarding their citizens against false convictions more than against crime itself shows up not only in the empirical differences between these two risks that their citizens run, but also figures prominently in the constitution and procedural rules of the modern state. There, with countable exceptions, one usually finds enumerated a host of protections against false conviction that typically include: a strong presumption of innocence, locating a heavy burden of proof exclusively on the prosecutor's shoulders; the right to reverse a conviction on appeal (sometimes, as in the US, absent a right of the state to seek to reverse an acquittal or to retry someone who has been acquitted); the exclusion of evidence about a defendant's character, unless he wants it introduced; and a defendant's unconditional right to silence. A similar indicator can be found in the height of the standard of proof used in criminal trials. This standard—whether 'proof beyond a reasonable doubt' (the usual standard in common law countries), or an 'intimate conviction of guilt' (prevalent in Roman-law countries) or 'being sure of guilt' (England's newly-adopted standard)—is invariably very demanding. The reason for a high standard of proof—the *only* reason for a high standard—is to shield the innocent from false conviction. High standards of proof do *nothing* whatever to reduce trial errors; they merely shift those errors in favor of defendants—whether guilty *or* innocent. In the process, they actually produce more errors than is either necessary or desirable. Finally, a brief glance at the procedural rules in most states reveals a huge number of 'adjustments' to the trial rules, many of which are designed by the judiciary to give significant probatory advantages to the defendant.[74] In short, the protections against false conviction are virtually all canonized as rights, sometimes even as constitutional rights. These rights, in turn, are zealously protected by the modern state.

Consider, by contrast, the state's commitment to protect citizens from the predations of others. While talk about the 'rights of victims' is heard occasionally, few of those rights have achieved full constitutional status. More significantly, violations of the rights of crime victims (most importantly, the right not to be a crime victim in the first place) rarely occasion the sort of outrage that accompanies the discovery that an innocent person has been falsely convicted. It is true, of course, that every modern state has criminal courts, large police forces and hefty budgets for criminal justice. But at this point we return to the bottom line: the data we shall examine leave no doubt that the modern liberal state is far, far better at shielding the innocent from false conviction than it is at protecting the innocent from violent crimes. This book will argue that this imbalance needs to be rectified.

One might conjecture that this striking asymmetry is due to the fact that it is vastly easier to avoid convicting the innocent than it is to eliminate crime. After all, if we combine a demanding standard of proof with appropriate sorts of procedural rules, we can be confident that relatively few innocent persons will be convicted. The problem of criminality, by contrast, appears vastly more complex and less amenable to simpler remedies. On this way of seeing things, states will inevitably fail in their responsibility to reduce crime drastically because that is an intractable social problem, largely outside of state control or at least beyond the financial resources of the state to solve, whereas protecting the innocent from false conviction is almost entirely under the thumb of the state itself. If true, this would be rather ironic since the core commitment of the state, according to the social contract, is precisely to protect its citizens from criminals. Protection from false conviction, while an important part of the contract, is, as it were, a subordinate clause, arising out of the primary commitment to protect citizens from felons.

The fact is that states and their courts could do a great deal more than they are now doing to discourage serious crime and to protect the innocent from the delinquent. Doing so would, however, require a deliberate decision to re-calibrate the balance that has been struck between the state's obligation to protect innocent citizens from the ill-intentioned and its obligation to protect the innocent from false conviction.

More specifically, this book will argue that there are effective methods for lowering the rate of serious crimes. Basically, these hinge on *convicting and incarcerating a higher proportion of the guilty than we now convict*. We will see that there is powerful evidence that higher conviction rates bring with them significantly lower crime rates. The trick, of course, is to figure out how to convict a higher proportion of criminals than we now do. Potentially, there are a variety of ways of doing that, among them: hiring more and better-trained police, incentivizing citizens who are crime victims to report those crimes to the authorities, making sentences more severe, educating young people about the evils of crime, developing more sophisticated forensic techniques for the detection of crime, and putting in place vigorous crime-prevention measures, to mention only a few popular proposals. But the probable effectiveness of such measures pales in comparison with a much more straightforward (and much more economical) solution to the problem of how to convict more wrongdoers: namely, tinkering with the standard of proof and the rules of criminal evidence and procedure.

Specifically, it will be my aim to explore the interconnections between the risks that make up Beccaria's social contract hypothesis, and to diagnose why modern societies have so consistently decided to valorize the avoidance of one of these risks over the avoidance of the other, and, finally, to propose that we re-think the balance between these two risks that we can expect a just state to strike. The thread of the argument leading to this conclusion is a complex one, somewhat difficult to follow and, by virtue of its complexity, inherently suspect. Still worse, the conclusions we shall reach are not what the politically correct conventional wisdom would have anticipated. For such reasons, I will try to make the steps of the argument as clear as I can. Along the way, our discussion will explore themes as diverse as the social contract, the obstacles to the control of crime, and will make a stab at re-defining rules for trial in a way that reflects the values explicit in the social contract better than current rules do.

Before we tackle those issues, however, we need to be clearer than I (or Beccaria) has thus far been about how specifically to operationalize the demands of the social contract. I shall do so by elaborating on an idea propounded by the brilliant mathematician and physicist Pierre Simon de Laplace early in the nineteenth century. While we don't normally expect creative scientists to make important contributions to legal theory, he did so in a book he wrote in the early nineteenth century on probability theory. As a strong believer that the law could, in a variety of ways, profit from understanding probabilities (he was especially interested in how we might calculate the reliability of eyewitness testimony), he ventured a kind of quantified version of Beccaria's social contract.

In his book about probability theory, Laplace (often described as 'the French Newton') considered a number of legal problems that he thought could be solved using statistical techniques. Specifically, he argued that the right way to resolve the evident tension between false convictions and false acquittals was by defining a standard of proof based on an appraisal of the harms resulting from the two erroneous verdicts. Specifically, he opined:

"[Finding the correct standard of proof for satisfying the demands of the social contract] reduces to the solution of the following question: does the proof that the accused committed the crime possess the necessary degree of probability so that citizens have less to fear from the errors of a tribunal if the accused is innocent and convicted, than from his new attempts at crime, and those of the unfortunates emboldened by his impunity, if he is guilty and acquitted?"[75]

More precisely, Laplace challenges us to design a legal system in which the risk to an ordinary citizen of being falsely convicted of a crime is marginally less than the risk of being the victim of a crime committed either by a). a guilty person who was falsely acquitted or b). by a third party who, far from being deterred by that acquittal of a guilty person, is animated to commit a crime himself.

A century and a half later, Robert Nozick in his classic *Anarchy, State and Utopia*, put a similar point this way:

> That system [of criminal justice] is
> most effective which minimizes the
> expected value of unearned harm to
> me, either through my being unjustly
> punished or through my being a
> victim of a crime.[76]

Nozick's thesis obviously is not identical to Laplace's but it is similar in important respects. What we should seek, Nozick says, is a legal system in which the *aggregate* risk of unearned harm resulting from either a). my being falsely convicted or b). my being the victim of an undeterred crime is minimized. What Laplace and Nozick share is the idea that, in deciding how demanding to make the standard of proof (and therefore how we distribute the two errors), we should take into account not only the risks and harms of false positives but also the risks and harms of false negatives.

Laplace's analysis is more nuanced than Nozick's. While Nozick's focus is almost entirely on the *deterrent* effects of the criminal justice system, Laplace (like Beccaria before him), while acknowledging the value of deterring third parties from committing crimes, sees the greater importance of *incapacitating* the known perpetrators of violent crimes so that they are not merely discouraged from committing criminal acts but literally prevented from such acts during their time behind bars.

On Nozick's analysis, we have to conclude that the current criminal justice system is an unmitigated disaster. While the annual risk to an ordinary citizen (aged twelve or older) of being falsely convicted of a violent crime in the United States is approximately 1-in-23,000, the annual risk of being the victim of a violent crime is about 1-in-150.[77] As we shall see in chapter 4, we are very far from minimizing the expected harm to innocent citizens.

Given the radical difference in magnitude between these two risks, it is hard to imagine any change in the justice system that would drastically reduce via deterrence the likelihood of being the victim of a violent crime. Cutting the false negative rate by half, say, would do relatively little to deter a great many violent crimes since it would remain true that the vast majority of violent crimes would lead to no conviction whatever. Prospective violent wrongdoers would still know that the odds of being incarcerated for a crime were low. It is also plausible to believe that many violent crimes are committed under duress or anger or while on drugs and that many of the perpetrators of such crimes probably don't engage—as deterrence theory assumes—in a rational calculation about their likelihood of being apprehended and convicted.

In short, Nozick's stress on deterrence doesn't seem very promising as the principal solution to the problem of violent crime; especially not when barely 23% of the violent crimes annually in the US lead to a conviction. By contrast, the sort of incapacitation that Laplace (and, before him, Beccaria) proposed as a key part of the social contract offers much more promise as a crime-risk reducer. The incapacitation of a higher proportion of truly guilty defendants than we now convict[78] would, as we shall see in due course, guarantee a significant reduction in violent crime rates.

If, as the Laplace version of the social contract requires, we need to ascertain and compare the harm done by the false negatives and false positives associated with the outcomes of criminal procedures dealing with violent crimes, then we need to compute two sorts of things: a). approximately how often each type of error now occurs; and b). the respective social and moral costs associated with each type. The next chapter will answer the first question. The second question will be addressed in chapter 4.

What I believe we can infer from Laplace's analysis is that there are three risks that need to be taken into account. The first one, which I will call R_1, is the annual risk of being falsely convicted of a violent crime; the second, R_2, is the annual risk of being the victim of a violent crime perpetrated by a felon falsely acquitted of a violent crime; and the third risk, R_3, is the annual risk of being the victim of a crime perpetrated by a felon who should have been incarcerated for a crime he actually committed but for which an innocent person was falsely convicted. As I interpret Laplace's analysis, he is suggesting that the state must seek to minimize the overall risk represented by those three dangers. If he's right, we must aim to minimize the risks of harms produced by the errors of judgment in the legal system; specifically, we should aim to minimize this risk:

Aggregate Risk of Judicial Adjudication of Crimes = $[(R_1$ x $H_1)+(R_2$ x $H_2)+(R_3$ x$H_3)]$, where H_1, H_2 and H_3 represent, respectively, the magnitude of the harms resulting from each of the three risks and R_1, R_2, and R_3 are their respective probabilities. To be clear, Laplace (and I) are not calling for a system that minimizes each of the two risks individually (for that would be impossible given their inter-dependence) but for a system that produces *the lowest aggregate risk and harm*. This book aims to show how we could, and why we should, pursue that end.

To explore this proposal, I will tackle a trio of serious hurdles. First, I will need to show that conviction rates are better predictors of the rate of serious crimes than are more fashionable hypotheses which suppose that the frequency of crime has little to do with conviction rates and is instead the result of (choose your favorite, according to your political predilections): poverty or unemployment or inequitable distribution of wealth or a bad educational system or a demographic spike in the number of young males in the population or social anomie or the loss of traditional values or broken homes or the divorce rate. Supposing that I can make plausible this first hypothesis (that relatively higher conviction rates lower crime rates significantly), a second hurdle will arise: what reason have we to believe that changes in criminal procedures will do much to alter the conviction rate? These first two issues are basically empirical questions, in principle resolvable by consulting the relevant data.

The last, and thorniest, problem is more philosophical, almost moral, in character. It amounts to meeting the challenge posed by this question: Even if it could be shown that higher rates of conviction lower crime rates, and that changes in trial rules can alter rates of conviction, how can I possibly propose that several procedural rules—and perhaps even the standard of proof itself—should be changed, knowing that such changes would involve treating the "rights" of the accused as negotiable and revisable rather than as inviolable and sacrosanct? In due course, I will deal with all three challenges. I begin with the first.

THE GENERAL CASE FOR CRIME MANAGEMENT AND REDUCTION

According to the social contract, the state undertakes to reduce crime. There would appear to be many ways to do so, of varying degrees of effectiveness. It puts in place a police force for patrolling the streets and apprehending criminals. It tries to regulate economic conditions, minimizing unemployment, and providing welfare and other safety nets to the poor (so that no one need commit a crime out of sheer economic necessity). It creates a justice system that tries and, where appropriate, convicts criminals, depriving them of their liberty, hopefully sending a message to others of like mind that this could be their fate too unless they change their ways. It builds prisons for incarcerating wrongdoers. Basically, systems of crime control consist of a mix of carrots and sticks, designed to reward those who obey the law and to penalize those who do not. This section will argue that one effective way—

arguably the most effective way—to keep crime rates within acceptable limits is by convicting a significantly higher proportion of those who commit crimes.

It is almost universally claimed that the United States already incarcerates too many people. That may well be so with respect to minor or even dubious crimes (especially drug-related crimes). As I read the data, however, that assertion is anything but true of serious felonies. Consider the fact that the number of convicted felons serving time in prisons in 2012 was 1.57m.[79] Of those, 54% (840k) had been convicted of violent crimes. That latter number (which includes in many cases persons serving long prison terms) is less than the number of violent crimes committed in a single year.[80] Given that the average sentence meted out for a violent crime is about 7.6 years, the fact that those now in prison for violent crimes constitute less than half of those who committed a violent crime in one year (and only 7% of those who committed violent crimes during the last 7.6 years), it is mind-boggling to suggest that we are imprisoning too many serious felons for too long. Of course, we would like in the abstract to have a smaller prison population just as we would like to have a lower incidence of violent crimes. But when the latter number is as high as it is, I don't see how anyone can hold that the number of violent felons now imprisoned has already reached or exceeded a number that is acceptable. Where violent crimes are concerned, we should be incarcerating more of the guilty and locking them away in prison for longer venues. It is worth adding that, while the felony conviction rate (and thus the prison population has grown dramatically (almost doubled) in the last thirty years, the conviction rate for violent crimes has remained more or less the same since 1986 (~40 convictions per 100k in the population).[81] While there may be some merit to the familiar complaint that we are locking away too many felons in prison, it is vividly clear that it cannot be said that we are incarcerating a super-abundance of violent felons.

To repeat, our immediate focus has been and will continue to be on the relation between rates of violent crime and rates of conviction. We will see that when conviction rates fall significantly, violent crime rates rise dramatically and that when conviction rates go up, the incidence of violent crimes generally goes down.[82] A useful point of entry into this topic is provided by a quick overview of criminal justice trends in the United States in the second half of the twentieth century.

Contrary to what you may have come to believe (since rival theories about the causes of crime are legion), economic measures do relatively little to lower the rate of such egregious crimes as murder, rape, kidnapping or armed robbery. Serious crime rates do not generally soar in times of depression or recession, nor fall dramatically in times of prosperity. For instance, during America's 'great depression' of the 1930s, serious crime rates were lower than they were in the 1920s and 1940s, times of comparative prosperity. There is general agreement among criminologists that joblessness and economic hard times per se are not powerful predictors of dramatic rises in serious crime, although they will explain up- or downticks in the rates of certain lesser crimes. Tellingly, the US saw its highest rates of serious crime in the twentieth century–a 500% rise over rates during the depression—during the period from 1965 to 1985, when the economy was growing, unemployment was relatively low, the country was the economic powerhouse of the world, great strides in civil rights were being made, and generous social welfare programs were in place. (This, recall, was the era Lyndon Johnson had dubbed the era of 'the Great Society'; he rarely pointed out that that phrase also captured the level of violent criminal activity.)

Figure 1. Crime and Expected Punishment for Serious Felonies, 1950-1998

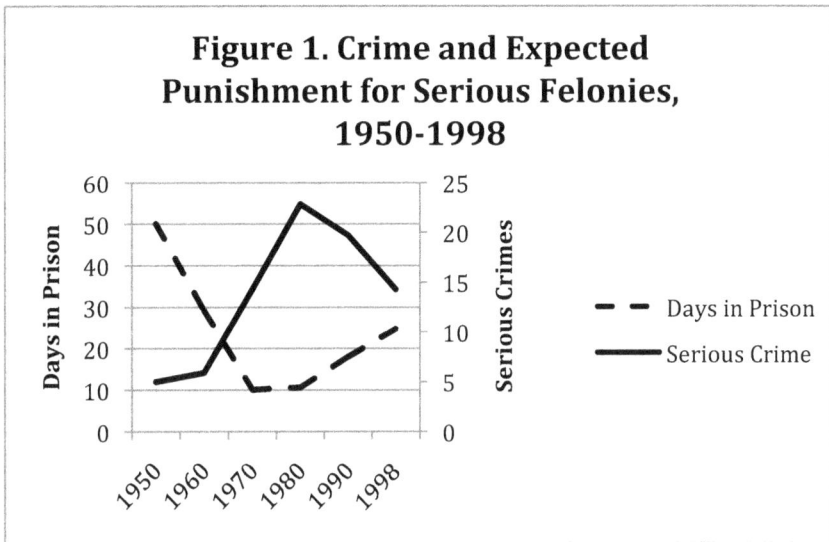

It will prove instructive to focus briefly on the half-century period from the mid 1950s to the late 1990s, for much was going on then that challenges traditional theories of crime control. Take, as our base line, 1950. In that year, as the solid line in Figure 1 shows, there were about 6 serious crimes (per 1,000 population), where a 'serious' crime is defined as homicide, rape, armed robbery, aggravated assault or burglary. A decade later the serious crime rate had climbed slightly to about 7 crimes. Then things began to get out of hand. By 1970, there were 12 crimes per thousand. A decade later, there were almost 23 serious crimes per thousand. In sum, between 1950 and 1980, the rate of serious crime rose by more than 380% over the base rate in 1950, despite the prodigious growth of police forces, generous social welfare programs, and a booming economy.

Eventually, the graph takes a mild turn for the better. By 1990, the rate was down to about 17 serious crimes per thousand and by 1997 it had fallen to more or less 15 per thousand. This latter pattern was clearly an improvement on that of the preceding two decades but was still 250% higher than the crime rate had been forty years earlier.

Two questions arise immediately: what caused the dramatic upturn in crime rates and (less urgently) what caused the milder decline after 1980? To find a plausible answer to the first question, consider the dotted line in figure (1). What we see here is a chart of the fluctuations in the *expected punishment* for a serious crime. The expected punishment (EP) is defined as the average time that a perpetrator spends in prison for each known crime. EP is most certainly not the average sentence meted out to someone convicted of the crime (that would be a much higher number). In 1950, the average person who committed a serious felony would spend 50 days in prison. By 1970, a serious felon would spend some 12 days behind bars. These EP numbers are so low because most felons were never arrested, many arrested felons were not charged, some charged felons were not convicted, and some convicted felons were not sent to prison or had their verdicts set aside on appeal, and most imprisoned felons served much less than their full sentences.[83]

The hypothesis under consideration here predicts that the crime rate will rise when the expected punishment declines and will decline when the EP rises. The data in figure (1) vividly bear out this claim. They show a *statistically significant* negative correlation between expected punishment and the crime rate. In 1950, the EP for a serious crime was 50 days in prison. Ten years later, this quantity had fallen 40% to 29.1 days. The crime rate between 1950 and 1960 rose by almost 20%. Then, between 1960 and 1980, things went haywire. The EP plummeted to 10 days' expected incarceration per crime, while the crime rate rose about 200%. Beginning in about 1980, the EP slowly began to rise, roughly doubling over the next 17 years. Meantime, and probably as a consequence, the rate of serious crimes fell by a third. It is data sets like these that explain why almost no one disputes that there is a powerful connection between expected punishment and the crime rate.

Figure (2) shows that a similar pattern is exhibited by homicide in this time frame. Decreases in expected punishment lead impressively to higher murder rates while increases in EP are followed by decidedly fewer murders.[84]

Figure 2. Murder and Expected Punishment, 1950-1998

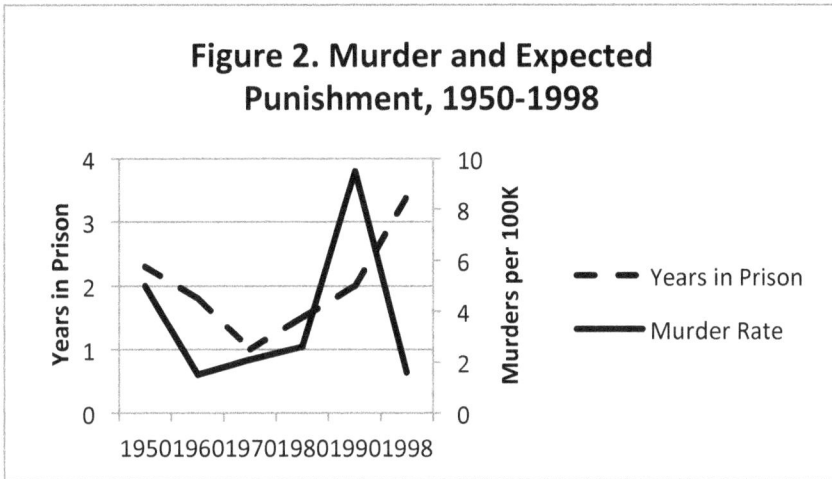

The EP is obviously measuring several things at the same time. Specifically, it is a function (among other things) of: the efficiency of the police in identifying and apprehending suspects, the effectiveness of the prosecutor in assembling a strong case, the skill of the jury in identifying guilty defendants, the severity of the sentence meted out by the judge or jury, the frequency with which verdicts are reversed on appeal, and the benevolence of parole boards in releasing prisoners before they have completed their sentences. The rich-texturedness of expected punishment thus takes us only part way towards our conclusion that conviction rates shape crime rates. Since conviction rates are only a part of the EP package, we need to look more directly at possible links between conviction rates and crime rates.

I propose to do so using the data such as those in Figures (2) and (3). In (2), we have a half-century of statistics about homicide in the US. In 1950, the annual homicide rate was about 2 per 100,000 in the population. The conviction rate for homicide (among those accused of the crime) was in the upper 60% range. Neither of these rates budged significantly for the next 15 years. Then, beginning in 1965, something interesting happened. Conviction rates, and thus expected punishments, for homicide fell in a five-year span from 67.4% to 34.9%, bringing with it a steep decline in expected punishment. At the same time, murder rates for whatever reason (and it is easy to speculate why), American prosecutors and juries around 1980 decided that too many murderers were escaping justice. During the next five years, rates of conviction and expected punishment slowly returned to their 1950 levels. Homicide rates fell by more than a quarter.

Much the same connection can be found in rape figures from the period. As Figure (3) shows, rape conviction rates peaked in the late 1980 at almost 2.5 rapes per thousand. In the early 1980s, they began to fall, as conviction rates rose. After a brief spike in 1990, they then fell precipitately, claiming fewer victims per thousand (roughly 1 per thousand). It is widely thought that the chief reason for the steep decline was the introduction of so-called 'rape-shield laws' in most states. The chief feature of these laws was to alter the usual rules of procedure governing rape cases, making it much easier to convict rapists than it had been earlier. That, of course, led to an increase in the conviction rate and EP rates and an associated decline in the frequency of the crime.

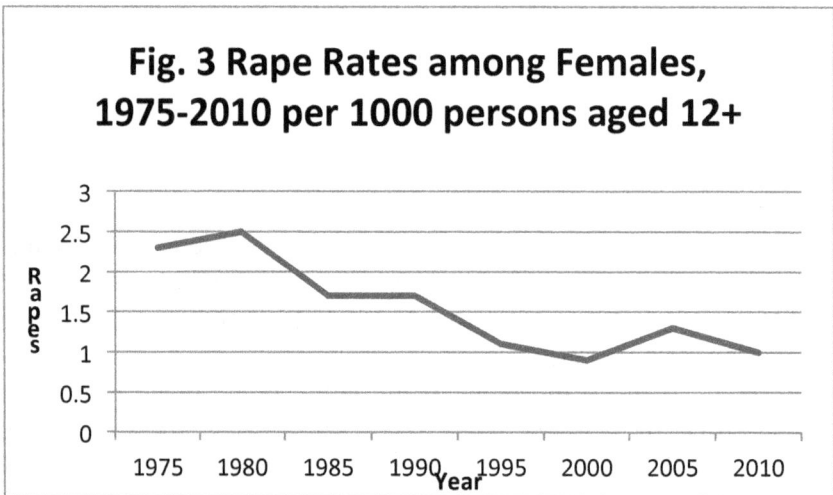

Fig. 3 Rape Rates among Females, 1975-2010 per 1000 persons aged 12+

The moral of the story seems clear: increasing the conviction rate generally lowers the violent crime rate, just as Beccaria predicted it would. [85] Contrariwise, lowering the conviction rate leads to more violent crime. That is *not* to say that the only way of lowering the crime rate is by convicting more of the guilty. Increasing sentences would doubtless have done something to lower the homicide and rape rates via longer incapacitation; so would decreasing the number of murderers and rapists who eluded police detection. It is no part of my brief to argue that raising conviction rates is the only way to control serious crime. It *is* important to my later arguments to show, however, that this is *a* way, and an effective one at that, to reduce the ordinary citizen's risk of ending up a violent crime victim. Figures 2 and 3 make that modest claim at least plausible.

While the evidence that I have cited is more impressionistic than robust, there are many detailed statistical studies leading to the same conclusion. They show, further, that the inverse relation between crime rates and conviction rates holds across a broad spectrum of countries. For instance, in a review of the relevant Dutch literature on this question, Catrien Bijleveld and Paul Smit conclude that "the conviction rate per offender ... [has] strong negative correlation with the recorded crime rate."[86] Carlos Alberto Carcach, surveying similar data from Australia, concludes: "The probability of imprisonment conditional on conviction is the one [and only] measure that has a consistently negative correlation with crime rates across all offenses."[87] In a classic study of crime in Britain, Pyle and Deadman studied the conviction rates between 1946 and 1991 and found that precisely this inverse relation between conviction rates and crime rates obtained.[88]

In general, rates of conviction prove to be good predictors of rates of serious crime (far better than any other, including the severity of sentences). If, for whatever reasons, a society begins convicting a smaller and smaller proportion of those charged with committing serious crimes, more and more people will evidently find the commission of such crimes worth the risk. Contrariwise, if the courts raise conviction rates, fewer crimes will be committed. This general correlation is borne out across the full spectrum of serious crimes and across a broad range of countries with different legal systems.

DETERRENCE OR INCAPACITATION?

In trying to understand more precisely how higher conviction rates lead to lower crime rates, there are two familiar but very distinct causal theories: deterrence and incapacitation. The former argues that higher conviction rates (and expected punishments) send out a warning that gives prospective felons pause about whether to commit crimes. If they expect a high likelihood of being caught and a long punishment, they will often think twice before committing a crime. The latter, incapacitation, has a very different focus. It doesn't suppose that high EP values would likely persuade would-be wrongdoers that crimes would be very costly to them. Instead, it focuses attention on the fact that, if conviction rates rise, then more serial felons will be apprehended and convicted, thereby literally preventing them from committing crimes, since they will be sitting in prison for several years. While both deterrence and incapacitation doubtless occur, I am more impressed by the data supporting the latter relation than the former one. Roughly my view boils down to the idea that if some deterrence occurs, splendid; but a much surer route to decreasing crime is, I believe, by incarcerating wrong-doers, especially serial offenders. The causal link between incapacitation and lower crime rates is much more direct and well-evidenced than is the deterrent hypothesis. I am not denying that deterrence does occur; it may well do. But when it comes to toting up the costs and benefits of higher rates of conviction, my principal focus will be on incapacitation. Locking away violent offenders—especially serial ones—is much more likely to lower crime frequencies than trying to frighten likely prospective offenders into living within the law.

The practical question obviously becomes: How do we bring about a higher conviction rate? Put simply, there are two ways to raise the conviction rate: a). arrest and bring to trial a larger proportion of those likely to have committed a serious crime and/or b). increase the rate of convictions among those who are arrested and probably guilty. Mechanism (a) is chiefly in the hands of the police, depending upon both their numbers, their resources and their competence and in the hands of the many victims of violence who refuse to report such acts. The second mechanism, (b), depends almost entirely on the efficacy of the courts in identifying and convicting those truly guilty arrestees who are actually arrested. Much of the rest of this book will be focused on the latter issue.

Beccaria, while lacking any hard evidence for his hunch, believed both that high rates of conviction would deter many would-be criminals from committing crimes and incapacitate those imprisoned from harming innocents. Convicted felons would serve as a warning to the much larger set of potential felons that there would be a steep price to pay if they disobeyed the law. Many modern authors are skeptical of the deterrence hypothesis, believing that would-be violent criminals are either incapable of making the requisite calculations of rational self-interest or are blissfully ignorant of the rates of conviction for the crimes they may be on the verge of committing.[89] For my part, I find the deterrence hypothesis intuitively plausible; if prospective criminals realize that they are highly likely to be caught, convicted and imprisoned for a serious crime, one would expect that to give some of them significant pause. Still, it is important to stress that the deterrence concept forms no essential part of the story that I am going to be telling here. This is because a). it is next to impossible to find a plausible technique for reliably assessing the amount of deterrence brought about by a certain form of policing and sentencing and b). as we shall see below, the vast majority of violent crimes go unpunished, which makes the deterrence threat much weaker than it would be if most felons were convicted. It is also true that so many factors (economic, educational, drug use, etc.) can impact crime rates that it is hard to be sure what has been the impact of various changes in criminal law policies. But, fortunately, there is a rival hypothesis to deterrence specifically, incapacitation—that convincingly explains the impressive link between conviction rates and crimes rates that is both more plausible than general deterrence and much easier to measure.

My hesitancy about factoring deterrence into the social contract derives from a belief that existing studies of the relation between incarceration and deterrence are generally badly designed. Typically, they look at what happens to crime rates in a given jurisdiction when there is a sudden, sharp increase or decrease in the length of the sentences meted out by the justice system in the jurisdiction. As we shall see in later chapters, there seems to be a strong link between a). reduced crime rates and tougher sentences and b). higher crimes rates and less harsh sentences. The problem, however, is that longer sentences result not only in some deterrence but likewise (and more importantly) in the *incapacitation* of more serial felons, a point that Beccaria likewise acknowledged. A serial felon free on the streets is apt to engage in repeated crimes; that same person, behind prison walls, can carry out no crimes on innocent citizens (save his fellow convicts). We have several independent routes to information about recidivism rates and can use those to gauge the impact of incapacitation on crime rates. It is vastly chancier to attribute a decrease in crime rates, following an increase in the sentencing schedule, to the decision of prospective offenders not to commit a crime, for fear of being sent to jail.

Even if deterrence were non-existent, it is clear that locking up those found guilty of committing crimes, at a minimum, prevents those prisoners themselves from committing crimes (except within the confines of prison itself) during their incarceration.[90] Even among those experts who have frequently voiced serious doubts about the efficacy of deterrence, many (e.g., Paul Robinson) concede that there is ample evidence to show that incarcerating sizable numbers of offenders lowers the crime rate.[91] The principal reason for this is that most serous felons sent to prison are *serial offenders*. They have typically been arrested numerous times before they go to prison and return to commit multiple crimes after their later release from prison. What imprisonment represents, at the very least, is a span of time when habitual offenders are not at liberty to indulge their chosen calling. Even if high conviction rates were to do nothing whatever to deter crime on the part of those who are free to walk the streets, they make it impossible for the incarcerated serial criminal—for the duration of his or her incarceration—to commit crimes.

If delinquents were not serial offenders, incapacitation would not be a very promising strategy. If a disposition to commit serious crimes were a randomly occurring trait in the general population, then locking away those who are known to have committed such crimes would predictably reduce crime by only a small amount (specifically, by that proportion of the general population that the prison population represents). But we have ample evidence that the vast majority of serious crimes are committed by recurrent (sometimes called 'habitual') offenders.

In 2002, for example, Logan and Levin published a study of approximately 275,000 prisoners released from American prisons in 1994.[92] Within that cohort, 93% had been arrested for a previous crime (prior to the crime they were then serving time for) and more than 80% had prior convictions going back even further. The *average* prisoner in this set already had nine previous arrests and four previous convictions before his current stay in prison. A quarter of them had been arrested at least 25 times prior to their current incarceration. (Some 18,000 of these prior arrests had been for homicide and 45,000 for rape or sexual assault.) More than 6% of these prisoners had been arrested more than 45 times prior to their current imprisonment. In short, many of those sent to prison are chronically serial criminals. You can zero in more closely on the seriality of our set of defendants arrested for a violent crime by looking at more recent data from 2009 in Table 3.

Table 3. Prior Offenses of Defendants Arrested for a Violent Crime, 2009[93]					
No prior arrest/ (conviction)	≥1 prior arrest/ (conviction)	1 prior arrest/ (conviction)	2-4 prior arrests/ (conviction ons)	5-9 prior arrests/ (conviction ons)	≥10 prior arrests/ (convict ions)
31% (47%)	69% (53%)	8% (12%)	16% (19%)	15% (12%)	30% (9%)

Further, most of them remain recidivists for a significant time *after* serving their time. Sixty-seven percent of these released prisoners were rearrested within three years after their release for having committed a felony (30 percent are known to have committed a felony within six months of their release), and about half of all those released were convicted of a new offense. Indeed, these 275,000 offenders were charged with more than 750,000 crimes within three years of their release. This cohort accounted, at a minimum, for more than eight per cent of the homicides and more than five percent of the rapes that occurred in 1995, the year immediately following their release. (And presumably they committed many other crimes that were not pinned on them by the courts since only about 22% of violent crimes result in a conviction and only about 37% even lead to an arrest.)

It is important to recall that we are speaking here of a relatively small proportion of prisoners, specifically, those released from US prisons in one twelve-month period. If we imagine a larger cohort of (say) those released over a period of three or five years, it is easy to project what the effect of their freedom would be on the rates of serious crime. Yet that is precisely what we are doing when we tolerate a conviction rate as low as it was in the 1960s and 1970s, when the vast majority of those arrested for serious crimes were not convicted and thus not incapacitated.[94]

The same phenomenon of the offender with numerous previous offenses to his credit shows up in other countries as well. One study commissioned by the British Home Office found that 51 percent of those sentenced to prison in the 18-20 year age group already had 10 or more convictions.[95] The same source reports on a survey taken in 2000 of a large group of British males who had just been sentenced to prison. One conclusion of that self-survey is that, on average, *each* of these criminals claimed to have committed "offenses at around 140 per year in the period at liberty before they were imprisoned."[96] Even if there was some boastful exaggeration here, and we accordingly reduce the estimate by an order of magnitude, we still have to conclude that sending a cohort of one thousand serial felons to prison for two years would prevent something like 28,000 crimes.

Studies by criminologists at Britain's Home Office estimate that the average felon in a British prison would, if free, be committing about 13 crimes per year (leaving aside drug-related offenses), if not for his incarceration. Models they have developed predict that a 15% increase in the conviction rate (meaning here: the number of convictions per crime) would, by virtue of incarceration alone, lead to a one per cent reduction in serious crime rates.[97] Supposing a ratio of that sort applies to the US

42

context, we can plausibly conjecture that by increasing the conviction rate for aggravated assault by 15% (from 148,000 to 170,000 per year), one could reduce the frequency of violent crimes by about 17,000 per year.[98] Even if about five percent of those additional convictions were false (as opposed to the current three percent), this would mean incurring an additional 1,100 false convictions in order to prevent some 22,000 crimes. Unless you would prefer to suffer as a victim of aggravated assault twenty times rather than be falsely convicted of assault once, the trade-off would appear to be worth it. The object of rehearsing these grim statistics is to underscore: a). that most of those currently in prison are habitual offenders and b). that many will resume their criminal activities soon after release from prison. There is thus every reason to believe that, if these felons had not been incarcerated (as a result of a false negative), the crime rate in the years immediately subsequent to their imprisonment would have been significantly higher than it was.

There is little room for doubt that convicting more criminals reduces crime rates by temporarily reducing recidivism. The crime statistician Daniel Nagin has concluded that "incapacitation effects make a substantial contribution to crime reduction" and that "the combined deterrent and incapacitation effect generated by the collective actions of the police, courts and prison system is very large."[99] In their book- length study of incapacitation, Zimring and Hawkins assert that empirical studies repeatedly bear out the hypothesis that "incapacitation is … an important, but by no means exclusive, means of social defense against serious crime."[100]

While most criminologists accept at face value the evidence that the imprisonment of felons, especially serial felons, does much to lower the serious crime rate via incapacitation, there are skeptics. Many of them subscribe to what we might call the ecological-niche model of crime. On this view, there are opportunities to commit crime and, when those currently active as criminals are incarcerated, a new cohort steps forward to fill the empty niche. Consider the crime of dealing in drugs. There is clearly a ready market for drug dealers. If the police and the courts manage to convict large chunks of the current dealers, there are probably others who will gladly fill their shoes, reaping the handsome profits to be made. Unfortunately, this hypothesis (once propounded by Émile Durkheim) explains far too much. Among other things, it predicts that crime rates will remain flat more or less whatever the police and courts do to incapacitate those currently involved in crime. This cannot be squared with the impressive correlations we have seen between changes in conviction rates and subsequent violent crime rates. The resigned fatalism about crime inherent in the niche hypothesis is simply inconsistent with the dramatic shifts in patterns of serious crime that we have examined here. More relevantly for our purposes, the vast majority of violent crimes are not the result of organized crime. Taking a rapist off the streets via incarceration is not likely to bring someone else forward to replace him.

Still, a note of caution is in order so that no one interprets my claims here more ambitiously than I intend them. My focus in the rest of this book will be entirely on the so- called 'serious' crimes. I believe that the evidence for the effects of incarceration on the rates of these four crimes is impressive. But this hypothesis, to which I am committed, leaves wholly open the question whether incapacitation works equally well for lesser crimes. I make no claims about whether (for instance) shoplifting, drug trafficking, white-collar fraud or car theft exhibit the same negative correlation with conviction rates that the serious crimes do. In defense of the limited scope of my claims here, I would add that it seems plausible to hold that the acid test for judging fulfillment of the social contract is whether the state can rein in the most serious crimes.

One further disclaimer is in order before we proceed further down the road I want to travel. The literature of criminology and of the philosophy of law is replete with rival theories about the *aim(s)* of punishment. Some see it as retribution or 'just deserts', others as rehabilitation. Some (like Beccaria) argue that the only acceptable rationale for punishment is crime reduction. I take no stand on that vexed question, content to observe that, whatever the ostensible purpose of the penal sanction, it is empirically true that incarcerating more perpetrators of serious crimes reduces the future frequency of those crimes. The robustness of this relationship, supposing it to be so, entails nothing whatever about the state's rationale for punishing felons. Pragmatist that I am, I take comfort from the fact that punishing many felons dramatically reduces my risks of being a victim of a serious crime. As someone sympathetic to the social contract, I think that curtailing serious crimes constitutes a crucial part of the state's fulfillment of its contractual obligations to protect its citizens. Still, I remain agnostic about the aims of punishment. For that reason, I say nothing in this chapter about the severity of sentences and their possible role in reducing crime (save noting that sentence severity appears to have less to do with crime reduction than likelihood of conviction does). In chapter 8, however, I will address the sentencing issue at length.

Chapter 3 False Outcomes and the Social Contract

> The first duty of the Government is to afford protection to its citizens. —Congressman John F. Farnsworth (1867)[101]
>
> [A]lmost all criminal defendants--including most of my own clients--are factually guilty of the crimes they have been charged with. The criminal lawyer's job, for the most part, is to represent the guilty, and if possible--to get them off. —Alan Dershowitz[102]

As we saw in chapter 2, there is wide agreement that one of the key provisions of the social contract we live by is that the state should make strenuous efforts to protect its citizens from being seriously harmed by their fellow citizens (especially those whom the state believes pose a risk to life and limb). In return for abandoning some of the liberties we might enjoy in the proverbial state of nature, we choose to live in a state with a rule of law, where the bad guys are sometimes punished and the law-abiding citizens are at least partially shielded from being victimized by those minded to do grievous harm to others.

There is likewise unanimity about a second key part of the social contract; to wit, that great efforts must be taken to lessen the risk that an innocent person, charged with a crime, will become a false positive. These two clauses of the implicit social contract are, as I have already explained, in serious tension. Many of the steps that we might take to reduce the risk of an innocent defendant becoming a false positive can dramatically impact our efforts at reducing violent crime. The harder we make it to prove a defendant's guilt, the more we guarantee that many of the guilty will escape punishment and recidivate. That not only leaves them on the streets to do further bad deeds but also encourages others to resort to crime, thinking that they can probably get away with it too. If, on the other hand, we make it easier to prove guilt, then the risk that an innocent person goes to prison rises.

Our society, including its legal scholars, its judges and its legislators, has failed dismally at initiating a serious discussion about how this acute dilemma should be resolved.[103] I believe that the issue can be reasonably aired and rationally resolved if and only if we compare the respective costs of the two principal risks that the legal system imposes on society: the harms resulting from false positives and false negatives. As we already noted, Lord William Blackstone, the famous English legal theorist, proposed in the middle of the eighteenth century that we should aim at a legal system that produces at least ten times more false negatives than false positives. That idea has been around (and dominant) ever since.

The absence of a reasoned version of this ratio is an even more serious matter than it might appear to be. Blackstone's core intuition evidently was that it is important to have in place a policy that makes us neutral as between whether a case ends in an acquittal or a conviction. Without such neutrality, we would have interminable debates about whether the system was fair and just. What would make us neutral about trial outcomes would be an assurance that the harms done over the long run by false positives and the harms done by false negatives were reflected in the frequency with which those results emerged. In short, we want a legal system that seriously takes into account the harms of *each* type of error and then insists that the trial system should be structured so that it produces outcomes in which the harms of the two errors are roughly balanced against their relative frequencies. (That is, the more harmful an outcome, the less likely we want it to occur.) Blackstone's idea has often been interpreted as telling us that if (say) the harm done by a false positive is really 10 times greater than the harm done by a false negative, then we should structure our trials so that we will have roughly ten times as many false negatives as false positives. On this premise, we want a system in which:

$$[(\text{Number}_{F+}) \times (\text{Harm}_{F+})] = [(\text{Number}_{F-}) \times (\text{Harm}_{F-})]$$

Because Blackstone opined that a false positive was ten times more harmful than a false negative, he concluded that a legitimate legal system should have ten times as many of the latter as the former. His intuition about linking harms and frequencies of error occurrence was right on the mark. Where he blew it was in his arbitrary and unexplained choice of a harm ratio of 10-to-1. He could scarcely have done otherwise, given the primitive state of then-available empirical information about what were the harms and the magnitudes of those harms associated with the two errors. By contrast, we are now in a position to reason much more convincingly about approximately what are the respective harms of our two errors. When we digest and internalize that information, we can replace his 10-to-1 hunch with a much more reliable measure. That ambitious task is precisely what we shall attempt to do in the next chapter.

The continuing interest in trying to fix the Blackstone ratio is scarcely surprising. If—and this is a big if—we can calculate what would be a normatively appropriate fraction for this ratio, then we could simultaneously determine what the criminal standard of proof should be and we could ascertain whether existing legal practices are compliant with the Laplacian version of the social contract (already discussed in chapter 2).

Table 4. Violent Crimes US 2008[104]	
Victims[105]	1.7m
Murder	16.2k
Rape	89k
Armed Robbery	441k
Aggravated Assault	835k
Other	330k
Annual risk to an American aged >12 of being a victim	0.64%
Crimes reported to police	848k
Suspects arrested & charged[106]	595k
Crimes reported but unsolved	253k
Convictions by trial[107]	30k
Convictions by plea[108]	333k
Cases dropped or dismissed	217k
Acquitted at trial	15k
Arrestees with Prior Arrests/Convictions[109]	411k (69%)

If, as the Laplace version of the social contract requires, we need to ascertain (and then compare) the harm done by the false negatives and false positives associated with the outcomes of criminal procedures dealing with violent crimes, then we need to determine two sorts of things: a). approximately how often each type of error occurs; and b) the respective social and moral costs associated with each type of error. The remainder of this chapter will deal with the first question. The second question will be addressed in chapter 4. Table 4 will serve as the starting point of our analysis. It summarizes several salient features of violent crimes in the US in 2008, a year that will serve as the paradigm case for analysis in the ensuing chapters.

Figure 4 summarizes some of the salient features of that profile. It shows vividly how the numbers shrink as one moves along the line from the crime to a final disposition.

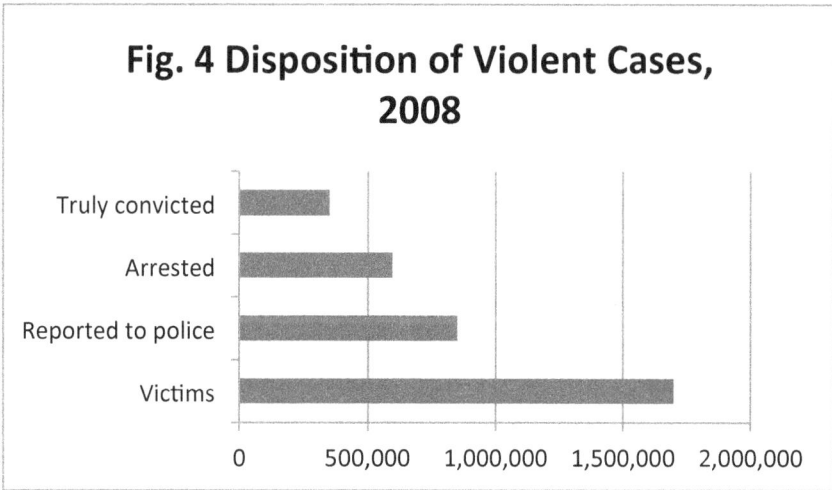

Fig. 4 Disposition of Violent Cases, 2008

Before we turn to assessing the values needed for the social contract calculation, a few words of warning are in order. The data we have just seen are precise and reliable. But, standing alone, they are insufficient to enable us to judge compliance with the contract. That latter task requires estimates of how frequently false positives and false negatives emerge in handling violent crime cases. As already noted, the government and the legal system seem to have a constitutional (lower-case) predisposition not to inquire into such matters, perhaps out of fear that collecting and revealing such information might lower confidence in the legal system. We shall have to dig out our own data. One important source of information about the frequency (and to some extent the causes) of false positives is the network of privately-funded Innocence Projects scattered around the country (and often based in university law schools). I shall draw heavily on their statistics. Much more problematic, and thus more speculative, will be our estimate of the frequency (and, in the next chapter, the harms) of false negatives. Although relatively little has been written on that subject, there are data sources which, if handled with some care, will enable us to make a plausible stab at divining the approximate frequency and costs of false acquittals. It must be stressed, before we take on that task, that the most we can hope for is a reasonable approximation to those values. Perhaps some day, the justice system itself will eventually realize that it has been very amiss on that front and put the situation right. Until that occurs, the criminal law has to be regarded as a dismal failure as a system of inquiry.

ESTIMATING THE FREQUENCY OF FALSE POSITIVES

As we know, a false positive occurs when a defendant is accused and convicted of (or confesses to) a crime that he did not commit. How, you might ask, can we possibly tell how many false positives there are in a large sample of trials and pleas? There is a general consensus that the answer to this question can best be found by looking carefully at the proportion of criminal convictions that end up in an exoneration of the convicted defendants. There have been numerous studies of this issue in the last couple of decades, many of them arising from the work of some 90+ Innocence Projects now active in many parts of the country. A key focus of this network has been DNA-based exonerations, of which there have been about 250 since 2000.[110] Such exonerations are rightly regarded as the most telling sort since the error rates associated with the use of DNA are generally tiny. Given that there have been more than 3m persons convicted of violent crimes since 2000, this number (250+) seems rather modest.

But it is important to understand that there are many exonerations beyond those that rely on DNA evidence. The routes leading to an official exoneration are diverse: key witnesses for the prosecution recant their initial testimony; third parties plausibly confess to the crime after the trial of an innocent; the post-trial discovery of signs of egregious police or prosecutorial misconduct in their handling of the evidence in the case; the incompetence or partiality of persons called by the prosecution as 'expert witnesses'; the discovery of exculpatory evidence not available prior to the conviction; evidence of a forced confession from the defendant; and misleading testimony by informants and eyewitnesses.

I have no quarrels with the idea that the frequency of exonerations can serve as a lead to how often innocent defendants are convicted. Indeed, I shall rely heavily on such data. However, it is often said that using exonerations as indicators of false positives drastically understates the frequency of false positives. After all, an exoneration often depends on the fortuitous emergence of exculpatory evidence not introduced at trial. Indisputably, there are some truly innocent defendants whose exonerating evidence has disappeared beyond retrieval. (Witnesses vanish or die or their memory of the events surrounding the crime has become fuzzy; sometimes the preservation of relevant evidence by the police is haphazard; and so on). In that sense, the data about exonerations serve—it is sometimes said—to indicate a *lower* bound on the frequency of false positives. Even so, a couple of studies have been designed in such a way that it is reasonable to infer that they capture the majority of the false positives for certain sorts of crime (especially rape and homicide).[111] Still, some researchers continue to suggest that the *known* exonerations are but the tip of the proverbial iceberg.

What such claims conveniently ignore is that many of the known exonerations, if taken as a token for the number of false positives, may well *overstate* the frequency of the latter. The reason why is easy to understand. Begin with an important home truth: an exoneration is *not* necessarily a proof that the exonerated convict did not commit the crime. It typically emerges after a convicted felon petitions for an exoneration hearing, has the petition granted, and then presents such new evidence of his innocence as he can. In deciding the new case, the judge (or in some jurisdictions the jury) must determine whether the exculpatory evidence shows that that there is probably a reasonable doubt that the defendant did not commit the crime. If the judge concludes in favor of the defendant, that is considered an exoneration and the defendant is released from prison and his slate is wiped clean. With any luck, he will get a hefty payment to boot for the state having wrongly convicted him.

But how strong an indicator of factual innocence is such an 'exoneration'? The answer to that question obviously hinges on the criteria used to decide whether to approve an exoneration request. Those criteria vary from state to state but the general practice is that, to be able to exonerate a convicted felon, the judge or jury must come to believe there to be 'clear and convincing evidence' that no rational person—considering the original trial evidence as well as the evidence newly presented by the petitioner—could be sure beyond a reasonable doubt that the defendant committed the crime for which he was earlier convicted.[112] If that seems rather a mouthful, it can be represented more succinctly as "an exoneration requires that the judge/jury be $\geq 70\%$ sure that the aggregate evidence is not strong enough to establish a $\geq 90\%$ probability that the defendant committed the crime."

Now, is satisfaction of that particular rule compelling evidence that the defendant is factually innocent? Of course not. Even if the judge could be 100% sure that no rational juror could believe that defendant's apparent guilt—including the new exculpatory evidence—reached the threshold of proof beyond a reasonable doubt, that does *not* establish the defendant's factual innocence. What's going on here is a common confusion between factual innocence and legal innocence. Obviously, if the newly recalculated apparent guilt of a defendant fails to reach the beyond-reasonable-doubt threshold, then the defendant should be freed from prison and declared *legally* innocent.

Legal innocence, as we have seen, is vastly different from factual innocence. Is the fact that someone has just been exonerated a strong indicator that he did not commit the crime? The answer is often clearly negative. Suppose that a judge concludes that the likely degree of guilt of a defendant seeking exoneration falls in the neighborhood of 75% or 80%. In those circumstances, he could be confident that no rational person would convict said defendant, since the usual standard is far from being satisfied. The defendant would be exonerated and so he should be in the sense that his level of apparent guilt does not satisfy the prevailing standard. But if the probability of the defendant's guilt is falls anywhere in the range between 50% and 90%, it remains likely that he is factually guilty (that is, he committed the crime) even though he is not legally guilty and will and should be exonerated. Just as an acquittal does not establish that the defendant did not commit the crime but only that he is legally innocent, an exoneration may well be quite compatible with the hypothesis that the defendant actually committed the crime. It is also worthy of note that 80% of exonerations emerge from cases tried earlier by jury, 7% from trials by judge and only 12% from plea bargains, even though some 90+% of convictions arise from the latter source.[113]

Sometimes, of course, the exculpatory evidence presented by the defendant will go so far as to make his factual innocence much more likely than his factual guilt. Many of the DNA exonerations fall in that category. But most exonerations are not so decisively in favor of defendant's factual innocence.[114] When they are not, and given the criterion for a favorable exoneration decision, one must be leery about accepting the thesis that exoneration is ipso facto a strong token of factual innocence.

Exonerations can emerge in other ways than the ones I have just described. They, too, sometimes seem to be less than ringing proofs of the defendants' factual innocence. For instance, a pardon offered by a state governor or the President is often counted as an exoneration. I will offer one concrete example of why I am skeptical that all or most exonerations involve proofs of factual innocence. The case is that of Robert Charles Cruz, which figures prominently as an instance of 'factual innocence' on the website of the Death Penalty Information Center.[115] In 1981, Cruz was tried and convicted of paying for a contract killing of his two business associates in Phoenix the year before and was sentenced to death. He appealed the verdict and it was overturned on a technicality. He was re-tried. A hung jury emerged at the second trial. The prosecutor re-initiated proceedings and, again, the jury was hung. At his fourth trial, Cruz was convicted unanimously but that verdict was overturned on appeal because there were no hispanics on his jury. Finally, in 1995, Cruz was tried once again and this time was acquitted. This sequence of events (two convictions, two mistrials and one acquittal) is widely cited as an exoneration, 'proving' Cruz's factual innocence.

While it is conceivable that Cruz did not, as the charges alleged, contract for the killings of his business associates, the two prior convictions point more strongly to Cruz's factual guilt than the one not-guilty verdict points to his factual innocence. How could one possibly argue that two convictions, two mistrials and one acquittal constitute anything close to a 'proof' of factual innocence? (Remember that even in the final trial, where Cruz was acquitted, the only legitimate inference we can draw is that the jury unanimously concluded that his guilt had not been proven beyond a reasonable doubt.) But that does *not* make it likely that he did not commit the crime, only that it is not certain beyond a reasonable doubt that he did so. Once again, cases described as 'exonerations' can often be dubious indicators of factual innocence.

Nonetheless, an exoneration still remains the most promising indicator of innocence we have to hand and I will employ it here, while insisting that the estimate itself may be either higher or lower than the true value. Here are the estimates arrived at in some of the best and most widely-cited studies of exonerations and false positives: Samuel Gross (2005 estimate), 2.1% false positive rate (FPR)[116]; Kalven and Zeisel (1966 estimate), 3% FPR[117]; Michael Risinger (2007), 3.8% FPR[118]; Samuel Gross (2014 estimate), 4.1% FPR[119]. The mean estimate here is 3.25%. Of the three best studies of false positives in England, the mean estimate was 2.3%.[120] Since I am mildly skeptical for reasons already indicated about whether all exonerations represent discoveries of false positives, I will for purposes of the calculations in this book assume that *approximately 3% of current convictions involve factually innocent persons.*[121] This assumption – that 97% of convictions involve the truly guilty—will loom very large in the arguments of this book since that percentage is the lynchpin for numerous interesting inferences. Other studies of a quite different kind bear out this conjecture. For instance, Ramsey and Frank interviewed some 800 judges, police officials, prosecutors and defenses attorneys, asking them to estimate how often false positives occurred in criminal prosecutions in their jurisdiction. Among the respondents, 96% of the police reported that the rate of false positives was ≤3%; among the prosecutors, 97% estimated ≤3%; 87% of judges thought the false positive rate was in the same range. Even among the only outliers, 40% of the defense attorneys opined the same thing. More than half of the defense attorneys agreed that fewer than 5% of those convicted were truly innocent.[122]

You might suspect that the known false positives, which generated our estimate of only 3% of them, are incomplete. After all, it is easy to imagine defendants who are genuinely innocent but who can't readily be exonerated because of (say) loss of evidence, or disappearance of an alibi witness. While that is certainly possible, it is at least as likely that the 3% false positive rate greatly overstates the frequency of that sort of mistake. Ponder this: as table 1 in chapter I shows, some 90% of convictions emerge not from trials but from plea bargains. When it is said that the false positive rate is about 3-4%, those estimates arise principally with exonerations emerging *from trials* not from pleas. Indeed, as one pair of Innocence Project gurus have pointed out:
"Overall, 8% of exonerees in our data were convicted by guilty pleas (71/873), a higher rate than in the 2003 Report – 6% (20/340) – but startlingly few for a system in which 95% of felony convictions are the products of guilty pleas."[123]

That is another way of saying that 92% of known false positives come from trials, while only 8% come from pleas, despite the fact that the overwhelming majority of convictions come from pleas. In another study of 466 recent felony exonerations, Gazal-Ayal and Tor report that 90% of false convictions emerge from jury trials even though trials produce only about 10% of total convictions.[124] If we suppose that the false positive rates in trials dealing with violent crimes is about 3%, it is clear that the false positive rate for pleas may be well below 0.1% and nothing like the 3% error rate that I am conceding to my opponents. To the best of my knowledge, there is *no* study of this question that presents data showing that the false positive rate for plea bargains is anything close to 3%. It seems natural to infer from such information that trials by jury (or judge) are much more likely to yield errors than plea bargains do.

Such a conclusion would strongly reinforce my thesis (to be explored in the next chapter) that false negatives generate much greater harm than false positives do. But rather than go that route—and in the interest of making my claims for revising the system appear generous to my critics—I will for these purposes grant that the false positive rate overall may be as high as 3% for both pleas and for trials, even while I entertain, and the evidence supports, very serious doubts that (where pleas are concerned) it is anything close to that.

ESTIMATING THE FREQUENCY OF FALSE NEGATIVES

False negatives occur under two circumstances: when a guilty defendant is acquitted at trial and when a guilty defendant has the charges against him dropped or dismissed by the judge or prosecutor. Almost no one tries to measure how often either type of false negative occurs. That is partly understandable, given the fact that the legal system prohibits a judicial investigation into the correctness of an acquittal since the double jeopardy principle guarantees that acquittals are fixed in stone. The relative invisibility of false negatives complicates my task in this section. Thanks in no small part to the general societal indifference to false negatives, there have been virtually no efforts to design empirical studies that would yield estimates of false acquittals. That means that my efforts here to estimate how often they occur must depend on a plethora of *indirect* indicators. With a bit of ingenuity, it is possible to find data that provide strong clues as to how often a guilty defendant is acquitted at trial and in the pre-trial process. The resulting inferences are not precise and I will try to explain why. As we look at various data sources not initially designed to measure false negatives, we will see that they nonetheless provide significant information about when and why false acquittals occur, thereby enabling us to make an approximate estimate of their frequency.

Lord William Blackstone (1723-1780) and his modern followers, independent of any data whatever, reckon that false negatives are (and should be) ten times more common than false positives. This is, on any analysis, an absurd notion, not least because it is often not even susceptible of implementation.

Consider the following scenario: suppose we have a series of 1,000 trials. Suppose that the verdicts are distributed as follows: 825 guilty verdicts and 175 not-guilty verdicts. Suppose, further, that 25 of the guilty verdicts are false positives (a 3% false positive rate). That means that the Blackstone ratio requires us to produce some 250 false negatives. But the total quantity of acquittals available is 175 (1,000-825). Even if *every* acquittal was of a guilty person, we would still be unable to find the 250 required by Blackstone's ratio. Well, that creates a bit of a conundrum. If this is mildly perplexing, bear in mind that I have elsewhere proven that most of the verdict patterns in American trials, like this hypothetical one, simply do *not* allow, not even in principle, satisfaction of the Blackstone demand of 10 false negatives for every false positive.[125]

A more subtle and realizable version of the Blackstone ratio would abandon the idea of ten false negatives for every false positive and instead propound the idea that what we want is that the *proportion* of acquittals that are false is ten times greater than the proportion of convictions that are false. In our scenario above, that would mean that we want a 30% error rate for acquittals, i.e., 63 false negatives. That outcome is conceivable, but it still leaves us with a ratio (of ratios) that is entirely an article of faith rather than a reasoned proposal about what we should be targeting. (I will say more about the ten-for-one idea in the next chapter.)

My discussion of how to estimate the frequency of false negatives will fall into two parts, reflecting the stark differences between the sources of errors in pleas and the sources of error in trials.

i). *Estimating the frequency of false negatives at trials.* As Table 1 made clear, trial acquittals represent a very small subset of overall acquittals. Specifically, of the 232k defendants who were arrested in 2008 for, but not convicted of, a violent crime, only 6% (15k) of the freed defendants were products of a trial. Conventional wisdom has it that most defendants acquitted at trial are probably factually guilty. After all, so the usual argument goes, these defendants wouldn't even be going to trial unless the prosecutor believed that he had a strong chance of persuading jurors that these defendants were guilty beyond a reasonable doubt.

While this argument does not involve any data (and we will soon be looking at one that does), it enjoys a prima facie plausibility. Even if the prosecutor sometimes overestimates the strength of his case against the defendant, it seems reasonable to suppose that most defendants winning an acquittal at trial have an apparent guilt in the range from about 70% to 90%. In such circumstances, that means, at a minimum, either that the prosecutor is an obscenely bad judge of the strength of his cases or that the jury concluded that the defendant is probably guilty but that the evidence is too weak to warrant a conviction. One's initial inclination in such circumstances is to suppose that at least half of those who are acquitted at trial actually committed the crime(s) they are charged with but the evidence allowed room for a rational doubt about defendant's guilt. Accordingly, one might assume that about half of those 15k acquitted at trial are guilty, giving us some 7.5k false negatives, even though my strong suspicion is that the true figure is higher than that. There are two powerful reasons for thinking that this simplistic assumption understates the frequency of guilt among those acquitted at trial. They are as follows:

a). One potential source for corroborating that hunch involves looking at some interesting data from Scotland. There, the justice system uses BARD as the standard, as in the United States, and trial by jury. However, the Scottish system consists of *three* verdicts rather than the usual two: 'guilty', 'guilt not proven' and 'not guilty'.[126] The intermediate verdict gives us a point of entry for trying to pin down the rate of false acquittals. A guilt-not-proven verdict is delivered when i). the jury is persuaded that the defendant is factually guilty (that is, $p(guilt) \geqq 0.5$) but ii). the jury is not convinced of that guilt beyond a reasonable doubt. Both the not-guilty and the guilt-not-proven verdicts count as official acquittals but they send decidedly different messages. In a study of criminal prosecutions in 2005 and 2006 done by the Scottish government, it turned out that 71% of those defendants tried for homicide and acquitted received a 'guilt-not-proven' verdict.[127] That means that about 7-in-10 acquittals for murder in Scotland involved defendants regarded by the jurors as having probably committed the crime.

b). A different way of estimating the frequency of false acquittals at trials emerges from the monumental study by Kalven and Zeisel of some 3,500+ jury trials in the US. The researchers asked judges in each of the trials that resulted in an acquittal whether, in the opinion of the judge, the case was 'close' (meaning the apparent guilt of the acquitted defendant verged on proof beyond a reasonable doubt) or whether it was a 'clear' acquittal (meaning that defendant's apparent guilt was well below the BARD standard). According to the responses to this question (dealing with 1,191 cases), judges indicated that, in their opinions, only 5% of the trials resulted in 'clear' acquittals; by contrast, 52% of the cases were, in the view of judges, 'clear for conviction'.[128]

Since our data in Figure 5 in the next chapter indicate that about one-third of trials for violent crimes result in an acquittal, the Kalven-Zeisel data would seem to entail that only about 15% of the acquittals are 'clearly' acquittals, while some 85% are, in the opinion of the presiding judge, close cases. If, as in our test case from 2008, there are some 15k acquittals, we can assume that more than 12k of them are close enough to warrant an assumption that these are probably factually guilty defendants, even if their apparent guilt fails to eliminate all reasonable doubts. (As I will show in chapter 6, we have good reason to expect that the ratio of truly guilty to truly innocent in the region below, but close to, the standard of proof is likely to be greater than 20-to-1.)

Putting the two data sets together (71% false negatives in Scotland; 80% in the Kalven-Zeisel study), it seems fair to say that most of those acquitted at trial of a violent crime were nonetheless regarded by the jurors and judges as probably guilty and thereby are reasonably assumed to be false negatives.[129] Accordingly, I shall hereafter assume that, among those 15k acquittals that emerged in trials for violent crimes in the US in 2008, some 11.2k (75%) were false negatives.

Duff and Findlay conjecture that one-third of all jury acquittals and one-fifth of all bench acquittals are of the form 'guilt not proven', that is, they involved defendants whom jurors (or judges) thought to be probably guilty but not guilty enough to remove all reasonable doubts.[130] Their estimate is more modest than mine because they don't reckon with the fact that a significant number of acquitted defendants will be truly guilty but nonetheless appear to have a degree of apparent guilt that falls just below the threshold for guilt.

Even though it is conventional wisdom that most defendants acquitted at trial are factually guilty (given the robustness of proof beyond a reasonable doubt), it has been argued by a few scholars that a sizable portion of acquitted defendants are factually innocent. For instance, Givelber and Farrell have published an entire book devoted to trying to make the case that the factually innocent are abundant among those acquitted at trial.[131] At the end of their book, however, they concede "we cannot establish through empirical research that many (or indeed most) of the acquitted are innocent." Nonetheless, they continue to assert that "the data are entirely consistent with this possibility." (p. 143) This is puzzling. The fact that existing data of any sort are merely 'consistent' with an hypothesis does not show that the hypothesis is probably correct, only that the data do not refute it. (The fact that there is additional sunspot activity this month is consistent with, but no support for, the hypothesis that I may be getting a cold!) The lack of a known refutation is not a powerful argument for the truth of a thesis as important as this one.

b). *False negatives in the dropping of charges (pre-trial acquittals).* The much more intriguing question concerns the true guilt or innocence not of those 15k defendants acquitted at trial in 2008 but of those 217k arrestees against whom charges were dropped or dismissed. Such decisions obviously came prior to trial, usually at the initiative of a prosecutor, sometimes at the initiative of a judge. We know that of those arrested by the police and charged with violent crimes in 2008, some 37% never made it to a trial or a plea bargain; the prosecutor or the pre-trial judge, in effect, acquits them.[132] But how many of them were truly innocent? Fortunately, there are two very large studies that shed substantial light on the answer to that crucial question. Both depend on the responses of thousands of prosecutors who were quizzed about the reasons why they dropped the charges that they did. One such study, analyzing FBI-initiated prosecutions nationwide, provides annual data about the reasons why federal prosecutors have dropped (or judges have dismissed) charges against those accused of a violent crime. The second study, undertaken by the Bureau of

Justice Statistics, looked at the same issue in state cases, where of course most violent crime adjudications take place.

What emerge from both studies are many cases that were dropped for reasons that may indicate defendant's innocence, or at least the relative weakness of the prosecutor's case against the defendant. I shall call these factors *innocence-indicators*. Both studies show that prosecutors have multiple reasons for the dismissal or dropping of charges against persons charged with a violent crime. Still, both data sets about prosecutorial decisions indicate that the dominant motive for dropping outstanding charges is *not*, as you might expect, a belief that the defendant is actually innocent.[133]

Sometimes, charges are dropped because of a defendant's willingness to testify for the state in the separate trial of an accomplice. Occasionally, charges are dropped because the prosecutor discovers that the statute of limitations expires before the trial can be scheduled or he discovers that the defendant, when the alleged crime occurred, was a minor and should be tried in juvenile court. Prosecutors will also often drop charges if the rulings in the pre-trial evidence hearing indicate that the judge will exclude what the prosecutors deem to be highly inculpatory evidence of defendants' guilt. When that occurs, the case against the defendant obviously becomes less compelling than it would have been if the relevant evidence were admitted. In fact, this was reported as the most frequent problem that prosecutors' offices ran into.[134] Commonly, prosecutors also cite limitations of personnel and financial resources to cope with all the cases on their docket. (So much for the common idea that prosecutors have virtually unlimited resources!) Charges are also likely to be dropped if a key witness for the state vanishes or changes her testimony (as the Bureau of Justice Statistics puts it: "the reason for this reluctance [to testify] was usually fear of reprisal, followed by actual threats against the victim or witness."[135]), or if the defendant was awarded bail awaiting trial and vanished, thereby becoming a fugitive at large.[136] Clearly, none of these reasons for dropping a case is, in any sense, an indicator of the defendant's innocence.

Oftentimes, of course, charges are dropped for reasons that imply the weakness of the case against the defendant. A detailed report about the many decisions made in 2010 by federal prosecutors – in deciding whether to drop charges against some 7.3k detainees arrested by the FBI—claims that in 20.5% of dismissals, there appeared to be a 'lack of criminal intent'; 7% of dropped charges were a result of the prosecutor's decision that 'no crime was committed'; and in another quarter of the dropped cases there were signs of 'weak or insufficient evidence.'[137] That boils down to saying that, in federal cases dealing with violent crimes, slightly less than half of all dismissals (48%) are motivated by factors other than a worry that defendant's guilt might not be provable at trial. (Recall, too, that 'insufficient evidence' does not mean lack of substantial evidence that defendant committed the crime but rather evidence the prosecution believes is probably insufficient to establish defendant's guilt beyond a reasonable doubt.)

This already gives us reason to suspect that about half of the cases where charges are dropped involve the abandonment of charges against defendants whom the prosecutor thought were probably factually guilty but was not at all sure that he could prove that guilt beyond a reasonable doubt. That argument becomes much more convincing when we remind ourselves of how defendants came to the prosecutors' attention in the first place. Typically, a person becomes the object of police investigations initially as little more than a suspect, perhaps among several others who strike the police as possible culprits. If, after further inquiries and the analysis of more evidence, police decide to file charges (thereby 'clearing' the case as far as the police are concerned), they are required to have grounds to believe that it is more likely than not that defendant committed the crime. To make the arrest official, the police must persuade either a judge or a grand jury (or both) that a rational person, confronted with the available evidence, would conclude that the defendant probably committed the crime.

Accordingly, by the time the prosecutor typically gets deeply into the act, he is dealing with a host of arrestees, each of whom is considered by the police, a grand jury and/or the arraigning judge to be more likely than not to be guilty on the available evidence. As the prosecutor begins assembling his case, some new evidence will often come to hand or be actively sought.

Sometimes, that evidence will be exculpatory, and persuade the prosecutor that defendant really did not commit the crime. Much more often, though, the decision point for the prosecutor arrives when, after having reviewed the evidence, he must decide whether the case against the defendant is strong enough to persuade a trial jury that the defendant is guilty beyond a reasonable doubt. Supposing, with many scholars, that this standard represents roughly a 90+% likelihood of guilt, this means that most of those now charged with a crime have an apparent guilt that falls in the very broad range from 50+% to something close to 100%. The prosecutor will generally cull those defendants in the range of 50-80% apparent guilt out of the class of those he intends to take to trial or to negotiate a plea bargain with.

Why would he do that? When apparent guilt is in that range, the prosecutor knows that it is unlikely that he will be able to persuade the defendant to accept a plea bargain and he also knows that, if he takes the defendant to trial, it will probably result in an acquittal. There are moral reasons as well that lead to the dropping of charges,[138] even against those whom the prosecutor believes to be factually guilty.

The second pertinent study on this vexing issue of the frequency of guilt among those defendants dropped out of the system prior to trial was published in 1992.[139] Unlike the FBI study, this one investigated state (rather than federal) criminal trials. It included some 40k cases. The researchers asked prosecutors why they had dropped charges in the cases (or why judges had dismissed charges) when they did. Three of the reasons given appear to be innocence-indicators: 'evidence issues', 'witness problems' and 'the interests of justice'. Some 35% of the dropped/dismissed cases were attributed to these reasons. That left 65% of the abandoned cases involving reasons implying nothing about guilt or innocence.[140] An earlier study of 17,500 arrests in Washington, D.C. federal courts indicates that the prosecutor dropped 3.6k cases but only a third of those dismissals (34%) were attributed to 'insufficiency of evidence'.[141]

Taking the mean between the FBI probably-guilty rate of 47% and the BJS value of 65%, we arrive at the estimate that about 56% of the dismissed and dropped arrestees were probably factually guilty. Even so, that number doesn't take us fully where we want to go. We're after a reasonable estimate of the number of *truly* guilty who have the charges against them either dropped or dismissed. The fact that the 56% of arrestees against whom charges were dropped are probably guilty does not yet give us a definite way of determining how many of them were actually guilty.

There is, however, a way of generating the result we seek. Remember that the defendants in this group were dropped or dismissed because of reasons that had nothing to do with signs of their innocence. Hence, we can reasonably suppose that the proportion of guilty among them would be about the same as the proportion of guilty among those who go to trial. (After all, there is no perceived evidential weakness in the case against them that distinguished them from those who do go to trial.) As the data in Table 4 make clear, exactly two-thirds of those who went to trial for a violent crime were convicted. We have already explained why we assume that 75% of those acquitted at trial are probably truly guilty. That seems to provide a plausible rationale for saying that, among those defendants who had the charges against them dropped for *non-evidentiary* reasons, approximately two-out-of-three (and probably more) are highly likely to be guilty. Hence, we shall assume that about 37% to 38% (that is two-thirds of the 56% of those whom were booted out of the trial system for non-evidentiary reasons) are factually guilty (and, if they had gone to trial, would have been convicted). This amounts to 81k false negatives. When added to the estimate of 12k probably guilty defendants among those acquitted at trial, this total suggests that, at a minimum, some 93k of the 595k violent arrestees are acquitted event though truly guilty. This suggests a false negative rate of ~40% (viz., 93k guilty out of 232k acquitted). As already indicated, this is a modest estimate of the frequency of false negatives. (See Figure 5.)

Figure 5. Verdicts and Errors in Violent Crimes Cases, 2008

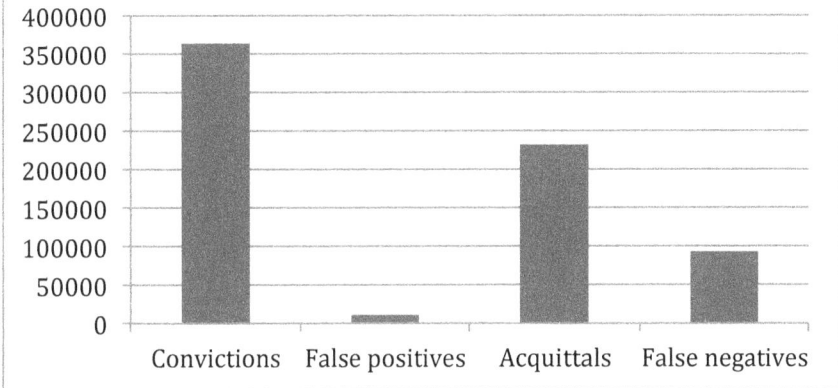

Having arrived at a mechanism for making plausible estimates of the frequency of false positives and false negatives (namely, a false positive rate of 3%, a false negative rate of ~38% among those against whom charges were dropped for reasons independent of their potential guilt and a false negative rate of 80% (12k out of 15k acquittals) among those who were acquitted at trial), I will examine in detail in chapter 4 how the Laplacian analysis (cited above) might enable us to introduce some degree of rationality into what is currently a highly emotional and uncritical discussion of how to strike a reasonable balance between false positives and false negatives.[142]

Before moving on to that key theme, it is worth pointing out that Cesare Beccaria was more than a little troubled by the dangers of false acquittals. While he favored a high standard of proof, he understood full well that such a standard would lead to many false acquittals and to high levels of unnecessary recidivism. His solution to that conundrum was intriguing. He held that a defendant—tried for a serious offense who appeared likely to have committed it but not likely enough to satisfy the then-prevailing standard of proof— should not receive the usual punishment for the crime but, if his guilt seemed relatively high, he should receive a much milder punishment than someone who was clearly guilty of a comparable crime. Such persons, he said, "place the nation in the fatal dilemma of fearing him [if he is freed and unpunished] or of punishing him unjustly [if convicted]."[143] Beccaria's solution to that conundrum was to 'banish' such likely felons, sending them out of the state for a set period of time.[144] Banishment, he thought, would protect the citizenry from the recidivist tendencies of such felons, while imposing on the latter a punishment much milder than they would have received had they been strictly convicted. (In the US, Kentucky, Georgia, Arkansas and Tennessee sometimes still use banishment as punishment, though never for apparent guilt profiles that fail to reach BARD.[145])

Chapter 4 How and Why the Current Rate of False Negatives Produces Much Greater Risk of Harm for Innocent Citizens than False Positives Do

My aim in this chapter is to estimate conservatively, in so far as the relevant data allow, the overall risks and harms caused respectively by false positives and false negatives. Working with the modest estimates of error rates from the last chapter, we now need to ascertain how much harm or risk of harm is imposed respectively by the two principal errors that routinely occur. Such calculations will enable us to see whether we are complying with the requirement of the social contract which insists that we should design trials so that they minimize the overall harm or risk of harm done to innocent victims resulting from erroneous verdicts. In brief, we have to calculate the amount of harm produced by individual cases of each type of error. Once we have a sense of the magnitude of each error, we can combine that with what we learned about the frequencies of these errors and then do the harm calculation that Laplace's model requires. It must be stressed that the calculations here are imprecise since much of the available data are less than robust. What will emerge from our musings is not exactitude but a plausible guess at the magnitude of the harms produced by the current system of justice.

For a start, let's return for a brief look at the data in Table 4. There are several interesting patterns there that strike one immediately. Among them: 47% of violent crimes go unreported to the police; 70% of the reported crimes are solved, at least to the satisfaction of the police, leading to an arrest; charges are dropped or dismissed against 36% of those arrested; of the remaining defendants (378k), 12% go to trial while 88% confess and accept a plea bargain; among the small set of defendants who do go to trial, the ratio of convictions to acquittals is 2-to-1. (Table 1 gives a brief capitulation of the three routes to conviction, making it vividly clear that the pleas are the principal drivers of current adjudication.) Intriguing as many of these statistics are, they don't yet get us to the chief points of concern in this book. To do that, we need to feed our earlier estimates of the frequencies of false positives and false negatives into these figures about the disposition of cases of violent crimes. (See Table 4 in chapter 3 for the details.)

As we have seen, The Bureau of Justice Statistics, based on victimization interviews, reports that in 2008 there were approximately 1,700,000 crimes of violence in the United States.[146] That boils down to slightly more than one violent crime victim for every 160 Americans aged 12 or older (assuming 250m in this age range in 2008). More than three-quarters of those crimes went unpunished; the remaining 23% led to a conviction. Since the average punishment meted out for someone convicted of a violent crime is approximately 7.6 years, and since so many offenders go unpunished, the average perpetrator of a violent crime is likely to spend barely 21 months in jail.[147] (This, situation, already discussed earlier as the 'expected punishment', is scarcely a potent deterrent to those minded to resort to violence.) In short, the chances of being the victim of a violent crime, despite the steep decline in the crime rate since the 1990s, remain unacceptably high. We have already worked out in the last chapter how often false positives and false negatives occur. What we need to do now is to clarify how much harm to innocents each of those errors produces.

FALSE NEGATIVE COSTS

The principal documentable harm resulting from a false negative is the harm wrought by the falsely acquitted felon during the time when—had he been truly convicted—he would have been incapacitated, and sitting in a prison cell somewhere.[148] We cannot begin to tote up the costs of releasing unpunished guilty felons without talking about recidivism among the falsely acquitted, that is, the criminal harm (and specifically the violence) likely to be done by those persons guilty of a violent crime but released without a conviction. More specifically, and especially if we are following Laplace's version of the social contract, we need to focus on the violent harms that these freed but truly guilty felons are likely to inflict during the time when, had they been convicted, it would have been well-nigh impossible for them to engage in such acts. In 2008, of the 595k persons arrested and charged for a violent crime, 232k either had the charges against them dropped or they were acquitted at trial. For reasons already indicated, I shall assume that approximately 38% (81k) of those persons against whom charges were dropped are false negatives, as are some 12k of those acquitted at trial.[149] So, we have, at a minimum, some 93k false negatives produced annually in the handling of cases of violent crime. As explained in the appendix to this chapter, it is reasonable (and *very* conservative) to estimate that these 93k false negatives released in 2008 will commit some 112k violent crimes during the time when they would, if convicted, have been incapacitated. (About 1k of these violent acts will be homicides and another 6k, rapes.)

This, then, is a first stab at estimating the aggregate annual costs of the current practices producing false negatives. If we look at individual instead of aggregate harms, we can say, very conservatively, that *the typical falsely acquitted-violent felon will commit at least 1.2 violent crimes during the span of what I call the Laplacian window* (in the case of violent crimes, the average sentence is 7.6 years).[150] According to a government study published in 2014, within five years of the release of those convicted of violent crimes, 71% had been arrested for a new crime. Nor did they waste any time: within 6 months of their release, some 25% had been re-arrested for a new offense.[151] Nor was this recidivism a new phenomenon. Of the 404k prisoners released in 2005, their history prior to their current incarceration indicated that the mean number of prior arrests was 10.6 and the mean number of prior convictions was 4.9.[152] Among released violent offenders in particular, 70% had prior arrests and 56%, prior convictions.[153]

Before we turn to look at the costs of false positives, it is important to stress how these recidivism data that I have been citing almost certainly understate the costs of false negatives enormously. Before I turn to propose some solutions to the out-of-control false negatives, I want to stress that the calculations I have made here have aimed to characterize the magnitude of harm from false negatives as conservatively as the data allow. While I will continue working with those numbers here, it is essential to say explicitly that, in fact, we have every reason to expect that the costs of false negatives (chiefly recidivist acts) are substantially greater than what I have calculated. There are four reasons that undergird this conclusion:

a). Statistics about recidivism are generally drawn from information about the frequency with which guilty offenders, when released from jail, are known to return to their criminal ways and resume their life as violent offenders. Such data often report how frequently a released offender is *arrested* for a new violent offense; other data commonly ascertain how often released offenders are *convicted* of a new violent offense. These ways of assessing the risks posed by repeat offenders guarantee that studies of repeat offenders will drastically understate the frequency of recidivism and therefore the damage done by such offenders. We have to remind ourselves that, for any type of crime, convictions are only a subset of prosecutions, which are a subset of those arrested, which are a subset of police inquiries, which are a subset of known crimes, which in turn constitute a smallish subset of committed crimes. Limiting the scope of recidivism estimates to those felons actually convicted of crimes thus tells only a small part of the story about the criminal activities of released felons.

Moving to our example of 1.7m violent crimes in 2008, it's crucial to remind ourselves that substantially less than 40% of those crimes led to the filing of charges (595k) and those led, in turn, to some 363k convictions. It is unimaginable that, given those 1.3m unsolved violent crimes in 2008, the only ones committed by the 93k false negatives are those for which they were eventually arrested and acquitted. (See Table 3.) Recall that the majority (53%) of those arrested for a violent crime were already established *serial* felons; 9% of them had 10 or more prior convictions to their credit; and 36% of them, when arrested, were either on bail, probation or parole for a prior felony.[154] The idea that few if any of the *unsolved* or *unreported* crimes of 2008 were perpetrated by those who were charged with, and then falsely acquitted of, committing a different crime is unthinkable. For that reason, actual recidivism rates must be significantly higher than what I assumed above. That is also why the Bureau of Justice Statistics has emphasized that "research indicates that [serial felons] commit more crimes than their arrest—let alone their conviction—records show."[155]

Table 5. Self-Reported Recidivism among Frequent Offenders[156]			
Violent Offenses per Time on Street	Juvenile	Young Adult	Adult
Per Month	0.1	0.16	0.2
Per Year	1.2	1.92	2.4

Since that is so, it would be a grave mistake to suppose that actual recidivism rates (usually limited to reporting convictions) are equivalent to prior conviction rates. Since only one-fifth of violent crimes lead to convictions, the risks posed by false negatives must be significantly higher than what I have assumed (which is that recidivism rates as measured by convictions must at least be doubled to produce a reasonable estimate of recidivism).

b). Such a hunch is further borne out by a different form of research that attempts to ferret out recidivism rates without counting arrests and convictions. Known as 'self-reporting' of criminal activity, studies of this kind involve interviews with convicted felons (usually while they are in jail) about their prior criminal history, including crimes for which they were arrested and those for which they were not. Such studies reveal that the typical serial felon claims to commit between 3 and 5 crimes for every crime for which he is actually arrested. Blumstein, in his classic and enormous study of serial felons in Washington, D.C., insists that self-reports from his interviewees indicate that they committed 14 robberies for every robbery arrest of theirs and 9 aggravated assaults for every assault arrest.[157] (See Table 5.) If these data are anything like correct, they entail that the violent harm ensuing from the release of truly guilty felons must be several times higher than I have calculated here, making the case for paying special attention to false negatives even more urgent. Further studies by the eminent British criminologist, D. Farrington, of self-reports from habitual offenders paint an even grimmer story. Their self-reports of criminal activity, ordered by different ages of the offenders, indicate the magnitude of the problem we are trying to assess. While studies of recidivism based on interviews are by no means foolproof, the National Research Council pronounces them 'reasonably valid' and 'acceptably accurate'.[158]

In sum, for 'the habitual offender', understood in this study as any offender with at least two serious felony convictions, depending upon his age, he is –when not incarcerated—committing between 1.2 and 2.4 violent crimes *per year*. By contrast, I have assumed that said felons are committing something like 1.2 violent crimes over a 7.6-year span. Since some 9% of those arrested for violent crimes in 2008 have a prior history of >10 known, prior felonies (and thereby qualify as chronic, habitual offenders), and more than half of those arrested have prior felony convictions, we can safely say that my estimate of the risks of harm posed by those who are false negatives significantly understates their likely pattern of violent crimes. We can reinforce this analysis by noting that active offenders (specifically those who make it a habit to commit armed robbery and aggravated assault) also report that they are arrested for only 7% of the armed robberies they commit and only 11% of their aggravated assaults. Even more troubling, in the literature of recidivism, are the multiple indications that the *severity* of the crimes that serial offenders commit increases in proportion to the number of prior crimes they have committed, especially if one is looking at the criminal careers of younger offenders.[159]

c). My calculation of the harm caused by the recidivist activities of the falsely acquitted also ignores the fact that almost certainly the released but guilty felons did additional harm besides committing *violent* crimes. Indeed, there is ample data showing that serial offenders commit far more property crimes than crimes of violence. Had that information been factored into our calculation, we would have seen an even larger bill of harm for our current policy that encourages false negatives.

d). There is also what we might call the multiplier effect that the available data don't really capture. It has two manifestations: many criminal acts, although they often count as one event in crime tables, involve multiple victims (think of the armed robbery of a couple on the streets); similarly many crimes have several perpetrators (think of an armed gang robbing a bank) even though the event usually counts as one event for bookkeeping purposes.[160] These two effects mean that there are significantly more victims than I have estimated, even for reported crimes and that there are significantly more perpetrators than crimes. Both effects have the result of underestimating the size of the victim pool and of underestimating the size of the pool of guilty culprits. In short, the harm resulting from crimes committed by falsely acquitted or dismissed felons is at least as great as I have calculated it to be. My postulate that the average falsely acquitted felon commits 1.2 violent crimes over 7.6 years is a deliberate underestimate of the true risks from recidivism.

FALSE POSITIVE COSTS

We now turn to consider the harm done by falsely convicting an innocent person of a crime he did not commit. Despite the striking decline in crime rates since the 1990s, there were 363k convictions for violent crimes in 2008. We have already argued that it is reasonable to estimate that approximately 3% of those convictions are false positives since, of the dozens of studies of exonerations and false convictions, only two report a false positive rate higher than 3% (specifically, Michael Risinger's 3.8% estimate and Gross' 4% estimate), while many report false positive rates of this sort well below 2%. Taking the 3% figure as a modest stab at it, we are talking about roughly 11k false positives annually resulting from the adjudication of violent crimes. That translates to about one false positive (for a violent crime) annually for every 22.7k adult Americans. This is vastly smaller than the risk of being the victim of a falsely acquitted, violent felon (1 in every 2,300 adults). If the legal system were to take either Nozick's or Laplace's version of the social contract seriously, it would be vastly more concerned about the victims of violent crimes committed by falsely-acquitted felons than about those wrongly convicted for violent crimes. Come to that, would you prefer a legal system in which you were some ten times more likely to be victimized by a falsely acquitted felon than to be falsely convicted of a violent crime?

That said, it is important to stress that the judicial system can hardly be blamed for all (or even for most) cases of violent crime, although it is tasked with trying to reduce such crime. After all, some 47% of violent crimes are never reported to the police.

The state can scarcely be held responsible for failing to mete out justice in those cases. Moreover, 21% of the violent crimes known to the police do not result in an arrest. Some of that failure can be blamed on the police but generally not on the courts.

Nonetheless, there is still plenty of blame left for which the judicial/court system must take the primary responsibility. I refer broadly to the problem of false negatives and the enormous harms that follow from them. To begin with, we need to shift from Nozick's crude version of the social contract to Laplace's version, not least because the latter spells out how to lay blame on the judicial system itself, when it is responsible for the errors. Recall that Laplace's view was that we should direct our attention to the crimes committed by those who were falsely released or acquitted by the system and compare that damage and risk with the harm done by the false positives of the legal system.

The calculation of the harms resulting from false positives is slightly more complicated than the false negatives calculation since there are *two* obvious sorts of harm resulting from most false positives: a). sentencing an innocent person to prison for (on average) 7.6 years[161] (or less if he receives probation or parole); and b). failing to convict the true perpetrator of the crime for which our false positive defendant took the rap. How might we sort out those costs? The first is more complex than the second. In terms of harm done to the innocent but convicted defendant, I shall simply suppose that 'the punishment [imposed] fits the crime'. That is, I take it as reasonable to suppose that the harm stemming from being convicted of, and punished for) a violent crime is proportionate to the harm that would have been done to one if he or she had been the victim of said violent crime. If your hunch is that the harm meted out to an innocent defendant by a false conviction is generally greater than the harm suffered by the victim of the crime, maybe you should think again. After all, how many of us would say that they would prefer to have been murdered rather than having been sentenced to 12 years in prison for a murder we didn't commit? Who would rather have been raped with violence than have been falsely convicted of rape and receiving the average 6-year sentence for that crime? Accordingly, being falsely convicted for a violent crime like rape or murder inflicts on the innocent

74

defendant what is intended to be approximately (or perhaps less than) the same harm that being a victim of that crime would suffer.

But what about the lesser violent offenses of armed robbery and aggravated assault? One might initially be inclined to believe that being a victim of such crimes is less costly than being falsely convicted of having committed them. But things are not so simple. Leaving aside the momentary fear and longer-term trauma that a victim of such crimes must feel when someone approaches—gun or knife in hand—saying "your money or your life" or if one is being beat up with a potentially lethal weapon, it is important to take into account that 38% of armed robberies in 2008 resulted in serious injuries to the victims as did 30% of the aggravated assaults. Some of those injuries had life-long effects.[162] For such reasons, I am inclined to think that it is not much of a stretch to assume that the harms imposed on the innocent but convicted defendant are roughly on a par with the harms associated with being the victim of a violent crime.

This is especially plausible in light of the fact that a non-trivial number of those false positives will be exonerated by the activities of Innocence Projects and by exoneration hearings. While it is rare for exonerations to emerge in the case of those sentenced to short prison terms, violent crimes tend to carry much longer terms, thereby allowing a shortening of the sentence and thus a reduction of the harm associated with a false positive to be significantly reduced via exoneration. It is important to add that there are numerous other features of the system that lower the harm done by a false positive, well below the costs that I am assuming for the calculation. They include the following factors: convictions can be appealed (and often are in the case of violent crimes[163]), sometimes leading to a complete reversal of the conviction (roughly 5% of convicted defendants who file an appeal receive this result[164]); approximately 2-3% of convictions for violent crimes lead to exonerations for the false positives, meaning release from prison; in most states, the sentencing judge or jury has the authority to impose a sentence of probation rather than incarceration[165] (even for convicted rapists and murderers), exercising this option about 12% of the time; finally, many defendants convicted of violent crimes receive parole (roughly

18%), well before the end of their sentence.[166] Clearly, if we were to take these factors into account, then our estimate of the cost of a false positive would decline dramatically since about one-of-three falsely convicted persons pays a price significantly lower than what I have calculated as the cost to the defendant of being made a false positive. That said, so as not to give the impression of making my argument easier for myself, I shall ignore all these reducing influences, thereby making my estimate of the costs of a false positive higher than they probably are.

So, to summarize where we go from here: our 'currency' for measuring harm, risk and compliance with the social contract is going to be harmful victimizations (whether of falsely convicted victims or of victims of violence committed by those who, but for a false negative, would be imprisoned). It is crucial to emphasize that the cost of a false positive goes beyond the injury to the falsely convicted person. It also includes the harm done to third parties, during the sentence of the falsely convicted, by the system's failure to find and to incarcerate the true offender. The well-known defense lawyer, Barry Sheck is widely quoting as saying: "Every time you convict an innocent person, a guilty person is out there committing more crimes and has to be stopped."[167] It is important to remind ourselves that the escaped true perpetrator of a crime is a key part of the cost of a false conviction, and I shall incorporate it into all my calculations. That said, it is interesting to note that Scheck—defense attorney that he is—has never bothered to point out that that every time you acquit an *innocent* person, 'a guilty person is out there committing more crimes and has to be stopped'.

Adding together the harm to the falsely convicted felon (1 victim unit) and the harm of the violent crimes committed by the uncaught felon (1.2 victims), we can see that the cost of a single false positive is approximately 2.2 victims. By contrast, the cost for a single false negative is roughly 1.2 victims. But that doesn't settle the question yet. In this sense, I fully concur with the widespread view that a false positive is more expensive than a false negative. That said, it is crucial to recall that we are aiming here to work out not only the respective costs of a single false positive versus a single false negative but, more importantly, the aggregate costs of all the false positives as opposed to the costs of all the false negatives.

(I have asserted that the harms associated with the typical false conviction have these two components: the sending to prison of an innocent person and the failure to incarcerate the true perpetrator. It is the combination of those factors that generally makes a false positive almost twice as costly as a false negative. It should not go unnoted, however, that in a *few* cases, the costs of a false negative are greater than those of a false positive. Consider one example of this conundrum: Smith is on trial for murdering Jones. Jones was indeed killed by Smith and with Smith's gun. However, Smith argues (correctly) that he was acting in self-defense. He is nonetheless convicted by the jury. In this case, we have a false positive but with no corresponding truly guilty perpetrator since the fact is that there was no crime and the jury erred by convicting Smith. In cases such as this, the cost of the false positive would be 1 victim (rather than 2.2 victims) and there would be no associated true culprit on the streets.[168] Because cases of this sort, where someone is falsely convicted of a violent crime when there was no such crime, are relatively rare, I shall adhere to my proposal to regard false positives as roughly twice as harmful as false negatives, even while acknowledging that the occasional false positive may do less harm than a false negative.)

There is one commonly cited factor that I have deliberately left out of the calculation of the costs of a false conviction; to with, the financial costs of keeping a convicted but innocent defendant behind bars. This is not a harm inflicted on the innocent defendant (although the harm of wrongful incarceration is clearly borne by him) but on the rest of society. Recent estimates of the cost to society of incarcerating a defendant—whether guilty or innocent—run in the vicinity of about $29k/year. In a study in the *Federal Register* in 2013, it was reported that: "The average cost [per inmate per year] of incarceration for federal inmates in Fiscal Year 2011 was $28.893.40."[169] (Similar if slightly lower expenses are reported within most state penal systems.) Obviously, this is not a trivial amount. But we should not forget that a substantial portion of those convicted of violent crimes were unemployed and receiving welfare when they committed their crimes. Since the average poor person in the US costs the government and thus the taxpayer approximately $21k annually, the additional annual cost of incarceration is roughly $8k greater than what the state would be paying anyway.[170] Against that we have to balance the saving in violent crime victims as a result of the incapacitation of serial felons. For such reasons, I don't attach a high cost to the expense of additional incarcerations.

One final point is in order. As often noted before, it has long been the deep-rooted conviction of the legal community that an ideal legal system is one in which the ratio of false negatives to false positives should be and is ten-to-one. If my assumptions are plausible, the data I've laid out actually give us a ratio of errors of approximately Blackstonian proportions (in the BR_3 sense). That is, we are assuming that the current system generates annually 93k false negatives and 11k false positives, yielding a ratio of slightly more than eight-to-one. The challenge facing us is that our earlier discussion of the respective costs of a false positive and a false negative showed them to be about 2-to-1 (specifically, 2.2-to-1.2). If that ratio is anything like accurate, then the ideal, Laplacian legal system would be one in which in which the ratio of errors was approximately 2-to-1. The fact that we are now producing in adjudicating violent crime cases a ratio of errors in the neighborhood of 8-to- means that we are a very long way from satisfying the demands of the social contract.

PLUGGING THE NUMBERS INTO THE CONTRACT

So, our core challenge boils down to this: how do the overall harms and risks from false positives in violent crime cases stack up against the overall harms and risks due to false negatives in such cases? We finally have the tools we need to answer that question. The 11k false positives occurring every year produce about 24k victim units (11k x 2.2). The 93k false negatives lead to 112k victim units (that is, 93.7k x 1.2). The annual harm enabled by the false positives and false negatives jointly is about 136k victims of violent acts (or the punishment for them), produced in adjudicating the cases of some 600k violent crime arrestees.

In other words, the set of false negatives emerging from the adjudication of violent crimes leads to 460% more harm than the

78

set of false positives does. Even if there were only half as many false negatives as I have conservatively estimated, it would remain true that false negatives would produce substantially more harm in aggregate than false positives do. (Table 6 summarizes the harm picture succinctly.)

Table 6. Data-Based Estimates pertinent to the Social Contract, 2008	
Estimated No. of false Positives (3%)	10.9k
Est. No. of False Negatives[171] (38% of 217k dismissals and 80% of 15k acquittals)	93.8k
Ratio of the Two Error Frequencies (F-s/F+s)	8.6 to 1
Aggregate Harm from False -s (1.2 victims ea.)	112k victims
Aggregate Harm from False +s (2.2 victims ea.)	24k victims
Ratio of Harms (Harms$_{F-}$/Harms$_{F+}$)	4.7 to 1
Total Victims due to Errors	136k victims
Risk of citizen becoming a False +	1 in 23k
Risk of citizen being violently victimized by a False-	1 in 2.2k
Ratio of the Two Risks (F- risk/F+ risk)	9.6 to 1
Risk of being the victim of a violent crime by the true perpetrator trial leading to a false positive	1 in 20k

This conclusion has multiple ramifications. Perhaps the starkest is this: a citizen's risk (1-in-23,000) of being falsely convicted of a violent crime is about one-tenth as great as her risk of being the victim of a violent act (1-in-2,200), perpetrated by someone who was arrested for the crime he committed and in the clutches of the legal system, only to escape prosecution or conviction. More than a thousand of the crimes committed by the false negatives are murders; another six thousand are rapes. Can the reader still be puzzled about why, in the first chapter, I voiced dismay at the inattention given to the problem of false negatives? The latter are unambiguously the larger and more worrying problem (in the sense of generating substantially more harm to innocent victims) and thus require more immediate attention than the much anguished-over false positives. That notwithstanding, false negatives and the harms they lead to remain largely under the radar of public and judicial sentiment.

My analysis does not dispute the traditional and familiar claim that a typical false positive is more harmful to society than a false negative. To the contrary, it buttresses up that hypothesis by giving it an empirical foundation. According to my metric, a false conviction (2.2 victims) is roughly twice as harmful as a false negative (1.2 victims). That justifies insisting that the state should make it harder to convict an innocent person than it is to acquit a guilty one. However, the current standard of proof, combined with various defendant-friendly rules of procedure, is creating a situation in which we have so many false negatives and so few false positives that the former are producing far more harm than the latter.

The reason for this disparity is not hard to fathom. A legal system that produces four-to-five times as much harm from its false negatives as from its false positives (when the actual ratio of those harms is about 2-to-1) is a system that is both making more overall errors and generating more overall harm than it would if it were producing errors in proportion to the harm ratio between those errors. Put more simply: if (with Laplace) we want to minimize errors and harms in our legal system, we should be producing roughly 2 false negatives for every false positive. Instead, we are producing approximately 8-to-1, and thereby generating far more errors than are either necessary or desirable.

To understand why this is happening, consider the following model: we are now falsely convicting 3% of those who are convicted. That entails that the ratio of truly guilty to truly innocent defendants in the region defined by the standard of proof is roughly 32-to-1. What about the region just *below* that standard? That population has to be very dense with truly guilty felons. Yet *everyone* with apparent guilt in that region just below the guilty/non-guilty threshold is acquitted. In short, with a very high standard of proof (and only a 3% false positive rate), we are engaging in the wholesale generation of false negatives, knowing full well that most of those acquittals are very probably guilty of the crime. Lowering the standard of proof so that it more nearly reflects the ratio of the harms resulting from the two errors would mildly increase the frequency of false positives while it would convert large numbers of (current) false negatives into true positives. If we have good reason to believe (as we do) that there are some 20 to 30 truly guilty defendants for every truly innocent one in the range just below the current standard of proof, it is obscene—even immoral—to insist that we should stick with a policy that, wittingly or unwittingly, lets some thirty truly guilty defendants off the hook for every truly innocent defendant that it saves from false conviction. Not even Blackstone would agree that it would be acceptable to let 25 or 30 guilty felons go free for every innocent defendant shielded from conviction.

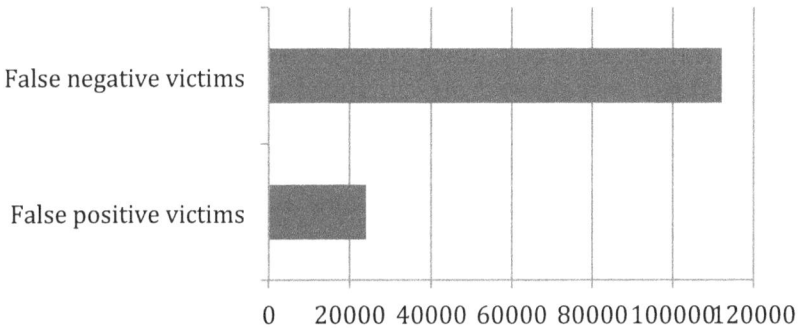

Figure 6. Harms Resulting from Erroneous Verdicts, 2008

Table 7. Summary of the Chief Errors in the Investigation and Prosecution of Violent Crimes	
Failures to arrest the guilty in reported crimes[172]	448k
Arrests of the innocent	155k
Acquittal/dismissal of the guilty	93k
Conviction of the innocent	10.9k
Total errors (out of 848k crimes reported to the police)	707k

The puzzle now facing us is straightforward (to state if not to solve): is there some way to lower the aggregate risk to the ordinary citizen of being either falsely convicted and/or being the victim of a falsely acquitted felon during the latter's Laplacian window? Answering that question will be the task of the next two chapters. For now, it is sufficient to say that what the social contract requires of us is that we minimize this value.

More specifically, we can define the Aggregate Risk of Judicial Adjudication of Crimes (ARJ) = $(R_1 + R_2 + R_3)$, where R_1 is the annual risk of being falsely convicted of a violent crime; R_2 is the annual risk of being the victim of a violent crime perpetrated by a felon falsely acquitted of a violent crime during his Laplacian window of 7.6 years; and R_3 is the annual risk faced by a citizen of being the victim of a violent crime committed by the true perpetrator of an earlier violent crime who escaped conviction by virtue of a false conviction of an innocent defendant.] The annual risk posed to the average American by the 2008 numbers is as follows:

$R_1 = 0.004\%$
$R_2 = 0.04\%$
$R_3 \eqsim 0.005\%$
Total annual risks = 0.05%

We calculated earlier the aggregate number of victims caused by failures of judicial adjudication as approximately 136k (Table 6). That means that the annual risk imposed on every one of us of meeting one or the other of these of fates is ~0.05%. If that risk seems relatively unthreatening, it translates into a *lifetime* risk of suffering one of these fates of 3.75%,[173] which is neither trivial nor unmenacing. (It is about the same as the likelihood of dying from a stroke, and is a considerably greater risk—by a factor of three—than that of dying in an automobile accident.) As we will see in the next two chapters, the current aggregate risk could be reduced dramatically by mildly changing the rules of trial.

Figure 7. Percent of Cleared Crimes, 2008

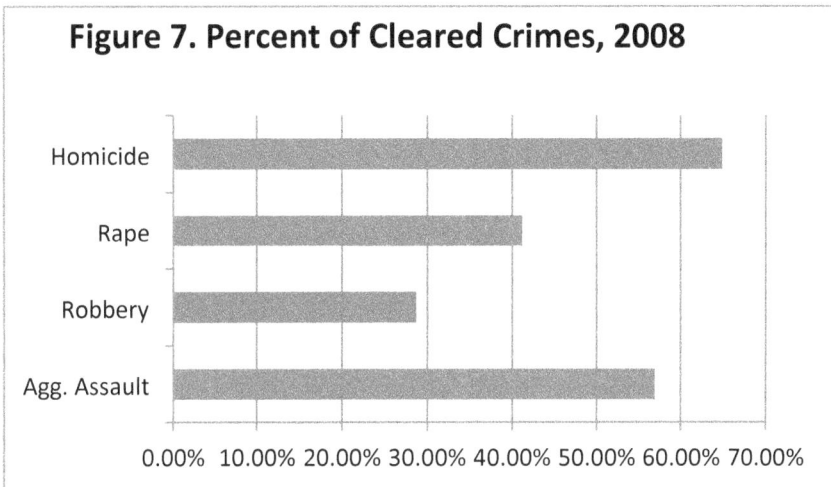

APPENDIX: VIOLENT RECIDIVISM

Computing the frequency with which acquitted but guilty defendants will commit violent crimes is far from being an exact art. Too few legal scholars have bothered to try to measure it. I shall adopt some simplifying assumptions that will enable us to estimate the approximate magnitude of that problem. I shall assume a). that truly guilty but acquitted defendants are as likely to commit crimes as are their fellow guilty defendants who were actually convicted but subsequently released; b). that official recidivism numbers, which generally measure the frequency with which released felons commit violent crimes, vastly understate the actual re-occurrence of criminal acts since i). there are some 5 unsolved crimes for every convicted felon, some of which are likely to have been committed by these serial offenders; and ii). extensive interviews of convicted felons in both the US and the UK indicate that the average felon commits between 2 and 5 violent crimes for every one for which he is arrested[174]; iii). my data are derived from two of the largest recidivism studies conducted by the Bureau of Justice Statistics, involving some 677k prisoners released from state prisons in 1994 and 2005.[175]

I begin with the assumption, already explained, that approximately 94k defendants, truly guilty of violent crimes, were released without conviction in 2008. The crucial question for us is: how likely are those 94k felons to commit new violent crimes during the time when, had they been properly convicted, their incapacitation would have prevented them from doing so?

The two studies I just mentioned give us slightly different answers to that question, not least because the crime rates in the late 1990s were higher than they were a decade later. I will calculate what each of the two studies would lead us to believe and then take the mean of those results.

The 1994 Release. Of those violent offenders released from prison in 1994, some 27.5% were rearrested within three years for a violent crime.[176] (Specifically, 1% of those released were arrested for murder, 2% for rape, 9% for armed robbery and 16% for aggravated assault.) Applying this violent recidivist rate to the 93k false negatives in our 2008 example, that amounts to 26k *known* violent crimes thought by the police to have been committed by this cohort over three years. For reasons already indicated (viz., the vast majority of violent crimes not being solved and the fact that numerous studies based on interviews with violent felons indicate that they usually commit several violent crimes for every crime for which they are arrested), I will assume that this group commits twice as many violent crimes as the police actually charge them with. That yields 52k crimes in three years. Extrapolating that forward leads to an estimate of the Laplacian window, through which we are looking, telling us that over 7.6 years, this group of falsely-acquitted felons will commit about 130k violent crimes.

The 2005 release. This project reports that during the 5 years after release from prison, 33% of those who served time for a violent crime had been re-arrested for a new violent crime.[177] If we apply these numbers to the 93k falsely acquitted felons from our 2008 study, we are talking about 31k felons being re-arrested for a violent crime. Doubling that number gives us 62k violent crimes committed in 5 years. Adjusting that to the 7.6-year length of the

Laplacian window, we have 94k violent crimes (on average, one for each released felon).

For purposes of the project of this book, I will take the mean between these two estimates as the vehicle for assessing the number of victims claimed by the false acquittals of violent offenders in 2008. That yields 112k victims of violent crimes who would not have suffered that fate if these guilty felons had been convicted and served their full sentences (approximately 1.2 victims of violent crimes for every false negative). I will likewise assume that each of the 10.9k false convictions will create a situation in which the real culprit—not apprehended because of the false positive—escapes punishment altogether and commits 1.2 violent crimes during the Laplacian window. (The 11k false positives will thus lead to some 13k victims of violent crimes. When combined with the (unfortunately) falsely convicted defendants, that produces 24k victims resulting from the false positives.)

It is crucial to stress, once again, how conservative my assumptions about degrees of recidivism are. One prominent study of habitual offenders conducted by Blumstein *et al.* and based on self-reports from those now in prison claims that the average such offender commits 0.15 violent crimes per month when he is not in prison. As Table 5 shows, that amounts to 1.8 violent crimes per year. That would imply that during the 7.6 year Laplacian window, the typical offender would commit some 14 violent crimes. I am attributing only 1.2 such crimes to him. In a second well-known British self-reporting study, which looks at recidivism rates for all crimes (and not just violent ones), the authors report that: "A survey of self-reported offending among males received into prison under sentence in early 2000, suggests that they commit [mostly non-violent] offences at around 140 per year in the period at liberty, before they were imprisoned."[178] A more recent US study concludes that "among the young, recently-released offenders who recidivate, each will commit 1.4 index crimes [felonies] per year."[179]

In case you feel uncomfortable assessing the harms of recidivism in terms of claimed victims, you might be interested in a detailed study of the subject by the Illinois Sentencing Policy

Advisory Council, couched in monetary terms. Their finding is that the 'average recidivism event' costs society $118k ($57k borne by the victim, $41k borne by the state and $20k in indirect costs).

Here again, these calculations make recidivism look more frequent and costlier than my conservative calculations assume. If the Blumstein and Halliday studies are anything like correct, they would entail that the 94k false negatives in 2008 led to somewhere between 1m and 1.3m violent crimes in the 7.6 years after their acquittal. My working estimate of some 112k violent crimes committed by the falsely acquitted recidivists during the Laplacian window is an order of magnitude lower than the self-reporting data would indicate. Using the alternative Illinois costing technique, that amounts to $13.2b in costs every year arising from the false acquittals of those guilty of violent crimes.

Part II A Pair of Solutions

> Underlying the question of guilt or innocence is an objective truth: the defendant, in fact, did or did not commit the crime charged. From the time an accused is first suspected to the time the decision on guilt or innocence is made, our criminal justice system is designed to enable the trier of fact to discover the truth…[180] –Justice Lewis Powell

The two following chapters will explore some promising remedies for the harms identified in Part I.

Chapter 5 Solution (A): The Case for Adjusting the Standard of Proof

> Acquitting the guilty and condemning the innocent—the Lord detests them both. *Proverbs* 17:15

Don't we all? The problem is, of course, that we know no workable way to avoid committing them both. *Proverbs* notwithstanding, we've plainly got to resign ourselves to making both sorts of mistakes. The trick, as we have seen, is figuring out how to balance those errors so as to produce results that are acceptable in the sense of minimizing the risk of harm to the innocent. Now that we have a reasonably good idea of the magnitude of the harms currently resulting from both false positives and false negatives (at least where violent crimes are concerned), we can begin tackling that challenge. The resulting harms are obviously enormous, claiming something like 136k innocent victims of violent crimes per year who are rendered victims by the error-prone machinery of the criminal justice system.

Who might have imagined that, in adjudicating 595k cases of arrestees (and convicting the defendant in 363k of them), the legal system would bear responsibility for visiting harm on so many innocents? An innocent person is harmed as a result of the court's findings in roughly one-quarter of all cases. Rather than just wringing our hands, however, it would surely be more constructive to explore whether there is anything we can do to reduce so much harm. Indeed, such a reduction, if one exists, is exactly what the social contract demands; we must minimize the aggregate harms to the innocent and, as we have already seen, we are currently far from doing that. The most obvious—but decidedly not the only—mechanism for altering the pattern of errors that occur in legal fact-finding involves altering the standard of proof. Before we turn to figuring out how we might adjust that standard, it would be useful to examine the spectrum of opinion about the meaning and adequacy of the current standard of proof.

Indisputably, there is no single factor as responsible for shaping the profile of judicial errors as the standard of proof is. A very high standard will predictably produce relatively few false positives and an abundance of false negatives. A very low standard would reverse that relationship. Many legal theorists seem to be content with the existing standard, evidently believing that BARD performs well; indeed –in the opinion of many well known legal theorists—it performs better than any rival would. (Both Tribe and Dworkin have vigorously defended this assumption.) A few prominent voices urge that it could and should be further improved on by ratcheting it up a few notches, meaning that they think the current frequency of false positives (3%) could and should be reduced. A small contingent of voices, including this author's, believes that BARD has outlived its usefulness and that it should be replaced by a standard that is both clearer than BARD (since there is little-to-no agreement about what a 'reasonable doubt' is) and less demanding in the level of proof that it exacts. This chapter will explore the merits of the debate between the defenders of the status quo, the perfectionists who want an even more demanding standard, and those of us who think the standard should be mildly lower (and vastly clearer) than it now is. We will also explore whether the defendant has an inalienable right (either moral or constitutional) to be tried by the BARD standard, as many of the defenders of the status quo—including the justices of the Supreme Court—insist.

THE STUNNING UNINTELLIGIBILITY OF THE CURRENT STANDARD

BARD has been around in Anglo-Saxon law since the end of the eighteenth century. By the middle of the nineteenth century, it was the prevailing standard in most American states. In 1970, the Supreme Court announced, on the flimsiest of grounds, that every criminal defendant has a *constitutional* right to be tried by BARD and that *every* element of the charges against him had to be proven beyond a reasonable doubt. The standard itself, however, remains notoriously un- or ill-defined. Ponder this quick run through its history over the last century.

Traditionally, reasonable doubt had been closely associated with the idea of 'proof to a moral certainty', a concept central to the writings of the philosopher John Locke (and others), who were trying to capture the traits of beliefs that were almost certain or virtually certain. In a case in 1994, the justices attacked that linkage. Justice Blackmun rejected it, because 'moral certainty' suggested that a finding of guilt could be grounded "on value judgments".[181] Justice Ginsberg agreed, saying that moral certainty "should be avoided as unhelpful in defining reasonable doubt."[182] How, then, *does* the Court define BARD? The unequivocal answer is that currently it does not and its long history of half-hearted attempts to define the idea would be comic if the matter were not so serious.

In 1894, for instance, a judge in a trial for polygamy in Utah was asked by jurors what a reasonable doubt was. His presumably straight-faced answer: "a reasonable doubt is not an unreasonable doubt."[183] The defendant was convicted. On appeal, the Supreme Court held that the trial judge's response "gives all the definition of reasonable doubt which a court can be required to give."[184] So, now that we know that a reasonable doubt isn't an unreasonable doubt, everything is clarified!

The Court further muddied the waters by announcing in 1962 that an Oklahoma judge in a criminal case had made a grave mistake when, in response to a juror's request for clarification of the standard, the judge responded that a doubt about guilt is 'reasonable' provided jurors can give a reason for it. The Supreme Court overturned the conviction of the defendant in the case, claiming that a "[jury] instruction containing the phrase 'a doubt that you can give a reason for' is wrong."[185] Just as a 'reasonable belief' is one for which one can give plausible reasons, it might be natural to think that a 'reasonable doubt' has to be a doubt that one has plausible reasons for. If, as the Supreme Court now allows, one might have a doubt about guilt but can't give any reason whatever for it, how can the *holder* of that doubt possibly decide the crucial question as to whether that lingering doubt is reasonable or not? Any first-year logic student could have told the Court as much; but then, to be blunt, the Supreme Court has rarely been very savvy about the logic of evidence. So, according to the Court, judges should not define 'a reasonable doubt' for jurors (even if they request such clarification) and the juror must decide whether his/her doubt is reasonable without worrying whether he has any reason for it.

You might, at this point, have begun wondering what a reasonable doubt is. We've been told that it is a constitutional requirement (even though BARD goes wholly unmentioned in the Constitution), that it isn't 'an unreasonable doubt', and that one needn't have a reason for it to count it as 'reasonable'. Beyond these insights, the Supreme Court generally refuses point blank to define it and urges trial judges to follow suit. Its new sham defense for its silence on this score is the assertion that the meaning of proof beyond a reasonable doubt is 'self-evident' and 'self-defining', adding that such concepts require neither definition nor clarification.[186] The Court conveniently ignores the fact that jurors often ask the bench to clarify what BARD means. That surely gives the lie to its purportedly self-evident nature. Beyond this nonsense, the Supreme Court's reticence to clarify the meaning of BARD raises acute issues of fairness or due process, since –absent any clear instructions whatsoever about the meaning of the standard—juries in different cases are apt to have quite different interpretations of the standard. (There is ample empirical evidence that both judges and jurors, when asked by researchers to define BARD, give quite divergent answers.)

I am aware of no serious legal scholar (with the exception of Laurence Tribe) who believes that this notion is anything other than opaque and ambiguous, hence open to a panoply of conflicting interpretations. You would think that might be a cause for concern, given that BARD is the defining line between legal guilt and legal innocence. For these reasons, re-thinking the nature of the standard of proof should be a top priority.

What I have tried to argue thus far in this book, however, is more drastic than the project of defining BARD with some clarity. We have powerful reason to believe that BARD (whatever its precise meaning, supposing that could be pinned down) leads to a situation in which the there is an overabundance of errors, unnecessarily imposing serious risks of harm on all of us. As I will try to show in this chapter and the next, there may be a way to remedy that situation. One solution would be to find a standard of proof that a). is clear or at least explained intelligibly to jurors, and b). will minimize the aggregate risks caused by the two errors associated with the social contract: falsely convicting the innocent and falsely acquitting the guilty. Struggling to define BARD more clearly is not what we need, since it is indisputable that a less demanding standard of proof will further our social contract commitments more effectively than trying to pin down this slippery notion will.

The tricky part of the exercise is not so much that of finding out what distribution of errors would satisfy the minimization demands of the social contract. We already know that a false positive produces about 2.2 victims, while a false negative produces 1.2 victims. As we shall see shortly, it is a small step from that information to figuring out what the appropriate level of confidence should be before jurors are entitled and expected to convict the defendant.

THE UTOPIANS

One perspective on the standard of proof, perhaps even the prevailing view in academic circles, says that we must minimize false positives *at all costs*. A few people think that we are already doing just that. Consider the opinions of two well-known justices on the Supreme Court. In 1970, Justice William Brennan (writing an opinion in the case that canonized BARD as the constitutional standard in criminal trials) wrote: "It is critical that the moral force of the criminal law not be diluted by a standard of proof that leaves people in doubt whether innocent men are being condemned."[187] Brennan went on to say in the same opinion: "It is also important in our free society that every individual going about his ordinary affairs have confidence that his government cannot adjudge him guilty of a criminal offense without convincing a proper factfinder of his guilt with utmost certainty."[188]

This, sadly, is pious rubbish, apparently intended for consumption by a gullible John Q. Citizen. We know perfectly well that, however demanding BARD may be, it does not and cannot guarantee a result with 'the utmost certainty' nor is there any intellectually honest way to assure the citizenry that the prevailing standard will eliminate all doubt about whether 'innocent men are being condemned'. The obvious and unavoidable fact is that, regardless of the standard we put in place, there will be false convictions from time to time. If citizens need to be sent any message, it is that errors in human affairs cannot be wholly avoided and that our intolerance for errors of false positives has to be mediated by a recognition that false positives are not a common occurrence but they will be with us forever. Instead, the Court seems to prefer reassuring bromides to honest transparency.

Thirty-five years after Brennan's opinion, Justice Antonin Scalia explicitly addressed the question of false convictions arising from proof beyond a reasonable doubt. Mildly more willing than Brennan to acknowledge that false positives do occur from time to time, he nonetheless thought the problem was so minor as not to need remediation since (he claimed) "the error rate [in felony convictions is] .027 percent—or, to put it another way, a success rate of 99.973 percent."[189] If Scalia's numbers were right, BARD would be the next best thing to perfection. Unfortunately, as the data from earlier chapters show, Justice Scalia got the error rate wrong by more than two orders of magnitude. As we saw in chapter 3, the best estimate of the frequency of false positives is in the neighborhood of 3%, meaning (using Scalia's terminology) that the 'success rate' was more like 97%. Thirty years ago, the well-known legal theorist Laurence Tribe sang a similar but more extreme tune, insisting that the BARD standard of proof is more demanding than *any* conceivable probabilistic standard could possibly be:
"The [criminal trial] system does not in fact authorize the imposition of criminal punishment when the trier recognizes a quantifiable doubt as to the defendant's guilt. Instead, the system . . . insists upon as close an approximation to certainty as seems humanly attainable in the circumstances."[190]
Can Tribe really believe that if a trier of fact is persuaded that the apparent guilt of the defendant is 99.99%, then he must vote for acquittal?

Several legal theorists share the cheery optimism of Scalia and Brennan about the power of BARD to minimize the occurrence of false positives. While they acknowledge, with Scalia, that such mistakes occur from time to time, they argue that the BARD standard represents the 'best effort' that we fallible mortals can make to avoid condemning the innocent. The best-known and most vocal proponent of this perspective is probably the famous Ronald Dworkin. In the opening chapter of his *Taking Rights Seriously*, Dworkin briefly contemplates the idea that "the proper goals of the criminal law include the protection of individual freedom [of the accused] as well as the prevention of crime" and even concedes that some people might think that it would be a good idea "to strike a balance between these two goals."[191] (This could be read as a less-than-precise formulation of the social-contract thesis I propounded in chapter 2.) Dworkin, however, will have none of it since he will brook no talk of compromises or trade-offs where the core rights of defendants are concerned. If the "moral principles" governing the protection of the accused were to be "dishonored" by considerations of crime control or the protection of prospective victims (heaven forbid!), it would be an occasion for "shame and regret."[192] In short, he insists that we wholly exclude the costs of false negatives and the victims they claim from the discussion of how high to set the standard of proof. All that matters for Dworkin is that we recognize that an innocent defendant has not just a constitutional but also a *moral* right not to be convicted. To honor that right, we must adopt the standard of proof that represents what he calls 'the best effort we can make' to avoid a false positive. Dworkin holds that morality requires that proof BARD must be the standard of proof in criminal trials because the criminal process must be "biased strongly against the conviction of the innocent" and BARD (in his opinion) introduces such a bias more surely than any other standard could.[193]

Dworkin readily grants that such a decision rule will lead to far more false negatives than a less demanding standard would but insists its use is necessary to "guard against a mistake [a false positive] that involves greater moral harm than a mistake in the other direction."[194] Since, in his view, the reasonable doubt rule represents the best and most strenuous effort that the legal system can take to avoid convicting the innocent, we are obliged to honor it, wholly ignoring the harms that result from such a demanding standard. Evidently, only the best will do, and never mind those innocents who suffer because of the hundreds of thousands of acquitted but guilty violent felons walking free, thanks to the insistence on the use of the most demanding standard we can concoct.

The second strain of utopian thinking about the standard of proof can be seen in the growing chorus of voices that insist— contrary to the views of Scalia, Brennan and Dworkin—that proof BARD is *not* tough enough. They are eager to replace it with an even more demanding standard. As one scholar puts it: "the state also bears a duty towards the guilty person, to refrain from convicting her as long as her guilt has not been proven *with the greatest certainty possible.*"[195]

Such proposals take a number of forms. These perfectionists differ in their specific articulations of what the new standard should be. Among those suggested so far: "beyond any doubt," "no doubt," "beyond all doubt" and even a return to "moral certainty." Tim Bakken, going so far out on a limb that he falls off, tells us that we need a new standard of proof, which "might encompass [proof of guilt]… to an absolute certainty… or a similarly high standard."[196]

Perhaps these advocates of an even more demanding standard should ponder the situation currently in Romania. Notorious for political corruption over decades, the current government has promised that it will aggressively tackle the corruption problem among politicians. Less enthusiastic about this reform than the general public, members of Parliament in June 2015 indicated that they would accept this crackdown only if Romania replaces its existing standard (BARD) with 'proof beyond all doubt' for corruption charges. Make a guess at how many corrupt politicians will be convicted under those circumstances!

It goes without saying that most of these proposals are hopeless. The idea that a rational jury can ever arrive at a verdict that admits not even a shred of a doubt belies the fact that full certainty about any reconstruction of contested past events is next to impossible. As the empiricist philosophers have been arguing since the time of Locke and Hume, honesty requires us to be fallibilists about our beliefs about the empirical world and to recognize the inevitability of error. In reaching a verdict about a contested belief, there will always be *some* residual doubt (no matter how powerful the evidence) and never a justified belief that the probability of defendant's guilt has reached the absolute certainty benchmark. Leaving aside the fact that scholars looking for an unerring standard are aspiring to what cannot be achieved, the advocates of such an approach are evidently blissfully indifferent to the fact that there would be few if any criminal cases that would ever satisfy their demand and that virtually every trial would end in an acquittal, often a false one.

AN IMMODEST PROPOSAL: RATCHETING DOWN THE STANDARD OF PROOF

As we have seen, a common response among legal theorists to the occurrence of false positives is to insist that we should raise the standard of proof, since (as many of them see it) we have a moral duty to do everything humanly possible to reduce false positives. A disinterested observer might suggest that a false positive rate of some 3% indicates that we are already doing a bloody good job of protecting the innocent defendant. After all, how common is it, in processes that hinge on frail human deliberation, to be able to boast that we are wrong only 1 time in 33? Medicine often cannot claim such a success rate, even where issues of life and death are at stake. Do only 3% of marriages fail? Do only 3% of automobiles get recalled for defective, fatality-producing flaws? My claim is that the perfectionist utopians are right that BARD has to be modified but they are profoundly wrong about the direction in which it needs to be changed. As we shall soon see in detail, the only way to satisfy the demands of the social contract is by minimizing the aggregate risk of being falsely convicted and being the victim of a violent criminal who was falsely acquitted. A lowered standard of proof would do just that. Here's why.

Almost forty years ago, two leading legal scholars, John Kaplan and Laurence Tribe, laid out ways of calculating the appropriate standard of proof by using plausible values for the utilities or costs of the various outcomes at trial. Because of limitations of space, I will give a simplified version of their original analysis. Roughly, the idea is that we want to set the standard of proof at that point of indifference where we are neutral as to whether a trial ends in an acquittal or a conviction. Kaplan's proposal was that the rational standard of proof was given by the formula:

$$SoP = 1/[1 + (cost_{F-}/cost_{F+})].^{197}$$

Plugging into this equation the costs (in terms of victims) of the two errors that we worked out in chapter four, we can see that a more rational standard of proof (in the sense of a standard that reflects the ratio of costs of the two errors, at least for violent crimes) would be given by:

$$SoP = 1/[1 + (1.2/2.2)] = 1/1.55 = 0.65.$$

If we were to accept Kaplan's analysis as sound, then the level of the criminal standard of proof should be closer to 65% than to 90% or 95%, as conventional wisdom has it. If you are skeptical whether jurors could readily calibrate their beliefs using numerical probabilities, there already exists an official 'non-probabilistic' version of a standard of proof widely used in the justice system that approximates to it. Called 'proof by clear and convincing evidence', it is utilized in civil law, in criminal hearings on the granting of bail in most states and in many exoneration hearings. It is usually understood as being in the region of about 70% confidence, intermediate between the weaker preponderance-of-the-evidence standard (>50%) and the much tougher BARD (≥90%). Tribe gives a more robust formula for calculating the height of the standard, that looks at the utilities of the four possible outcomes at trial: true and false positives and true and false negatives.[198] On virtually any *plausible* assignments of utility values to those four outcomes, a standard of proof in the 90-100% range fails to capture the utilities and disutilities of those outcomes.[199]

The object lesson seems to be clear: we are now utilizing a standard of proof much more demanding than it should be, since it leads to far greater risk of harm in aggregate than many lesser standards would. BARD (understood as a surrogate for about 90% confidence) would make sense as a standard of proof for violent crimes just in case the harm done by a false conviction was about ten times greater than the harm done by a false acquittal. There is no way that such an assessment of harms can be plausible, in light of the data rehearsed earlier on the recidivism of violent felons.

I am proposing that it would be sensible policy, as the social contract suggests, to set the standard of proof at that point where we minimize the risk to the average citizen of either being violently victimized by a falsely-acquitted felon or being falsely convicted of a violent crime he didn't commit. To set the standard higher (or lower) than this would mean that the standard is putting all of us at greater risk of harm than is necessary. This point of equilibrium defines the threshold at which the justice system can neither be said to be convicting too many innocent defendants nor acquitting too many guilty ones. Viewed from this perspective, it is vividly clear that the current standard of proof is too high. As I have already shown, the promiscuous acquittal of, or dropping of charges against, many very probably guilty defendants (because their apparent guilt is perceived as below the BARD standard) is generating much more harm than the occasional conviction of innocent defendants does.

For utilitarians or consequentialists, the calculations I have rehearsed should put an end to the fiction that BARD encapsulates an informed and realistic assessment of the true utilities of the outcomes of a trial. It is simply indisputable that more harm to innocent persons arises from using BARD than would result from the introduction of a less demanding standard.

CLOSE CASES AND THE 32-TO-1 CONUNDRUM

We can get a clearer idea of why the lowering of the standard would produce much less overall pain by considering two possible alternative scenarios or thought experiments. Let us suppose, first, that BARD were modified slightly *upwards* as the Utopians demand. Suppose, specifically looking at our paradigm case from 2008, that it were raised enough to reduce the number of false positives by about 10% (from its current level of 10.9k false positives in cases of violent crime to about 9.9k false positives). This would have the undoubted merit that it annually saves a thousand innocent defendants from the fate of being punished for a violent crime they did not commit. But there is a huge downside to this seemingly minor modification. As we have seen, the false positive rate with the existing standard is 3%, meaning that there are roughly 32 guilty defendants for every innocent defendant in the region marked out as the 'conviction zone' by BARD. If we raised that standard mildly, we would find ourselves in a range where the ratio of guilty to innocent defendants was more like 40-to-1, that is, there would be about 40 true positives for every false positive in the conviction range (that is, the area defined by the standard of proof and above). That's another way of saying that raising the standard of proof sufficiently to convert 1,000 current false positives into true negatives would inevitably mean converting some 40,000 true positives (using the current standard) into false negatives. Specifically, convicting 1k fewer innocent persons than we now do annually for violent crimes would mean converting the true convictions of some 40k genuinely guilty felons into false acquittals. The cost of that move is easy to compute, given our calculations from the last chapter: the conversion of 1,000 false positives into true negatives would reduce the harm associated with such false positives by some 2,200 victims (2.2x1,000), while the conversion of 40,000 true positives to false negatives would produce some 48,000 new victims (40,000x1.2). In short, this seemingly modest, upward-trending adjustment to the current standard of proof would *increase* the aggregate number of victims by about 45,000 over current levels.

Figure 8. Distribution of Apparent Guilt

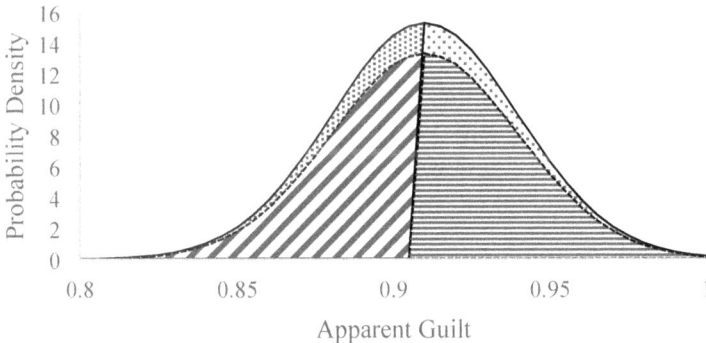

Figure 8 reflects the patterns found in our data from 2008. It pictures some 93k false negatives and some 11k false positives among the 595k arrestees. The area with sloped lines represents the false negatives; the area with solid horizontal lines represents true positives; the area to the left of the standard with dark dots represents true negatives; and the area with lighter dots represents the false positives. Clearly, moving the standard higher slightly reduces the frequency of false positives while dramatically increasing the frequency of false negatives. Moving the SoP downwards to the left has the reverse effect; it modestly increases the number of false positives while heavily reducing the number of false negatives.

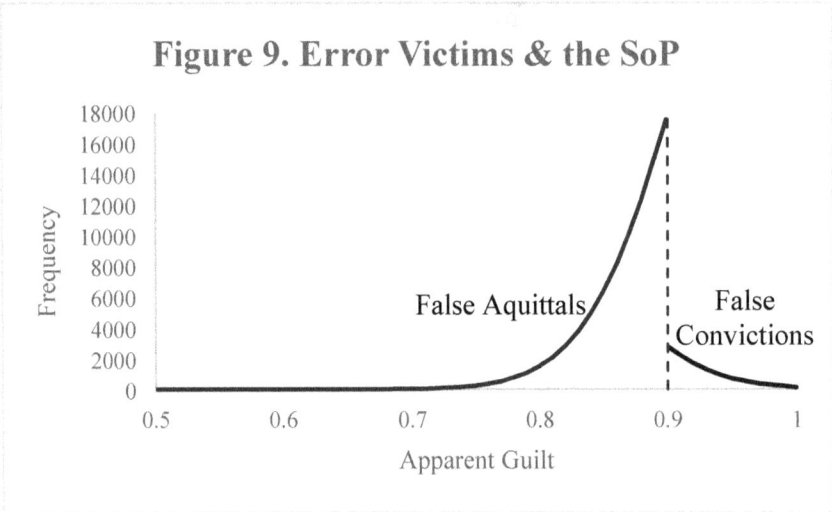

Figure 9. Error Victims & the SoP

Figure 9 shows the same effect, to wit, a very heavy concentration of truly guilty felons relative to truly innocent ones at higher standards (90% and above) and a very low concentration of truly innocent defendants in the same region.

Figure 10. Distribution of Apparent Guilt

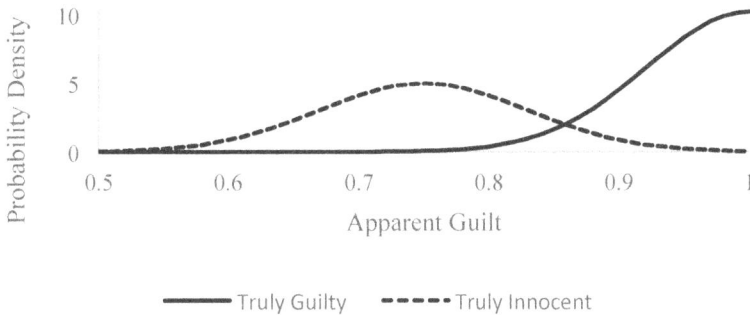

Figure 10 expresses the difference not in terms of those at trial but in terms of the *harms* that result from a very high standard. Moving the standard higher than at present moderately reduces the harms from false positives while moving the standard modestly lower drastically reduces the harms resulting form false negatives. It drives home the crucial fact that most truly guilty arrestees are heavily clustered around the region we take to be defined by BARD. If BARD is in the vicinity of about 90-95%, then we can see that there are roughly 40 guilty defendants for every innocent one. Moving the standard slightly to the left of that point, say around 85-90% and the ratio of truly guilty to truly innocent falls to about 10-to-1. Move it slightly higher (say to 98%) and that ratio becomes more like 40-to-1.

Why does all that matter? For the crucial reason that, if we tinker even modestly with the height of the standard of proof, we end up with *very* different error ratios. If we make the standard more demanding, we are turning about 40 or 50 true convictions into false acquittals for every false conviction we turn into a true acquittal. Similarly, if we lower the standard of proof from its current level (to say 88%), we are turning more than 12 false negatives into true positives for every false positive we produce. Because so many of the guilty defendants are clustered so near the standard of proof and so few truly innocent defendants are to be found there, the idea of raising the standard of proof still further –

which is a very popular proposal in the legal literature or our era—would exact an enormous price in additional false negatives in return for a very modest reduction in the number of false positives.

Figure 9 shows that the false acquittal rate goes up dramatically as the standard of proof is elevated because the ratio of truly guilty to truly innocent rises significantly. It graphically illustrates that, the more demanding the standard, the more likely it is that a truly guilty defendant will get off the hook by having what would be a true positive under BARD become a false negative under the tougher standard. By contrast, the false conviction rate drops precipitately as the standard rises since fewer and fewer innocent defendants exhibit a guilt profile sufficient to satisfy the rising demands of the higher standard. The most important moral to draw from the chart, however, is the relation between the two curves. *Every* shift of the standard of proof to the right or to the left alters the distribution of errors. While a modest rise in the standard of proof reduces the false positive rate from an already low to an even lower level, that same shift in the standard brings dramatic increases in the proportion of the truly guilty who are falsely acquitted. On the other hand, lowering the standard slightly increases the false conviction rate (but much less dramatically than if it is increased by a shift to the right of the standard), while mildly lowering the rate of false acquittals.

Consider, by contrast, specifically how things would change if we *lowered* the standard of proof by a comparable amount so as to increase the false positives from 10.9k to 11.9k. The increase in the number of false positives would lead to 2,200 new victims, while the conversion of some 25k false negatives into true positives would reduce the harm currently occurring by some 30k victims. The aggregate impact of this mild reduction of the standard of proof would be approximately 28k fewer victims of violent crimes than are produced by the current standard. Table 8 illustrates how the calculation might go.

Table 8. Risks of Violent Harms Annually Produced by Current System and its Variants[200]				
	False Positives	False Negatives	Harms	Aggregate annual risk[201]
Current system	10.9k	88k	130k victims	1-in-1.9k (0.052%)
Mildly raised standard	9.9k	128k	176k victims	1-in-1.43k (0.07%)
Mildly reduced standard	11.9k	63k	102k victims	1-in-2.5k (0.04%)

To those who insist that we should be raising the standard, my reply is simple: modestly lowering the standard would produce far fewer victims than the current system and some 74k fewer victims than a modest elevation of the standard would. When Dworkin self-righteously tells us that it would be an "occasion for shame and regret" if we took into account the costs of false negatives in setting the height of the standard of proof, *he* is the one who should be ashamed of himself. As even Lord Blackstone would have conceded, transforming more than 32k true positives into 32k false negatives (which is what results if we raise the standard by enough to reduce the false conviction rate from 3% to 2.7%) is an extravagantly high price to exact for converting 1k false positives into 1k true negatives.

Along similar lines to Dworkin, the legal scholar Katherine Goldwasser says emphatically: "a reduction in criminal false negatives cannot [be used to] offset false positives."[202] If the existing 32-to-1 ratio does not persuade her that we have already given far too much emphasis to reducing false positives (by wholly ignoring the costs generated by such a reduction), I have to conclude that she fails to understand that the raison d'être for a standard of proof is precisely to have a decision rule that will distribute outcomes in accord with their respective costs. Saying, with Dworkin, that we should wholly ignore the costs to those innocent victims of violent harm caused by those who were falsely acquitted, indicates that Goldwasser has little grip on the logic of the standard of proof. The function of the standard is not to make it as hard as we can possibly imagine to prove the guilt of a defendant but to insist on a threshold for conviction that correctly reflects the risk of harms associated with the two errors. Taken literally, her approach would entail that the only acceptable standard was one that never led to false convictions. As we know, the only way to achieve that is by acquitting every defendant.

As the victim profiles associated with our three scenarios make very clear, the social contract, as described in chapter 2, would hold that the *joint* risk of (a). being the victim of a falsely acquitted felon during his Laplacian window and b). of being false convicted of a violent crime would be much lower under what I have called the 'mildly reduced standard' scenario than it would be under current practices or under a regimen with an even more exacting standard than BARD. That entails that, under the terms of the social contract, we should be reducing the standard of proof without hesitation. The existing standard is bad enough in terms of producing unnecessary harm to victims and ought to be lowered. But the fashionable and emotive pleas for an elevated standard, or 'doing the best we can possibly do to avoid false convictions' would expose all of us to much greater harm of being an innocent victim than is either necessary or tolerable.

The three scenarios we have just been exploring (the existing standard, the mildly elevated standard and the mildly reduced standard) represent more or less what has long been called the region of 'close cases', meaning that they appear to fall quite close to the existing threshold for a conviction. Almost all the cases that actually go to trial are perceived by at least one (and often both) the parties as close cases. A defendant who thinks he has a reasonable chance of winning will generally opt for a trial over a plea bargain. A prosecutor who thinks he has a reasonable chance of winning will proceed to trial if he cannot reach a plea bargain agreement. If a defendant perceives his case as weak, he will almost certainly elect a plea bargain, provided he can get one. A prosecutor who sees his case as weak will generally drop charges altogether. The regions just below and just above the threshold of proof (BARD) are the ones involving cases that are especially sensitive to precisely how the standard is understood by the jurors. We also have strong reason to believe that each region is very heavily populated with truly guilty defendants. As we saw in our paradigm look at violent crimes (2008), more than 350k guilty defendants (and about 11k innocent ones) fall in the small range between BARD and full certainty. It would be extraordinary if the number of defendants fell off dramatically just below the standard since the density is so high just a few points higher. (For instance, could we really believe that there are some 350k guilty defendants in the range between 90% and 100% apparent guilt, and only a few to be found in the region from (say) 85-90%? Subtle adjustments to the standard and to other rules of trial can make all the difference as to whether a defendant falling in the range close to the standard will be acquitted or convicted.

BARD AS A RIGHT?

It will immediately occur to readers that the US Supreme Court has declared that trial by the BARD standard is a constitutional right and moral theorists like Dworkin have claimed it to be a moral right as well. How, then, could we even consider changing this deeply entrenched and highly canonized right of defendants? The fact is that neither the Supreme Court's argument for the BARD standard nor the moralists' argument is anything more than question-begging.

Consider, first, the claim (promulgated in 1970) that BARD is a constitutional right we are bound to uphold and revere. In its opinion that canonized BARD as constitutional (*In re Winship*), the Supreme Court gave two reasons for asserting it to be a constitutional requirement. The Justices most certainly did not claim to be able to find any passage in the US Constitution that mentions any standard whatever, let alone proof beyond a reasonable doubt. (That is scarcely surprising since BARD only became widely used well after the framing of the Constitution and Bill of Rights. Its framers cannot have had reasonable doubt in mind, since that standard was not yet in place in the common law.) Early in the nineteenth century, common-law countries began to use BARD (or, as they often called it, 'moral certainty'). How then can it be a *constitutional* requirement?

The first argument used by the high court was that it is demanded by the due-process clause of the Constitution. That insists, among other things, that there must be fairness in trials. The Court in 1970 noted, correctly, that BARD was widely used in criminal trials. The *Winship* case that brought BARD to the Supreme Court had involved a New York statute allowing for a lower standard of proof in the handling of cases in juvenile courts. The Court argued that, since BARD is already used in the vast majority of trials, it would be unfair to abandon it for a select group of defendants (namely, juvenile offenders).

This is no argument whatever for the thesis that the reasonable doubt standard is better than others; it is simply an argument based on fairness and due process. It amounts to the claim that the prevailing standard—*whatever* it is—should be used across the spectrum of criminal offenses. But it is transparently clear that this argument would be no argument against the *replacement* of the BARD standard, provided that the new standard were likewise applied across the board.[203]

The second effort from the Court to justify BARD—apart from citing its widespread current use—likewise falls flat on its face. The Court argues that it is self-evident that a false conviction is costlier than a false acquittal. (Self-evident or not, as this book shows, there is plenty of empirical evidence to sustain that claim.) The mistake arises when the Court implies that, if indeed a false conviction is more harmful than a false acquittal, it follows that we need the BARD standard. That manifestly does not follow. The Court's bald claim that a false conviction produces more harm than a false acquittal entails only that an acceptable standard of proof must be one apt to produce more false negatives than false positives. I have no quarrel whatever with that claim. But *any* standard of proof greater than 50% will arguably satisfy that demand. The Court simply acted as if a necessary condition for an adequate standard (namely, that it produce more false negatives than false positives) suffices as a sufficient condition for picking out BARD as the uniquely appropriate standard. Clearly it does no such thing; necessary conditions are most certainly not sufficient conditions.

There is thus *no* clause in the Constitution that would prohibit the wholesale re-definition of the criminal standard of proof, so long as it were—in accord with due process—applied uniformly and would guarantee, over the long run, the production of significantly more false acquittals than false convictions. On these grounds, clear and convincing evidence, for instance, would be as constitutional as BARD and, of no small significance, much less prone to produce the huge number of mistakes that BARD does.

This still leaves us with the 'moral' argument for BARD than Dworkin was so fond of. Recall that he asserted that it would be a "source for shame and regret" if the defendant were tried by any standard lower than BARD, especially if (as I have proposed) the lowering of the standard were to be driven, in part, by an appraisal of the costs to society of false negatives. Can Dworkin possibly believe that hewing to a rule that would enable 30 guilty defendants (mostly serial offenders) to go free at the price of one fewer false conviction is a policy that we should be proud of? How can a moral theorist of the law be so indifferent to the rights of prospective victims who stand to suffer grievously from such a policy? I think the appropriate response to Dworkin's elephant tears can be found in an opinion by Justice White. He wrote: "Due process does not require that every conceivable step be taken, at whatever cost, to eliminate the possibility of convicting an innocent person. Punishment of those found guilty by a jury, for example, is not forbidden merely because there is a remote possibility in some instances that an innocent person might go to jail."[204]

It seems vividly clear that the existing standard of proof (along with other rules of evidence to be examined in the next chapter) is generating an error profile that creates significantly more harm than is either necessary or desirable.

The problem, however, is that BARD is so ill- or undefined that it is difficult to imagine how it could be mildly lowered. While we could perhaps instruct jurors to convict only if defendant's guilt had been proven 'nearly (or almost) beyond a reasonable doubt', this only seems to compound the degree of unclarity already exhibited by the existing standard. As an alternative, one could consider (a la Kaplan) defining the standard as a degree of probability (say, 80%). The trouble here is that there is plenty of empirical research indicating that ordinary citizens don't have a very solid grasp on how to calibrate their degrees of confidence quantitatively.[205] Beyond that, the Supreme Court has made it vividly clear on several occasions that it would not tolerate a standard of proof couched in terms of probabilities.

Accordingly, if we are to move away from a situation where, at the point of the standard, there are some 32k guilty persons for every 1k innocent ones, we need to tackle the problem in ways that —without imposing an even more confusing version of the standard of proof than we now have—nonetheless allow us to bring the humongous number of false negatives under greater control. To repeat: the problem is that, while mildly scaling back the standard of proof would in principle lead to far fewer victims than the current standard does, there is no obvious way to define a standard that will be mildly weaker than BARD. The existing legal system basically works with three common standards: the preponderance of the evidence, clear and convincing evidence and BARD. Obviously the preponderance standard will not do since it fails to acknowledge the fact that a false positive is more costly than a false negative. Clear and convincing evidence does acknowledge as much (not to mention that it would also comply with the social contract's emphasis on taking seriously into account the respective costs of the two errors). But the likelihood that those who shape judicial rules would accept a shift in standards as drastic as the move from BARD to clear and convincing evidence (generally thought to be in the region of 70-75% confidence in guilt) is low. The puzzle thus becomes how, if at all, does one define a standard slightly less demanding than BARD that would be both intelligible to jurors, and acceptable to the courts. While I do not deny that such a task is possible, I think its prospects of wide acceptance would be low, however desirable its implementation would be.

If so, that leaves us with a serious conundrum: if current practices are patently violating the social contract by ignoring the costs and frequency of false negatives, how might it be possible to reduce significantly the abundance of such errors without imposing a profound and controversial change in the official standard of proof? The next chapter will explore in detail how we can meet that challenge.

Chapter 6 Searching for a Solution (B): Burden-Warping and the Skewing of Errors in the Defendant's Favor

> Under our criminal procedure the accused has every advantage.... Our dangers do not lie in too little tenderness to the accused.... What we need to fear is the archaic formalism and the watery sentiment that obstructs, delays, and defeats the prosecution of crime.–Judge Learned Hand (1923)[206]

We have seen that existing practices in criminal law lead to the infliction of more violent harm on innocent victims than is either necessary or desirable and that, if we were to lower the standard of proof modestly, there would be significantly less harm to the innocent. But the standard of proof is by no means the only factor contributing to the high levels of false negatives and comparatively low levels of false positives currently in play. Nor is adjusting the standard of proof the only mechanism available to us for reducing the harms to the innocent now caused by the abundance of false negatives.

Many of the rules of evidence and procedure (whether those in place or those recently proposed) can exert a dramatic impact on the frequency and distribution of errors. Some rules (the relevance rule or the rule admitting expert testimony on DNA or fingerprint evidence) reduce the frequency of *both* false positives and false negatives by making a true verdict—whether a conviction or an acquittal—more likely. They are obviously a highly desirable epistemic commodity. Other rules (for instance, some parts of the hearsay rule) raise the likelihood of *both* sorts of errors and should be drastically re-written. The more interesting and controversial rules fall into two other classes:

i). Those that give a probatory advantage to the defendant, thereby reducing the frequency of false positives but increasing the frequency of false negatives. (These are what I will call 'burden-enhancers'.) They make it harder to convict the guilty *and* the innocent.

ii). Those that give a probatory advantage to the prosecution, thereby reducing the frequency of false acquittals and increasing the frequency of false positives ('burden-reducers'). They make it easier to convict the guilty *and* the innocent.

As this chapter will show, there are vastly more burden-enhancers than burden-reducers.[207] Their cumulative weight (combined with the mighty distributional power of the standard of proof itself) is such that, as we saw in chapter 4, only 3-in-100 convictions (11k in 363k) are false positives while approximately 2-in-5 acquittals (93k out of 232k acquittals) are false negatives.

For such reasons, we will use this chapter to examine what I call the burden of persuasion. As I am using the term here, the 'burden of persuasion' is not, as often understood, a mere synonym for standard of proof. It is broader than that, denoting a measure of how difficult it is to convict the truly guilty. While a high standard of proof certainly contributes mightily to that end, it is by no means the only element in a trial that makes it harder than it should be for the prosecutor to prove the guilt of truly guilty defendants. As we will see in this chapter, there are dozens of rules of evidence and procedure that give an epistemically unjustified probatory advantage to the defendant. By contrast, a burden-reducer has an effect similar to lowering the standard of proof; a burden-enhancer has an similar effect similar to what raising the official standard of proof would have.

While the standard of proof and burden-enhancers (or reducers) can have similar results, they function very differently. The standard of proof sets the level of confidence necessary for a conviction, full stop. It says nothing about what evidence is to be admitted nor about the trial procedures to use. A burden-enhancer, on the other hand, can jigger with the kinds of evidence that will be admitted or excluded at trial; it can tell jurors what probative significance, if any, they should give to a particular kind of evidence; and it can shape the rules of trial procedure so as to give other asymmetric advantages to the defendant.

American criminal law is replete with burden-enhancers (arguably more than in any other legal system in the world) and has several burden-reducers. It follows that if we are interested in reducing the level of current victimization caused by trials, we can do so either by lowering the standard of proof (which, as we have seen, would be a difficult task to take on) *or* by adjusting some of the burden-enhancers to dim their impact on the distribution of errors. Alternatively, we could use some combination of the two so as to minimize the joint risks of false positives and victimization by falsely-acquitted felons during the time when they should be in prison.

There is also ample evidence that adjusting these burden-modifiers can dramatically change the outcomes of trials. A particularly striking illustration of the magnitude of those changes comes from a look at the impact of so-called rape-shield laws, introduced in most states in the 1970s and 1980s. That family of rules eliminated—for rape cases alone—two burden-altering rules. Prior to that, it was commonplace for judges to exclude evidence of the prior arrests and the prior convictions of those accused of rape on the grounds that such evidence was 'unfairly prejudicial', in short, inflammatory. Among other changes that they introduced, the rape-shield laws allowed as unproblematic the admission of prior bad acts on the part of a rape defendant. They also encouraged by exclusion what had earlier been the practice of admitting information about the prior sexual history of the victim. The principal motives for the latter change was to grapple with the concern that, if a rape victim knows that her sexual history would be likely to come out at trial, she might be inclined not to file charges at all. Shortly after the introduction of these changes, there was a statewide study of the impact of those laws on rape conviction rates in Michigan, among the first states to adopt this change in legal procedures. What they found was that "there was a post-reform increase in rape convictions per month" in Michigan from 8 forcible rape convictions (before the reform in the law) to 21 (immediately after its introduction).[208] No surprise: they also found that rape frequency declined.

Given that some 90% of convictions emerge not from trials but from plea bargains, one might think that the fine points of legal trial procedure are relatively unimportant. Such a claim would be misleading because negotiations about plea bargains are driven by both parties' knowledge of what evidence would and would not be admissible and what jury instructions would be doled out during a trial, should one occur. The defendant's willingness to opt for a plea bargain in lieu of trial usually will depend upon how he and his counsel reckon he would fare during a trial. If strongly persuaded that he would be acquitted at trial, he will have little incentive to enter plea bargaining. For that reason, the rules of trial procedure cast a long shadow over both the prosecutor's and the defendant's negotiating positions about what concessions the state would make, and how amenable the defendant would be to accept a plea deal.

As we shall see shortly, some of these burden-altering rules exclude prosecutorial evidence that is unquestionably relevant to the case. Others give the defendant effective control over various features of a trial in ways that work to his advantage. Then there are those rules that require judges to instruct jurors not to draw perfectly reasonable adverse inferences from some of the evidence that has been admitted or from certain events in the trial itself. Each of these practices gives asymmetric advantages to the defendant not enjoyed by the prosecution, making a false acquittal more likely than it would be without such burden-enhancers. So that readers can get a grip on just how many obstacles to conviction the rules of procedure put in place, I shall briefly cite numerous examples (by no means all) of the probatory advantages given to defendants.

BURDEN-ENHANCERS

1. Exclusionary Rules:
• Exclusion of relevant evidence directly obtained from defendant by police without a warrant or probable cause. (*Mapp v. Ohio*[209])

This rule arises from the judiciary's view that its role is "to police the police" and can and often does lead to the exclusion of highly relevant and inculpatory evidence. As even the Supreme Court concedes[210], however, nothing whatever in the Constitution mandates the exclusion of such evidence nor was it excluded before the 20th century.[211]

• Poison Fruit Doctrine, i.e., the exclusion of relevant evidence emerging *indirectly* from an illegal search. (*Silverthorne Lumber v U.S.*)[212]

While the prosecution cannot introduce evidence illegally seized from the defendant, the latter may introduce evidence that he or his agents have illicitly acquired.

• Likely exclusion of relevant prior convictions and arrests (prior crimes of defendants are excluded in ~90% of the cases where the defendant does not testify and in ~50% of cases where he does testify).[213] (FRE 609)

No one disputes that prior criminal activities such as are contained in records of arrests and convictions are generally pertinent to determinations of guilt in the current case. That notwithstanding, information about prior crimes is usually excluded (especially if defendant does not testify) because judges fear that jurors may give it more weight than it should have.

• Exclusion of 'unfairly prejudicial', relevant evidence, if the prejudice is thought by the judge to be greater than the probative value of the evidence. (FRE 403)

It is obvious that evidence for the prosecution will generally be prejudicial to the interests of the defendant. This rule allows for the exclusion of virtually any evidence that the judge considers to be "significantly more unfairly prejudicial than relevant', whatever that might mean.[214] Since there is very little robust empirical evidence measuring how prejudicial various sorts of evidence are, judges are left largely to their own intuitions to resolve this tricky balancing act.

• Numerous exclusions of relevant, hearsay evidence. (FRE 802,803)

Some types of hearsay evidence are admissible but many of the exclusions involve evidence that most of us would consider pertinent and relevant to the case.

• Exclusion of evidence about the character of the defendant, unless a non-testifying defendant wants it introduced. (FRE 404, 405,406)

Here, the concern is simply this: if character evidence is relevant (and it must be, since the courts will readily admit it if the defendant wants to introduce it and will invariably admit it in cases involving alleged rape), why should one party, but not the other, be able to exclude it?

• Exclusion of non-Mirandized confessions, even if corroborated by other evidence. (*Miranda v. Arizona*, 1966)

The courts grant that defendant does not possess a constitutional right to be read his *Miranda* rights but their insistence on such a policy is another instance of the courts' decision 'to police the police'.

• If the defendant refused to cooperate with police in their investigations or refused to answer their questions, the jury generally cannot be informed of this behavior. (*Doyle v. Ohio*, 1976)

• **The d**efendant usually fully controls exclusion of testimony from many so-called 'privileged witnesses' (except for spouses).

Even if those witnesses (doctors, clergy, psychiatrists, lawyers, social workers, counselors) have pertinent evidence arising from their conversations with the defendant and wish to testify, they can be silenced by the defendant, however relevant their testimony might be.[215] Worse yet, jurors are generally not informed when the defendant exercises his privilege to silence privileged witnesses, despite the fact that many jurors would consider it relevant to know that defendant blocked the testimony of someone who may have known something about the crime and the defendant's role in it.

• A voluntary admission of guilt by the defendant to the police (even after being Mirandized) can be retracted by the defendant, thereby becoming inadmissible at trial, unless there is independent evidence corroborating the confession.

2. Prohibition of Appropriate Inferences by Jurors:

• If a judge decides to allow the admission of a testifying defendant's prior crimes, he will generally give an instruction to the jury that they must ignore their awareness of those priors for any purpose other than raising doubts about the truth of the defendant's testimony. By contrast, a non-testifying defendant's prior convictions can be introduced only if the prosecutor can show that their probative value is greater than their 'unfairly prejudicial' character. (FRE 609)

• The jury is instructed to draw no adverse inferences from defendant's silence at trial, despite the fact that, through most of American legal history, jurors were encouraged to draw adverse inferences from the silence of the defendant, if they believed the defendant's refusal to tell his side of the story was a partial indicator of guilt. (*Carter v. Kentucky,* 1981)

Courts concede that defendant's failure to testify is relevant information; indeed, in civil cases, the defendant's silence can serve as the basis for an inference that defendant has something to hide. But in criminal cases, the current regime is that all the actors in the drama (judges, lawyers and the jury) must wholly ignore the fact that defendant did not testify.

3. Procedural Asymmetries Favoring the Defendant:

• There can be no appeal of acquittals, even if the trial leading to defendant's acquittal involved egregious, defendant-friendly but erroneous rulings. (Fifth Amendment[216])

This is a particularly heavy thumb on the balance scale. If a defendant is convicted in a trial due to what an appellate court later thinks are erroneous rulings by the trial judge, his conviction is properly set aside unless it can be shown beyond a reasonable doubt that the errors were 'harmless'.[217] If an acquittal, the verdict cannot be appealed, regardless of any egregious errors the judge may have committed. This issue will be discussed in detail in the next chapter.

• Defendant is allowed to present his case and his testimony *after* the prosecution rests its case (and, if he wishes, after all his own witnesses have testified), thereby being able to shape his testimony to his advantage while all the other witnesses, including the victim of the crime, are generally sequestered prior to giving testimony so that they cannot shape their testimony to fit the testimony of others. (FRE 615[218])

Very few legal systems in the world allow the defendant to withhold testimony until every other witness has gone on record. In many jurisdictions (Germany for instance), the defendant is often the *first* witness to testify in a trial. England, Australia and Scotland have similar policies. In several American states (e.g., Michigan), the victim of the crime is not allowed to hear the trial until *after* she has given her testimony. Surely, a fairer arrangement would be either to insist that both the defendant and the victim testify early on (thereby hearing the rest of the trial) or allowing the victim's testimony –like the defendant's—to be offered after the testimony of other witnesses.

• Defendant can present character evidence to impeach prosecution witnesses while still blocking the admissibility of evidence of his own character (if he does not testify). (FRE 608)

• For many crimes, including some violent ones, the law stipulates a point in time beyond which the defendant cannot be prosecuted (the 'statute of limitations'), however inculpatory the evidence.

In most states, murder and rape have no statutory limits. (In those states with limits on rape prosecution, the outer limit is normally 15 years.) However, when it comes to armed robbery and aggravated assault, most states insist that prosecution is prohibited beyond three to five years after the date of the crime. (The outer limit for the prosecution of misdemeanors is normally two years.) The usual reason for the preventing the prosecution of 'old crimes' is that the quality of the evidence (esp. eyewitness memory) deteriorates with time. But, if that is so, it's fair to ask why murder and rape cases generally have no time limits attached.

• A defendant who has been acquitted at trial will rarely be tried for the *different* offense of perjured testimony (a felony), even if there is powerful new evidence that his trial testimony was false. (*Ashe v. Swenson* [219])

To put it mildly, this rule encourages the defendant to lie during his trial, since there is little threat of a legal price to pay if he does so and wins an acquittal, despite the fact that any other witness who can be proven to have lied can be and sometimes is later charged with perjury.

• The prosecution is required to share exculpatory evidence with the defendant; the defendant, in most states, is not required to share inculpatory evidence with the prosecution. (*Brady v. Maryland*, 1963)

• In some instances, the standard for *admissibility* of evidence proffered by the prosecution is satisfaction of BARD instead of satisfying the preponderance standard (the usual evidential standard for the defendant).

• Recently revised rules for line-up identifications (now adopted in many jurisdictions) make it more probable than it used to be that eyewitnesses will fail to identify truly guilty defendants.[220]

• After trial, the defendant can seek to overthrow his conviction on grounds of the incompetence of his lawyer; prosecutorial incompetence leading to an acquittal cannot be the basis for an appeal.

• In many jurisdictions, defendants may reject more prospective jurors without cause (a 'peremptory challenge') than the prosecutor can, thereby giving the defendant more control over the composition of the jury than the prosecutor enjoys.

This is a patently asymmetric rule with no epistemic rationale whatsoever. Indeed, it can be argued that neither party should be allowed to exclude prospective jurors 'without cause'.

• Jury unanimity is required (with a few exceptions in a couple of states).

This often leads to hung juries and either very expensive retrials or the dropping of charges. You might think that this rule is party-neutral, since it applies alike to both available verdicts. It is not; in two-thirds (64%) of the cases of a hung jury studied by Kalven and Zeisel, the majority of jurors voted guilty. In only 24% of the cases did the majority favor an acquittal.[221] They also report that in 42% of the hung juries with a majority in favor of conviction, there was a super-majority of 10-11 votes supporting a guilty verdict. The jury was nonetheless hung and the case declared a mistrial because of the unanimity requirement. (In some jurisdictions in the US, 20% or more of trials end in a hung jury.[222]) During appeal of a conviction, the prosecution can produce no new evidence that has come to light since the trial, even if it is highly inculpatory and indisputably relevant.

Every felony conviction at trial can be appealed if the defendant wishes unless the defendant's lawyer certifies that all apparent errors favoring the prosecution were 'frivolous'. (the *Anders* rule) Even then, the court will review the case to see whether the counsel's withdrawal was 'harmless'.

If a conviction is appealed because of an alleged trial error and the appellate court agrees that an error occurred, a new trial will be ordered unless it is clear beyond a reasonable doubt that the error was 'harmless'.

• 'Discovery' is a process in which each side shares some information about the case it intends to present with the other side prior to the trial itself. Its implementation is not (as it should be) automatic. Instead, the defendant alone decides whether discovery will take place.

This asymmetry is particularly offensive. The discovery process is highly desirable epistemically since it means that both parties will go *into* the trial well prepared and with a good idea of the case of their opponent. Leaving the choice about whether to have discovery in the hands of the defendant allows the latter to decide whether he wants to spring a surprise.

• The judge in a jury trial may declare an acquittal on his own authority and without consulting the jury, thereby terminating the case. By contrast, he cannot declare a conviction, however overwhelming he thinks the inculpatory evidence is. He may also reverse a jury conviction, while he cannot undo a jury acquittal.

• If either party has a statement made pretrial by a witness who subsequently testifies, the party with that statement (either as notes or a recording) must share it with the other party. If the defense fails to comply, then the testimony of the defense witness will be struck from the record. If the prosecution fails to comply, a mistrial may be declared. (*Fed. Rule of Crim. Proc.* 26.2)

• In a bail hearing, when the prosecutor requests denial of bail for reasons of the dangerousness of the defendant, it is not sufficient that the former prove this danger to be more likely than not. He must prove it to the standard of 'clear and convincing evidence'.

SOME BURDEN REDUCERS

• The prosecution usually has far more resources, financial and otherwise, for the collection of relevant evidence.

This disparity often leads to the idea that a criminal trial can be likened to combat between David and Goliath, with a lone and often indigent defendant fighting against an all-powerful state. What it ignores is the fact that in a criminal trial the state carries the *full* burden of establishing defendant's guilt beyond a reasonable doubt. The defendant is required to prove nothing (unless he chooses to adopt what is called an 'affirmative defense'); the state, everything. The Biblical analogy is especially far-fetched since the defendant, unlike poor David, does not have to slay his adversary to win. It would be absurd to say that a 'fair trial' requires both parties to have equivalent resources for producing evidence, given where the burden of proof unambiguously falls. [223] In short, although this is a burden-reducer, it merely reflects the fact that the full burden of production of evidence, according to the law, falls on the prosecution.

• The prosecutor has enormous discretion in shaping the specific charges brought against the defendant.

• The prosecutor can sometimes strike deals with accomplices of the defendant for securing inculpatory testimony. Likewise, he can grant immunity from prosecution to witnesses who would otherwise invoke the 5th amendment, thereby forcing their testimony. The defendant can request that the judge do the same; but the latter is not obliged to do so.

• The defendant generally may not require the victim of the crime being tried to agree to a pretrial interview with defense counsel.

• In many states, if the defendant adopts an 'affirmative defense' (e.g., insanity, self-defense, provocation), then the burden of proof falls on him to prove that defense (usually to a preponderance of the evidence) and not on the prosecutor to prove BARD that the defense story is false. In federal courts, the prosecution must prove guilt BARD even when the defendant adopts an affirmative defense.

• In a trial for rape or sexual assault, the prior sexual history of the testifying victim is automatically excluded from examination. By contrast, the prior criminal history of the defendant is introduced unproblematically.

These two clauses of the so-called rape shield laws go directly against existing practices in the prosecution of all other crimes. They were put in place specifically with a view to making it easier than it had been before to secure convictions of alleged rapists.

I trust it is clear that every one of the rules that I have called burden-enhancing gives the defendant, whether innocent or guilty, a probatory advantage, thereby lowering the likelihood that the defendant will be convicted. It is this feature that inclines me to urge the reader to think of these asymmetric, advantage-granting rules in the same way that I have urged we should think of the standard of proof; to wit, as mechanisms for altering the likely outcomes of a trial to the defendant's advantage and the distribution of errors. If the defendant wants to silence the privileged witnesses (e.g., his lawyer, his priest, his social worker, his psychiatrist) he can, without the jury ever learning that he has done so. By contrast, the prosecutor can, in most trials, silence no witness. If the defendant wants to spring a surprise on an unprepared prosecutor, he can do so by declining 'discovery'; if, on the other hand, he fears a surprise from the prosecutor, he can demand discovery. And so on. There is strong reason to believe that if a few of the burden-enhancing rules were to be made less asymmetric, more truth-conducive and less coddling of guilty defendants, then the distribution of errors would shift in the direction of producing both more true positives, fewer false negatives, and fewer victims.

But, one is inclined to ask, by how much? Unfortunately, most of the rules cited here have not been the subject of careful empirical analysis to see what their actual impact has been on the frequency of convictions and acquittals. In a few cases, however, we do have pertinent data. Consider the most famous of the exclusionary rules; the one saying that any evidence seized from the defendant without a warrant or probable cause cannot be introduced into evidence. Until 1914, illegally seized but relevant evidence was freely admitted by both state and federal courts. In that year, *Weeks v. U.S.* held that federal courts must thenceforth exclude all such evidence. States were still free to admit such evidence if they liked until 1961, when the famous *Mapp v. Ohio* ruling led the Supreme Court to insist that states as well as federal courts must exclude illegally-seized evidence.

This new policy elicited, of course, cheers from the defense bar and howls from prosecutors. For at least the next thirty years, there was intense debate in the legal community as to whether this new policy was having a deleterious impact on crime control. Several scholars tried to investigate the issue empirically. In 1988, the American Bar Association issued a summary report based on these various empirical studies of the effect of excluding such evidence.[224] It reached the conclusion that:

"Overall in jurisdictions with prosecutorial screening between 0.2% and 0.6% to 0.8% of adult felony arrests are screened out because of illegal searches. Adding together data on each of the stages of felony processing (police releases, prosecutor screening, and court dismissals), we find that the cumulative loss resulting from illegal searches is in the range of 0.6% and 0.8% to 2.35% of all adult felony arrests."[225]

If we take the average estimate from the ABA meta-study, we should expect that the exclusionary rule leads to the dropping of charges in about 1.5% of serious felony cases.

Having to drop approximately 1.5% of the criminal cases against probably guilty felony arrestees may seem like a drop in the proverbial bucket, until one considers that in our 2008 example described in previous chapters, the mean ABA estimate entails dropping charges annually against some 9k defendants, most of whom are guilty of violent crimes. More importantly, we need to bear in mind that we have enumerated above more than thirty other rules of procedure that are each likely to have a modest impact on driving down the number of convictions. In a few cases, the impact of these rules on outcomes would probably be greater than that of the exclusionary rule (e.g., prohibiting the appeal of acquittals[226], or requiring a unanimous vote from a jury or excluding evidence of prior crimes). In others, the impact would be significantly less, for instance, the rule allowing the defendant to prevent testimony from 'privileged witnesses'. What cannot be denied, however, is that in aggregate, these rules unquestionably make it significantly harder to convict the guilty than BARD already makes it. Harder than it should be, if our interest is in seeking true verdicts.

If each of the thirty-some-odd burden-enhancing rules mentioned above has even one-tenth the impact that the exclusionary rule does, we are speaking about some 27k probably guilty violent defendants going free each year (and leading to about 32k victimizations of innocents), thanks to the procedural indulgences and idiosyncrasies of American criminal law. If the burden-enhancing rules were eliminated, victimhood from annual crimes would be significantly reduced. This is especially the case if, as we have seen, a huge number of truly guilty defendants are clustered just below the cut-off delineated by BARD. In those close cases, we could expect to convert about 30 cases of false negatives into true positives for every new false positive accrued.

To make matters worse, the judicial rationale for many of the burden-enhancing rules is wholly unconvincing. Consider, briefly, two examples. The first has to do with character evidence. Traditionally, evidence of a defendant's character was freely admissible (as character evidence of other witnesses continues to be except victim-witnesses in rape cases). The current rules freely admit good character evidence proffered by the defendant (in his own testimony or through character witnesses). But if he does not offer evidence of his own character, then the state cannot introduce any negative evidence of a non-testifying defendant's character (except in trials dealing with sexual crimes). In short, while the law acknowledges that both good and bad character evidence are relevant (otherwise such evidence wouldn't be admitted at all), it gives the defendant full control over whether evidence about his character and his habits will be admitted. In my view, the rules governing character should be drastically revised without hesitation, thereby opening the door to the possibility of convicting more guilty defendants than at present.

As a second example of the dramatic effects of these procedural innovations, consider the *Carter* rule, saying that, if the defendant declines to testify, jurors must be sternly instructed to draw no adverse inferences from defendant's silence. Before its introduction, a classic study drawn from some 4,000 cases in the late 1950s and early 1960s found that 17% of criminal defendants did not testify at their trials.[227] Some thirty years later and once *Carter* had been in place for a while, in a study by the National Center for State Courts, the authors reported that the proportion of non-testifying defendants had leapt to 52%.[228] This three-fold increase in the class of silent defendants exhibits how drastically some of these burden-enhancing rules have altered previous legal practices. Can there be anyone—apart perhaps from a few

Supreme Court justices—who believes that a trial is more likely to produce a true verdict if the defendant keeps his mouth shut than if he testifies?

But, it might be argued, some of these burden-enhancers have been deemed 'rights' by the Supreme Court and defendants' rights are supposedly not negotiable, however undesirable they may be epistemically. That is nonsense. Very few of these rules are set in constitutional stone (and even if they, that is amendable). Most of them have been invented in the last sixty years by the Supreme Court, often based on rather flimsy arguments. Whole chapters could be written on how ill-motivated several of these rules are. By way of illustration, I shall limit my commentary to two sets of inter-related burden-enhancers: the new policies about defendant's silence and even newer rules about the admissibility of eyewitness evidence from lineups.

THE SILENCE CASE

There are five distinct rules—four of them dating from the period defined by the 1960s to the early 1980s—articulating a defendant's right(s) to silence. The oldest of these, known as 'the right against self-incrimination', can be found in the Bill of Rights. It was drafted at a time when several European powers were still utilizing judicial torture to extract confessions from defendants. Our Founding Fathers wanted none of that and wrote the Fifth Amendment to protect defendants from such horrors. I have no quarrel whatever with the claim that defendants should not be coerced into either talking to the police or testifying in their own trials. It's the subsequent glosses on what that 'right' means that ought to raise eyebrows. There are four classic cases since the 1960s that have drastically re-defined the meaning of the right to silence.

In *Griffin v. California* (1965), the Court argued that neither the prosecutor nor the judge could mention during the trial the fact that a defendant had not testified in his own defense. This seems a rather curious principle. Even if none of the principal actors in the trial alludes to the fact that the defendant has not taken the stand, is it even remotely conceivable that the jurors would not themselves take note of this fact? Do they need a prosecutor to remind them that the defendant did not testify and if he does remind them, is that an unfair thing to say or a violation of defendant's right to silence? Consider a similar right. Defendant has a clear right to testify if he wishes. Suppose he exercises that right and that the prosecutor later in the trial mentions defendant's testimony. Would anyone in their right mind then say that the defendant's right to testify had been violated because the prosecutor drew the jury's attention to his testimony? Obviously not. Why, then should we suppose that a defendant's right to silence is compromised if the judge or prosecutor mentions that silence?

After *Griffin* came *Miranda v. Arizona* (1966), a case that gave us the familiar litany, delivered at the moment of arrest, when a defendant is told that he has a right to silence, a right to an attorney during his interrogation, and so on. *Griffin* and *Miranda* both left open the possibility that the prosecution could inform the jurors that the defendant had refused 'to assist the police in their inquiries'. That possibility was quickly scotched in *Doyle v. Ohio* (1976), which prevented the state from informing jurors of the defendant's non-cooperation during interrogation. This was a more alarming development than *Griffin*. It is one thing to say that the prosecutor cannot tell jurors what they already know perfectly well (viz., that defendant was silent at trial). It is quite another to keep from them arguably relevant information that they do not know and that some of them might think (if they knew it) was relevant to their deliberations.

Finally, and most importantly, there was *Carter v. Kentucky* (1981), which gave the non-testifying defendant the right to demand that the judge give to the jury a special instruction, telling them firmly that they must wholly ignore defendant's silence and draw no adverse inferences from it. *Carter*, in particular, was a very sharp break with previous American practices. It had traditionally been the canonical practice that jurors were not only allowed, but often encouraged, to give whatever probatory weight to defendant's failure to testify that they thought appropriate.[229] *Carter* aimed to bring such obvious and reasonable inferences to an abrupt halt. The Court, in its ruling, acknowledged that *Carter* would encourage a guilty defendant's trial silence and prevent the

125

drawing of what would often be perfectly rational adverse inferences by jurors. Nonetheless, it argued, a 'right is a right'.

Its rationale for this drastic change, despite these obvious drawbacks to *Carter*, was the Court's fear that factually innocent defendants might sometimes have reasons for wanting to avoid testimony (e.g., fear that their demeanor on the witness stand would prejudice the jury against them). In short, the explicit expectation of the Court was that *Carter* might shield the occasional silent but innocent defendant from being falsely convicted, due to a jury's adverse inference from his silence. That may be so. But the majority on the court didn't bother to ask itself—as it virtually never does any more—how often an advantage-conferring rule like this one would let guilty defendants off the hook, thereby leading to false negatives.

Here is a sample model instruction now used by judges to preclude jurors from attaching any significance to defendant's silence:

"The defendant chose not to testify in this case. Under our Constitution, a defendant has no obligation to testify or to present any evidence, because it is the Government's burden to prove a defendant guilty beyond a reasonable doubt. A defendant is never required to prove that he or she is innocent. Therefore, you must not attach any significance to the fact that a given defendant did not testify. No adverse inference against a defendant may be drawn by you because he did not take the witness stand, and you may not consider it in any way in your deliberations in the jury room."[230]

The logic here is bizarre. Jurors are told (correctly) that defendant "is never required to prove that he or she is innocent." That fact is then said to entail ('therefore') that jurors must attach *no* significance to defendant's silence. But there is a logical disconnect here. The fact that defendant need prove nothing does not mean that his failure to use his own testimony to rebut inculpatory facts established as highly plausible by the prosecutor should simply be ignored. The enabling of the one person in a trial who probably knows more about the alleged crime than anyone else to keep his mouth shut without having to pay a price for exercising that privilege is wholly incompatible with the idea that a criminal investigation is an attempt to get as full an account of the relevant facts as possible. As Justice Stewart pointedly observed in *Carter*: "The one person who usually knows most about the critical facts [in a case] is the accused."[231] Recognizing that fact is salient, the Court nonetheless decided to give the defendant a cost-free option of not testifying.

It is worth comparing the new no-inference-from-silence jury instruction with the instruction in the earlier *Griffin* case that prompted the court to rule that adverse inferences from silence must be blocked. Here is what the judge in that case said to the jury, which the Supreme Court regarded as unacceptable:

"It is a constitutional right of a defendant in a criminal trial that he may not be compelled to testify. Thus, whether or not he does testify rests entirely in his own decision. As to any evidence or facts against him which the defendant can reasonably be expected to deny or explain because of facts within his knowledge, if he does not testify, or if, though he does testify, he fails to deny or explain such evidence, the jury may take that failure into consideration as tending to indicate the truth of such evidence and as indicating that among the inferences that may be reasonably drawn there from those unfavorable to the defendant are the more probable. In this connection, however, it should be noted that if a defendant does not have the knowledge that he would need to deny or to explain any certain evidence against him, it would be unreasonable to draw an inference unfavorable to him because of his failure to deny or to explain such evidence. The failure of a defendant to deny or explain evidence against him does not create a presumption of guilt or by itself warrant an inference of guilt, nor does it relieve the prosecution of its burden of proving every essential element of the crime and the guilt of the defendant beyond a reasonable doubt."[232]

This seems a sober, thoroughly level-headed appraisal of the situation with a silent defendant. His silence in and of itself need signify nothing about his guilt. But, depending upon the circumstances of the case, his failure to speak about matters that appear to implicate him, and about which it is reasonable to suppose he is knowledgeable, makes it natural to infer that his silence carries some indication that he has no plausible story to tell. As recently as 1947, the U.S. Supreme Court itself said as much in

Adamson v. California: "It seems quite natural that when a defendant has opportunity to deny or explain facts and determines not to do so, the prosecution should bring out the strength of the evidence by commenting upon defendant's failure to explain or deny it."[233]

What the Court had held to be 'quite natural' for a century and a half, it now regards as a grievous violation of a defendant's rights, all because (in the Court's opinion) the occasional innocent defendant might prefer not to testify.

The *Carter* rule evidently had a dramatic impact on the structure of trials. In the 1960s, the vast majority of defendants gave testimony, thereby opening themselves up to cross-examination by the prosecutor. When jurors were allowed to draw adverse inferences from silence, nine-of-ten defendants without prior convictions testified and three-quarters of defendants with priors testified. (See Table 9.) Three decades later, thanks in large measure to *Carter*, those numbers had shrunk to three-of-five and to less than half respectively. Unless you hold that the defendant's own story about the crime is of little or no evidential significance to assessing his guilt, you have to believe that this burden-enhancing rule has had deleterious, error-inducing effects.

Table 9. Pre- and Post-*Carter* Testimony Practices		
Giving Testimony	1966[234]	2000[235]
Defendant with no record	91%	62%
Defendant with a record	74%	45%

Similar stories can be told of many of the other burden-enhancers. What was once accepted policy and truth-conducive practice is now often laid to one side and great pains are taken to change the rules of procedure if the Court suspects that some innocent (and, unfortunately, many guilty) defendants might escape the conviction that they would once have received, back in the days when jurors were generally not told what inferences they could and could not draw, when most relevant evidence was freely admitted, and when the rules gave far fewer asymmetrical, procedural advantages to the defendant. Many senior judges and legal scholars evidently believe that if the amendment of some existing rule might make a false conviction less likely, then such a change is automatically justifiable, without worrying about how many true positives—achievable by the present version of the rule—are apt to be transformed by the new rule into false negatives.

This indifference to the trade-offs question is almost as frequent as the insistence on a very high standard of proof, in both cases regardless of the consequences. Never mind that this approach confuses and confounds the whole question of the distribution of errors. In theory, it is the standard of proof that should be the mechanism for distributing errors, while the rules of evidence and procedure should be party-neutral and truth-conducive. Many scholars happily ignore that bright line in the sand by arguing that, besides a very tough standard of proof, we need plenty of burden-enhancing rules that will further skew errors in the defendant's favor.

THE MOVEMENT TO TRANSFORM THE STRUCTURE OF ADMISSIBLE LINE-UP EVIDENCE

If the defendant-friendly silence question has now been incorporated into law for about a quarter century, there is currently a movement afoot to grant defendants—guilty or innocent—yet another advantage. Psychologists have recently done dozens of studies on how the police run lineups and their proneness to erroneous identifications. Evidence from lineups is important because it is via the line-up that a witness to a crime who saw, but is not acquainted with, its perpetrator can decide whether a police suspect is or is not the person she witnessed committing the crime. Typically, the lineup has had a familiar form: it consists of five or six persons (or sometimes five or six photos) resembling the witnesses' description of the perpetrator, who are lined up so that the witness can view them (usually one of the group will be the police suspect). The witness examines them in what is called a 'simultaneous lineup' and then informs the police whether anyone in the lineup was the felon whom she saw committing the crime. If she identifies the one of the six whom the police already suspect to be the perpetrator, this eyewitness identification will both increase their confidence that they have their man and almost certainly the person who fingers him will be called as an eyewitness in the trial that may follow. If she does not pick out the police suspect as the culprit, then the case against him may well be dropped, absent strong eyewitness evidence of his guilt.

The researchers I mentioned have collected extensive data on the reliability of such eyewitness testimony and many of them have proposed that the structure of such lineups should be changed. Their proposal is for a so-called 'sequential lineup', which involves the witness in seeing individually and in sequence the half dozen (including the police suspect) who, on traditional practices, would be standing together against the wall (or in photos on the same page), waiting for the witness to compare and contrast them (the simultaneous lineup). Studies done by several psychologists have attempted to measure the success and failure rates of both types of lineup. (A failure can obviously be of two types: a failure to identify the truly guilty party if he is in the lineup; and the false identification of a party who is not guilty (but was nonetheless regarded as the likely suspect by the police). Researchers have noted that, while both types of lineups—simultaneous and sequential—may lead to mistaken identifications, the sequential lineup is less likely to result in the witness fingering an innocent person than is the simultaneous lineup.

This difference has attracted a great deal of attention from those preoccupied by the problem of false convictions. They observe, correctly, that the sequential lineup leads to fewer false IDs (12%) than the simultaneous format produces (20%). That would obviously make a false conviction more likely to emerge from a traditional lineup arrangement than would result from the use of sequential lineups. This has led many people and organizations to apply strong pressure on legislators, police and prosecutors to abandon the traditional format for lineups. The movement has already had a dramatic effect in the US; many states and large-city police departments have already replaced simultaneous lineups with sequential ones. This is widely seen as a victory for those concerned to protect the innocent from a false conviction.

While the cause may seem noble, the facts suggest otherwise. Even though it cannot be disputed that the new sequential format is less likely to make false IDs of innocent persons, the data make clear that the simultaneous lineup significantly *increases* the likelihood that truly guilty defendants going through a lineup will be *correctly* identified by the eyewitness (specifically, simultaneous lineups lead to a correct ID 50% of the time while sequential lineups pick out the true culprit only 40% of the time). In short, traditional lineups are more likely to pick out the truly guilty than the new-fangled sequential lineups are. What drives the movement to convert from the former to the latter is that, as already noted above, studies indicate that the simultaneous lineup is likely to mistakenly pick out an innocent person in the lineup (20% false ID rate) while the sequential lineup has a false ID rate of about 12%. Obviously, falsely identifying an innocent person in a lineup makes it more likely that he will be convicted while correctly identifying a guilty person makes it more likely he will be convicted. The problem arises with the trade-off. Proponents of sequential lineups are willing to trade-off a significant number of correct IDs of the guilty (thereby making their conviction more difficult) in return for reducing the frequency of false IDs of the innocent. There is general agreement among researchers that simultaneous lineups make *fewer total errors* but there is also agreement that sequential lineups result in fewer false positives. This takes us back, of course, to the vexed Blackstone question of how many true convictions we are willing to lose in order to reduce the number of false convictions.

One large determinant of the answer hinges on the question of how many of those going through the lineup process are the true culprit. Supposing that 60% of lineups contain guilty persons, then 1,000 simultaneous lineups will generate 300 correct IDs and 80 false IDs; while a sequential lineup will produce 240 correct IDs and 48 false IDs. By going from the current format to the sequential one, we lose 60 correct IDs and cut the false IDs by 32. That seems a fair trade-off, since a false positive is roughly twice as costly as a false negative. The situation is much more extreme if, as seems likely, the frequency of guilty defendants in lineups is closer to 80% than 60%. Here, the results are as follows:

simultaneous lineups produce, among 1,000 lineups, 400 correct IDs (.50 x 800) and 40 false IDs. A sequential lineup would produce 320 correct IDs (.40 x 200) and 24 false IDs (.12 x 200). Under these circumstances, by going over to the sequential format, we lose 80 correct IDs and 16 false IDs.[236]

Proponents of sequential lineups conveniently ignore that this technique comes with a relatively high price tag. Neither the 60% guilty nor the 80% guilty hypotheses necessarily apply to our case of violent crimes in 2008. But the results for that sample are easy to compute. We have already seen reason in chapter 4 to conclude that, of the 595k arrestees for violent crimes in that year, some 445k (75%) of them were truly guilty. If we apply what we now know about correct and false ID rates of the two types of lineups, we can reasonably conjecture that, had a thousand of them been involved in simultaneous lineups, the number of correct IDs per thousand would have been 375 (750 x .5) while the false IDs would have been 50 (250 x .2). The comparable results from 1,000 sequential lineups would have been 300 (750 x .4) true IDs and 30 (.12 x 250) false IDs. Supposing that most of these cases involved eyewitnesses, the use of the traditional lineup technique would have produced 75 more true IDs and 20 more false IDs than a sequential method would, had the latter then been in place. That means that, given current patterns of guilt among the arrested, more harm to innocents results from the sequential than from the simultaneous lineup.

The core point is that the advocates of the new form of conducting lineups are apparently wedded to the idea that *any* measure that reduces the false conviction rate is to be preferred over its rival(s), no matter what the cost paid in lost true convictions may be. When and if the new sequential method becomes dominant (as appears likely during the next decade), it will be one more item to add to our earlier list of procedural rules that are burden-enhancers, in that they make it more difficult for the prosecutor to secure convictions of the truly guilty, thereby making a false acquittal of the guilty more likely than it need be.

PROCEDURAL RULES FOR THE EPISTEMICALLY CHALLENGED

Just as we saw in the last chapter that many legal theorists regard BARD as unique among possible standards of proof by generally shielding the innocent defendant from conviction, so do many scholars and jurists bring that same sensibility to bear in assessing many other rules of evidence and procedure. In particular, there is a large family of rules that these guardians of the innocent believe need to be changed in order to provide the guarantees that flow from the Kantian commitment to treat defendants as ends rather than means. Among the proposals recently made are: allowing every defendant who offers a confession to the police to retract it if he wishes, even if it was a voluntary confession (Ayling[237]): permitting the defendant to ignore the hearsay rule and freely introduce hearsay evidence(Stein and Goldwasser[238]), while insisting that the prosecutor should be constrained by the current hearsay exclusions; lowering the standard for admissibility of evidence for the defendant (Friedman[239]); and permitting the defendant to call "experts" who do not meet the standard definition of expert witnesses (Stein).

The arguments driving these proposals all exhibit the same structure: existing rules lead from time to time to false convictions; by changing those rules we could lower the frequency of false convictions; of course, there also would be significantly more false acquittals (indeed far more false acquittals generated than false convictions eliminated); but that is alright because we all agree that a false conviction is worse than a false acquittal. So as not to be seeming to caricature mercilessly the position under discussion, a few choice quotations may be in order. Corey Ayling: "outlawing confessions would be justified even if the net result were to free more guilty persons than innocent ones."[240] Katherine Goldwasser: "to exclude [otherwise doubtful] defense evidence (and thereby increase the risk of erroneous conviction) solely out of concern about the risk of an erroneous acquittal is flatly unacceptable."[241] Alex Stein and Daniel Seidmann chime in: "The wrongful conviction of an innocent defendant (a "false positive") is much costlier than the wrongful acquittal of a criminal (a "false negative"). Therefore... a reduction in criminal false negatives cannot offset false positives."[242] The degree of indifference shown here to false negatives is quite stunning, given that every false acquittal not only represents a crime that goes unpunished but probably several crimes that go unprevented. It is clear that this camp does not see crime control as any significant part of the function of evidence law. The social contract evidently reduces, for them, simply to an agreement to keep the innocent (and many of the guilty) out of jail, albeit at a high cost.

Their commitment to taking rights seriously—*if and only if* they are rights belonging to criminal defendants, not to prospective victims—blinds them to seeing that the adoption of any given procedural rule—just like the adoption of a standard of proof—reflects a decision between competing priorities: convicting the guilty, acquitting the innocent, keeping the hands of the state clean, respecting the autonomy of defendants and witnesses, and so on. If, with Stein, Kitai and the others, we take the view that the overwhelming priority in settling on the rules of trial is to protect the innocent defendant from conviction, we have started down a slope that offers no traction, since there is virtually no procedural rule that cannot be weakened still further so as to avoid convicting the occasional innocent defendant. Doing the best we possibly can do to protect the innocent from false conviction is a fool's game, since the best we can do would inevitably end up acquitting virtually every guilty defendant.

The utilitarian, by contrast, accepts that the use of BARD and other rules of trial is itself a compromise between our desires not to convict the innocent and to convict the guilty and reflects our wish to strike a balance between protection against crimes and against false conviction. Deontologists do not like that way of putting it, because—loyal Kantians to the end—they loathe the thought of such mundane tit-for-tat. But the obvious question to put to them is: Why stop at BARD or any other rule of trial? If our overweening concern is to protect the innocent from conviction, there are indefinitely many ways we could tinker further with the system so as to make it ever more acquittal-prone. My response is brief: *if* BARD could be justified as the appropriate standard in a criminal trial, that is because we can show that it strikes the right balance between reducing crime and protecting innocent defendants from false conviction, not because it represents the best protection we could possibly offer the innocent defendant. If existing procedural rules are acceptable, that is not because they represent the best the state can do to protect the interests of the innocent defendant but because they are conducive to finding out the truth about a crime. As one might expect, these defendant-friendly asymmetries mean fewer convictions than would otherwise occur. Unfortunately, the legal community has done few studies of the impact of most of these new procedural innovations.

It is also important to remind ourselves of what I called the 32-to-1 rule in the previous chapter. Let's focus our attention specifically on that set of defendants (both innocent and guilty) whose apparent guilt is just below the BARD threshold. Suppose, further, that many, if not most, such defendants have taken advantage of one or more of these burden-enhancers available to them. If they narrowly escape conviction thanks to such rules, they would obviously have been convicted if these rules were not in play. Suppose, finally, for the sake of the discussion, that 11,000 defendants find themselves in this happy situation of having narrowly escaped conviction by utilizing one or more of these burden-enhancers. Given what we know about the relative frequency of false positives, we can infer that some 330 (3%) of these acquitted defendants are truly innocent, while some 10.7k of them are truly guilty, but acquitted, thanks to the burden enhancers. Both sets would have been convicted but for one or another procedural rule getting them off the hook. This leads to an outcome that imposes—via an abundance of false negatives—vastly more harm on the innocents in the broader community who would have gone unharmed had these burden-enhancing rules not been in place. Once again, the social contract is largely ignored by the law and those who write or interpret it. It is a phony arithmetic that suggests that saving some 300+ innocent defendants from the harm of a false positive justifies the release of some 10.7k guilty but unconvicted defendants to the streets. The balancing of serious risks required by the social contract has been wholly ignored while judges and legislators have conjured up rules that protect vastly more guilty defendants from conviction than innocent ones.

Two last points before moving on. In the previous chapter, I discussed the formulaic proposals that Kaplan, Tribe and many others (including this author) have made for defining the standard of proof in terms of the ratio of the respective costs of errors (Kaplan) or the ratio of utilities of the four possible outcomes (Tribe).[243] Those decision-theoretic mechanisms make sense as a way of figuring out how high the standard should be set, subject to one proviso: that the standard of proof alone is the factor affecting the distribution of errors. However, as we have seen here, the rules of procedure and of evidence are chock-a-block with rules that exclide relevant evidence, give asymmetric advantages to one party, and discourage legitimate inferences by jurors. In aggregate, the burden-enhancers significantly outweigh the burden-reducers. The undeniable result of that situation is that the error profiles of trials will *not* mirror what we would expect to be the error profile associated with whatever Kaplan- or Tribe-derived standard of proof we might impose. The *de facto* ratio of false negatives to false positives will inevitably be different from, and probably higher than, what the standard of proof (supposing we were able to put in place a clear and coherent standard) alone would lead us to expect. Calculations of the Tribe-Kaplan sort would give us an acceptable level for the standard of proof *if and only if* the rules of procedure were party-neutral and truth-conducive. We could make them that way if we were prepared to reduce the existing asymmetries by eliminating most of the burden-enhancers and burden-reducers. Lest this proposal seems utopian, we should add that most other legal systems have managed to come much closer than the American one to rejecting procedural rules that asymmetrically impose large obstacles to finding out the truth.

One last observation concerning the rules of procedure is in order. Clearly, my focus in this chapter has been on procedural rules that either lower the rate of false positives while raising the rate of false negatives (burden enhancers) or raise the rate of false positives while lowering the rate of false negatives (burden reducers). It is crucial to stress before leaving this subject that not all rules of procedure have these impacts. The ideal rule of procedure is one that simultaneously lowers the rate of *both* false positives and false negatives, thereby reducing the overall error rate. There are many such rules already in play. Among them: the requirement that all and only relevant evidence must be admissible; that expert testimony is admissible if and only if it is known how reliable the methods used by the experts in question are; and that both parties possess the power to subpoena testimony from those they wish to call as witnesses. Each of these rules, and several others besides, are truth-conducive and symmetric, giving comparable advantages (or disadvantages) to both parties. These rules reduce both false positives *and* false negatives. If all the rules of procedure had these traits, then we would have a situation where the distribution of errors would be directly linked to the standard of proof. But that could come about only if legislators and judges had the integrity to strip out of the rules all the burden-enhancers and burden-reducers. Until and unless that is done, there can be no grounds for believing, as the US Supreme Court routinely insists[244], that the principal aim of a criminal trial is to find out the truth about a purported crime. The Germans get it right when they say unambiguously in their rules of procedure that: "In order to establish the truth, the court … shall extend the taking of evidence to all facts and means of proof relevant to the decision."[245]

Chapter 7 The Ways Double Jeopardy Undermines Legal Inquiry: Jumping on the Anglo-Saxon Bandwagon

> The central purpose of a criminal trial is to decide the factual question of defendant's guilt or innocence. —US Supreme Court[246]

In the preceding chapter, I mentioned that one of most striking defendant-friendly rules of criminal procedure is what is usually known as the principle of double jeopardy. While scarcely found outside the reach of Anglo-Saxon law, this principle has been part of the English-speaking tradition for many centuries. It appears explicitly in the Fifth Amendment of the US Constitution ("[N]or shall any person be subject for the same offence to be twice put in jeopardy of life or limb.") but many other Anglo-Saxon counties have recently dropped or drastically weakened the scope of double jeopardy. Canada, England and Wales, India, and several states of Australia now allow appeals of acquittals under certain circumstances (especially if new, inculpatory evidence of guilt arises after an acquittal at trial). And so they should.

As an epistemologist, I come back to the supposition that the primary task of a criminal proceeding is to find out the facts of the matter with respect to two crucial questions: Did the alleged crime occur? And, if so: Did the defendant commit it? Through most of the long history of the common law, the answer given by the jury to these two questions was generally dispositive. There was no general machinery for appealing *any* verdict, whether a conviction or an acquittal. In the late nineteenth century, both England and the United States broke with the traditional assumption that the jury's was the last word on such matters. Specifically, higher courts introduced the notion that if a person was convicted, and if he believed that his conviction depended upon some mistake made in his trial (usually by the presiding judge), he could seek redress from a higher court, arguing that the mistake in question was responsible for the supposedly erroneous verdict. If the appellate court found merit in the defendant's argument, the jury's verdict could be set aside and a new trial ordered. If not, the guilty verdict would stand.

This innovation was both bold and commendable. If we once grant, and it is surely undeniable, that judges sometimes err in their application of the law to the cases before them, then the creation of appellate courts permitted the system to catch and correct some of the mistakes that had hitherto gone undetected. In the US alone, this principle has saved hundreds of thousands of persons from suffering punishment for crimes they probably did not commit. In epistemic terms, this initiative allowed the legal system to catch and correct many mistakes (including many false positives) that would have previously gone undetected, when no appeal was possible.

But, to a truth-seeker's eye, this reform was blatantly too timid. For if it is true that judges often make mistakes, it is inconceivable that such mistakes occur only in trials leading to conviction. Judges presumably are as likely to make mistakes in trials leading to acquittal as in trials leading to conviction. (In fact, I will be arguing later that there are reasons to believe that there are systemic pressures that lead judges to make errors favoring defendants more often than errors disadvantaging defendants.) Had those nineteenth-century reformers successfully advocated the availability of appeal for *both* sorts of verdicts, there is no room for the slightest doubt that many of these false acquittals could have been caught and corrected, just as many false convictions have been. Nor can it be doubted for a moment that the aggregate number of erroneous verdicts would be significantly less than it is under a regimen that permits only one-sided appeals. If our principal interest is in maximizing the likelihood of a true outcome to a trial, defendant and prosecutor alike should be able to appeal verdicts that they can show to hinge on erroneous interpretations of the law by trial judges.

So far, there is absolutely nothing novel in my argument. It is an utterly obvious statement of the epistemic consequences of a policy of asymmetric appeals. It boils down to the mundane observation that more false acquittals will occur in a system without appeal of acquittals than would occur in a system incorporating a symmetric appellate mechanism. Without two-sided appeals, we are committing unnecessary mistakes, many of which could, on review, be caught and corrected. Obvious though this truism may be, this is already a powerful argument for correcting the asymmetry in question and allowing appeals of either verdict.

Still, this is *not* the most powerful argument for doing so. My aim in this chapter is not to show that the current asymmetric policy allows more false acquittals than necessary to go unchecked—that I take to be completely obvious—but that this asymmetry has other unsettling epistemic consequences, even more deleterious than this one. To discover what those undesirable side effects are, we must engage in a subtler analysis of the *long-term* consequences of the appellate asymmetry.

It will be helpful to distinguish between two quite different things that happen in the appellate process: a). the judicial system is charged to identify and rectify specific mistakes made in particular cases, where the term 'mistake' generally means a failure to follow existing rules of evidence or procedure. We might term this procedure, *learning of its mistakes*. At the same time, the machinery of the appellate process b). allows the judiciary *to learn from its mistakes*. By that, I mean that courts gradually learn that certain existing rules of procedure and evidence constitute obstacles to finding out the truth. Such discoveries often eventually prompt emendations in the rules themselves. These are very different roles and it is crucial to be aware of them both. This duality of roles can appear paradoxical. On the one hand, appellate courts are looking to insure that lower courts scrupulously follow existing rules. On the other hand, those higher courts must be constantly alert to the ways in which existing rules—which they are charged to enforce—are flawed. But this paradox, if paradox it be, is not unique to the criminal justice system. It is at the core of every enterprise and activity seriously committed to the idea that one can and must learn from one's mistakes.

More than a century ago, the American philosopher of science, Charles Sanders Peirce, argued that any robust, non-dogmatic system of inquiry into empirical questions must contain mechanisms that enable inquirers to discover both sorts of mistakes. When Peirce referred to mistakes, he did not only mean specific conclusions erroneously reached by the application of the methods or rules in question. On the contrary, Peirce thought that what a system of inquiry must allow for is systematic discovery, over time, of the ways in which *the existing rules* guiding the system are bad or inadequate rules, that is, how they thwart finding out the truth about the objects or processes under investigation.

In the case of science, which was Peirce's principal concern, this meant that inquiry should be so constituted that it was capable of finding out if existing rules or methods were conducive to the truth or if, to the contrary, they were often responsible for generating erroneous beliefs. He maintained that one of the great virtues of science was that is was a system capable of discovering when its rules were systematically leading it astray. By discovering such fallacious procedures, and modifying them, Peirce argued that scientists, in effect, were continuously *learning how to learn*. The rules of scientific method, for him, were not commandments cast in Mosaic stone, but a set of fallible guesses about how best to interrogate nature. Because of the existence of various feedback mechanisms in science, we can often discover when those guesses are misleading us and we can change them for the better. Peirce's point was that in the ideal system of inquiry we are not only learning about specific mistakes we have made in the acceptance or rejection of particular hypotheses. We are, more importantly, learning about how the very rules that constitute the current anatomy of inquiry fail to be optimal. This self-correction was, for Peirce, a necessary condition for judging any system of inquiry to be genuinely empirical.

I want to ask here whether the legal inquiry system has these features that Peirce regarded as essential for any genuine system of inquiry. Specifically, I want to focus on the logic of the appellate process with this set of epistemic questions in mind.

Legal systems like the American one allow for the appeal of convictions. This means, of course, that superior courts are routinely presented with situations in which persons are claiming to have been wrongfully convicted. A simpleminded version of what goes on in such appellate discussions is that they result in a determination by superior courts of whether the rules currently in place were assiduously followed in particular trials.

But that is not all that is going on; it is not even the most important thing that is going on in the appellate process. As the history of 20th-century American jurisprudence vividly reveals, higher courts, when they accept an appeal, are not simply deciding whether a given case was conducted and decided according to the existing rules. Courts are likewise, and more importantly, looking for and sometimes discovering ways in which the *current* rules conduce to false convictions. On discovering that existing rules persistently lead to the conviction of the apparently innocent, circuit and supreme court justices frequently propose modifications of the existing rules and procedures so as to make them less likely to conduce to errors of the sorts they see coming across their benches on a regular basis. This is precisely the sort of feedback mechanism that Peirce had in mind when he talked about authentic systems of inquiry. One learns from one's mistakes not only that the mistakes occurred but also that their occurrence was made more likely by the use of certain rules or procedures which are themselves open to review and modification. This is genuinely *learning how to learn*.

In the legal case however, at least in the United States, unlike the scientific one, such learning is decidedly *one-sided*. The system is continuously reviewing convictions, diagnosing their causes, and tinkering with or adjusting the rules so as to reduce the likelihood of false convictions in the future. That is doubtless a good thing; but it is *not* an unmitigated good because tinkering with the rules so as to reduce further the occurrence of false convictions may lead to new rules that produce vastly more false acquittals than the existing system does. In a genuinely self-corrective system of inquiry, such retrograde changes could be quickly identified because they would show up in the form of enhanced numbers of false acquittals. However, where appeals are uniquely one-sided, there is no feedback mechanism for discovering whether a given change in the rules—motivated by a concern to protect the innocent from false conviction—has inadvertently made the prospect of false acquittals much more likely.

Obviously, the asymmetric appeals process is not only more likely to identify the causes of false convictions than of false acquittals; it is also likely to introduce new rules or revisions of old rules that, while reducing the frequency of false convictions, may vastly increase the frequency of false acquittals. If you doubt this, think of the effect of the *Miranda* rule introduced in the 1960s. The Warren Court was convinced that the earlier rules governing confessions—basically variants on the notion of voluntariness—were leading occasionally to the admission of false confessions and thus producing false convictions from time to time. Under the *Miranda* regime, by contrast, research indicates that the frequency of false acquittals may have jumped significantly while it is not clear whether *Miranda* reduced false convictions to any significant degree. Paul Cassell has conducted extensive empirical studies of the effect of *Miranda* on conviction rates. Among his conclusions: "each year the number of crimes that go unsolved because of *Miranda* is between 56,000 and 136,000 violent crimes and 72,000 to 299,000 property crimes."[247]

There is a second problem, related to, but distinct from, this one. Given the asymmetry of appeals, there is no comparable process going on with respect to learning about the rules that conduce to mistaken acquittals. If the courts don't bother to look for false acquittals in lower court rulings, their causes will usually remain shrouded in mystery. Absent judicial review of acquittals, judges have nothing other than judicial folklore to fall back on in deciding whether existing rules could be modified so as to make false acquittals less likely. Absent a systematic scrutiny of cases resulting in acquittal, the legal machinery can produce little more than uninformed hunches about either the frequency of such errors or about which current rules of evidence may be responsible for producing such errors as do occur. In sum, we have much less information than we should about what causes false acquittals and no mechanism for ascertaining whether recent modifications to those rules have increased their frequency.

Return for a moment to the parallel with science. Suppose that scientists were able to discover when they had erroneously *accepted* an hypothesis but could never tell when they had mistakenly *rejected* an hypothesis. Such a state of affairs would mean that science was only partially a self-corrective system, since one entire family of mistakes went wholly unscrutinized. Unable to learn when they had made mistakes of this sort, and thereby unable to adopt remedies to minimize such errors, this part of science would have to be regarded as dogmatic and insufficiently sensitive to the need to learn from our mistakes. I believe that precisely the same judgment must be applied to any legal system that, as a matter of policy, declares one whole family of potential mistakes to be inaccessible to judicial scrutiny. Where there is no such scrutiny, no learning is going on and where there is no learning, there is no scope for self-correction. Error-prone rules go undiscovered and the system fails to learn from its mistakes or improve itself.

There is one final epistemic consequence of the asymmetry of appeals that I want to discuss briefly. It deserves separate treatment in its own right so I will try to state the problem succinctly. I take it to be a plausible psychological thesis that no professional practitioner of any empirical craft—whether it be science, medicine or the law—wants to commit mistakes, if he can avoid doing so, for to do so raises questions about his professional competence. I likewise assume that, if one does make mistakes, one would prefer that they passed unnoticed rather than that they be drawn prominently to public attention. In the adjudication of a typical criminal case, the judge is called on to make dozens, sometimes even hundreds, of rulings. Apart from ruling about the admissibility of evidence and about the behavior of counsel, he likewise must decide what instructions to give jurors on matters of the law. Allowing for certain exceptions, these rulings are not subject to judicial review during the trial. On appeal, however, *all* the rulings of a judge are subject to scrutiny—provided, that is, that the defendant is convicted. If he is acquitted, however, the erroneous rulings of the judge will never come to public attention. In that sense, a less than fully competent or fully, self-confident judge, of which there are doubtless some, has a vested interest in the defendant's acquittal under an asymmetric review system. If a given case requires many rulings that are close calls, the prudent judge will understand that ruling in the defendant's favor—thus increasing the likelihood of an undeserved acquittal—is less likely to bring him into the spotlight of appellate scrutiny than if he errs in favor of the prosecution—thereby increasing the chances of a conviction and thereby an appeal.

If the current system were replaced with full symmetry with respect to appeals, this temptation to rule in the defendant's favor would immediately disappear. If a judge knows that *any* verdict can be appealed, he has no motive for skewing his rulings in favor of defense or prosecution. There is much more that could be said about this topic but no discussion of the epistemology of appeals would be complete without at least an acknowledgment of this defendant-friendly bias built into the one-sided appellate structure.

To this point, my analysis has been couched entirely in epistemic terms. I believe that the epistemic case for permitting repeals of acquittals is unassailable. If we want the judicial system to be able to learn from its mistakes, if we want to detect flaws in existing rules of procedures and evidence, if we want to avoid the guilty going free because a judge has egregiously misinterpreted the rules or misapplied the law, then permitting appeals of acquittals is the natural response.

But, of course, the justice system is not driven by epistemic values alone. There are moral and political dimensions associated with the criminal law and, when it comes to the question of appeals, Americans butt directly up against the insistence of the Fifth Amendment to the Constitution: "... nor shall any person be subject for the same offense to be twice put in jeopardy of life or limb." In sum, enabling appeals of convictions would appear to be specifically forbade by the Constitution. Can it be argued that the right to protection from double jeopardy automatically trumps the powerful epistemic arguments in favor of symmetric appeals?

Without pretending to be a constitutional lawyer, I still have to say that the situation seems to me a good deal less clear-cut than this thumbnail argument would suggest. On at least three momentous occasions in the history of appellate law, justices of the Supreme Court have devised ways around the seemingly impregnable guarantee against re-trial. Let's remind ourselves of those circumstances. All three occurred in the nineteenth century. The first was the decision to apply double jeopardy protection to *all* criminal trials even though Constitutional language specifies explicitly that this guarantee only applies to capital crimes. (Recall the "jeopardy to life or limb" language.) The second was the invention of the notion of a mistrial. When, for instance, a jury is deadlocked or when the judge decides that an egregious error has been committed by the prosecutor or the defense during a trial, he will declare a mistrial, thereby permitting the prosecution, if she wishes, to initiate a new trial. On its face, the notion of a retrial conflicts directly with the double jeopardy clause. This was got round by arguing that the first trial was not really a trial at all but a 'mistrial'. The Constitution does not, it was said, guarantee no re-trial after a mistrial. The third, and most inventive, deviation from the language of the Fifth Amendment came with the invention of appeals for convictions. Here, the first trial is not a mistrial but a genuine trial, albeit one in which, in the opinion of a superior court, serious errors occurred. How then can an appellate court order open the door to a second trial when it decides that a conviction emerged from a flawed trial? The usual response here is that a retrial requires a waiver by the defendant of his right not to be tried a second time. Provided that he waives that right, the right has not technically been violated by a retrial. Retrials after flawed acquittals could not be justified on the same grounds since, we have to suppose, acquitted defendants will not rush to waive their right to protection against a second trial.

The US Supreme Court has made it clear on countless occasions that double jeopardy functions to promulgate errors favoring the defendant. Notwithstanding, the Court holds the constitutional prohibition against second trials to be ironclad. As the justices wrote in a famous double jeopardy case in 1984:

"The constitutional protection against double jeopardy unequivocally prohibits a second trial following an acquittal, [because the] public interest in the finality of criminal judgments is so strong that an acquitted defendant may not be retried even though the acquittal was based upon an egregiously erroneous foundation. If the innocence of the accused has been confirmed by a final judgment, the Constitution presumes that a second trial would be unfair."[248]

This passage means precisely what it says. Even if a witness was suborned by the defendant, even if the judge made incredible errors in the defendant's favor, an acquittal will still stand. What,

146

we need to ask, would be "unfair" about a second trial, supposing as the Court does, that the defendant was acquitted for "egregiously erroneous" reasons in the first? Why would it be "unfair" to refuse to let a defendant off if he won acquittal in a trial that was wrongfully conducted? And, if it comes to that, why should we suppose that the public interest in finality is greater than the public interest in a just verdict?[249] To the contrary, it seems unfair to society to let a patently flawed acquittal stand just as it is unfair to let a flawed conviction stand. Apart from the fairness issue, defenders of double jeopardy have used other equally dubious arguments. Here is how Martin Friedland, author of a well-known book on double jeopardy, formulates the core case against retrial after acquittal:

"[If two trials were permitted,] an innocent person will not have the stamina or resources to fight a second charge. And, knowing that a second proceeding is possible, an innocent person may plead guilty at the first trial. But even if the accused vigorously fights the second charge he may be at a greater disadvantage [because he will normally have disclosed his complete defense at the former trial]. The prosecutor can study the transcript and may thereby find apparent defects and inconsistencies in the defense evidence to use at the second trial."[250]

This strikes me as a series of non sequiturs. If it is true that some innocent persons "lack the stamina or resources" to endure a second trial, then we should prohibit judges from declaring mistrials, since those usually require the defendant to start over again from scratch. If it were true that many defendants do not have the stomach for a second bout, we should not expect to see the high proportion of federal felony convictions appealed, since winning an appeal often entails retrial. As for Friedland's suggestion that the innocent defendant, faced with the prospect of a second trial, might plead guilty immediately, this seems wildly implausible on its face. As unpleasant as one trial, let alone two, must be, that prospect has to pale in comparison with the unpleasantness associated with most criminal punishments.

Most telling of all is the last argument Friedman reprises. It voices the worry that, if retrial were allowed (which of course it already is after a mistrial or an overturned conviction), then the prosecution would know the second time around much about the defense strategy and might even be able to detect "inconsistencies in the defense evidence." We're evidently asked to infer that it is a bad thing, a moral failing, if the prosecution detects an inconsistency in the case offered by the defense. If one has the slightest inclination to see the purpose of a trial as getting at the truth, one would surely welcome rather than deplore the opportunity for *either* side to be able to expose incoherencies in the case presented by the other side. That is precisely what the adversarial system is designed to foster. Only a zealous member of the defense bar, single-mindedly concerned with his client winning rather than with whether truth emerges, could expect the rest of us to take seriously the argument that a prime advantage of a system permitting only one trial is that its allows defense inconsistencies to go undetected and unchallenged. This feature is not a virtue of the present system but an unmitigated vice.

Note, again, what happens when a mistrial is declared or when a conviction is reversed. Typically, a new jury is empaneled and the procedure begins again from scratch. The defendant loses quick finality and is made to bear additional expense. The prosecution now knows the defense strategy. Despite all that, double jeopardy concerns do not protect the defendant from re-trial after a mistrial. Why should those concerns suddenly kick in when a defendant is acquitted in a trial riddled with errors favorable to him?

Another argument commonly heard in defense of double jeopardy involves the idea that if the state were not limited to one shot at a defendant, then it could harass someone indefinitely, bringing them to trial over and again on the same charge until it either found a jury that would convict or drove the defendant mad. That is a red herring in this context. The proposal under consideration is not that the state should be able to re-charge someone with a crime indefinitely many times. It is simply that an acquittal, like a conviction, should be open to judicial review. If the appeal of an acquittal is unsuccessful, that is, if no serious errors occurred in the original trial, then that would put an end to the state's power to harass the defendant, as least where the crime in question is concerned.

If there is some conceptual space for accommodating the Fifth Amendment to a system of two-sided appeals, I think it probably resides—as I have already hinted—in a clarification of the notion of what a trial itself is. Instead of thinking that a trial ends when the jury (or the judge in a bench trial) delivers its verdict, it is easy enough to conceive a trial as terminating when and only when the appeals of the verdict, if any, have been settled. So construed, double jeopardy protection would not preclude appeals of acquittals, while it would continue to safeguard citizens from unrelenting harassment from the state, which almost certainly was its initial motive. As for the argument that appeals of convictions would undermine the notion that the jury's decision is the final word, the fact is that this notion is already in tatters. The current policy of permitting appeals of convictions undermines it. So, too, does the policy of allowing the trial judge to overthrow a jury's conviction on his own authority. In sum, the replacement of present policy in favor of symmetric appeals would require some creative semantics on the part of the high court, but no more than they have already brought to bear on a host of other vexed constitutional questions. Let us recall, very briefly, some of the relevant jurisprudence specifically on the notion of double jeopardy. Originally, constitutionally, double jeopardy applied only to capital crimes. The Constitution's language on that point is very clear. The Court found a way to apply it not only to noncapital felonies but even to misdemeanors. Originally, double jeopardy applied only to federal trials. The court fixed that problem too. Originally, double jeopardy precluded retrial after either a conviction or an acquittal. The Court dissolved that symmetry in the late nineteenth century. For such reasons, I am not moved by the argument that it would be impossible to reconcile the Fifth Amendment with a system permitting the appeal of acquittals.

I will close this chapter with a perceptive observation from the leading scholar of the history of double jeopardy, Akhil Amar, since he puts my conclusion more succinctly than I could: "Insulation [from appealing an acquittal] is an arbitrary windfall to the guilty, not a carefully structured scheme to protect the innocent.

A defendant has no vested right to a legal error in his favor."[251] What Professor Amar does not stress, and what I have tried to highlight here, is that treating acquittals as beyond correction not only allows many guilty parties to escape justice but it also prevents the judicial system from becoming self-corrective in the sense required of any system of inquiry that claims to be able to learn from its mistakes.

Part III Error Management beyond the Trial or Plea

The next chapter will focus on the leading errors of the justice system that occur prior to trial and after conviction and will suggest how they can be drastically reduced. The last chapter will pull together the various reforms proposed in the book.

Chapter 8 Additional Court-Related Sources of Reducible Harm: Bail, Sentences, Probation and Parole

Apart from false positives and false negatives (the latter mostly generated by an inflated threshold for a finding of guilt, aided and abetted by a plethora of defendant-friendly rules of procedure), there are other powerful ways in which in which the decisions of the justice system augment unnecessarily the risk of harm to innocent and undeserving victims of violent crimes. In this chapter, we will look briefly at two important sources of such risks (both related to the special circumstances of recidivism): a). the widespread non-compliance with the spirit of 'truth-in-sentencing' (specifically, via the use of probation in lieu of incarceration for punishing many of those convicted of violent crimes and the use of parole for shortening the time a convicted violent felon spends in prison); and b). the generous granting of bail to dangerous arrestees, some of whom are charged with such violent crimes as murder and rape and who proceed to commit such crimes while on bail.

As before, our focus will be entirely on those accused (in the case of bail) or convicted of violent crimes (in cases of probation and parole). We begin by noting that, according to a California study of recidivism among those released early from prison in that state, "people on parole or probation commit only [sic] one in six [17%] of violent crimes."[252] The 'only' here is more than a little disconcerting since, if the pattern in major California cities is replicated in the rest of the country, it would mean that, nationwide, probationers and parolees commit something like 283k violent crimes every year—crimes they obviously could not have committed if incarcerated. Such numbers, constituting one-in-six of all known violent crimes, scarcely warrant an 'only'. These numbers include *all* prisoners released in 2012, not just those convicted of violent crimes. Given that 57% of those released had been convicted of violent crimes,[253] we can estimate that, if the rest of the nation exhibits the same pattern as California, some 161k violent crimes committed each year are perpetrated by violent felons on parole or probation.

Almost certainly, the actual situation is much worse than these numbers suggest. The recidivist activities reported in California include only those crimes whose perpetrators authorities have identified and arrested. Given that we are ignorant of those who committed some two-thirds of violent crimes, there is every reason to suppose that the actual recidivism damage due to early releases is closer to 300k per year than the number of *known* recidivists cited in California. Such a level of victimization is almost thirty times greater than all the harm done by the 11k false positives emerging from the adjudication of cases of violent crimes. Once again, we have to ask ourselves why the latter outcome produces so much public hand-wringing when its toll of victims is literally minuscule in proportion to the costs of errors emerging from dubious decisions about parole and probation. Shortly, we will look in more detail at the parole/probation situation.

BAIL

Bail has been around for a long time in the Anglo-Saxon world.[254] Commonplace in England in the Middle Ages, the law then governing bail said that it should be routinely granted except for offenses designated by England's Parliament as not admitting bail (usually capital cases). In the US, the Judiciary Act of 1789 made all non-capital crimes bailable. In such cases, the only legitimate grounds for denial of bail awaiting trial was evidence that the individual would probably not return to face trial, i.e., that he would become a fugitive from justice. In 1984, Congress stipulated —and the Supreme Court later agreed—that bail was not a right, not even in the case of non-capital crimes and that bail could be legally denied, provided the prosecutor could show clear and convincing evidence that giving freedom to the prospective bailee would likely constitute a significant *danger* to the community. That remains in most states the prevailing practice. Specifically, if a prosecutor wants to block the granting of bail to an arrestee, he must prove by 'clear and convincing evidence' that the arrestee is dangerous (or a likely candidate for flight). In theory, this new arrangement *should* produce a bail system in which few bailees charged with violent crimes will do significant harm to others during their average 229 days awaiting trial.[255]

Unfortunately, however, successfully predicting the dangerousness of giving freedom to those accused of violent crimes is evidently anything but easy. According to one very elaborate study of the behavior of those accused of a violent crime and released on bail: 18% of those charged with murder, 52% of those charged with rape, 44% of those charged with armed robbery and 64% of those charged with aggravated assault are released on bail.[256] On average, well over half of arrestees charged with a violent crime are released on bail.

Although dangerousness is supposed to be a legitimate ground for denying bail, courts are more than a little obtuse in the ways they assess potential dangers. If you doubt that, consider this: in 1994, state courts released on bail 56% of those defendants who were facing a new felony charge for a crime committed when they had been free on bail for an earlier crime.[257] In other words, a very recent act of abusing bail evidently is apparently not seen as a sufficient reason for denying bail to someone charged with having committed a violent felony while on bail! If judges are not persuadable that it is probably dangerous to grant bail to a felon who is a known bail-jumper and is currently charged with a crime that he probably committed while on bail for a previous crime, there is not much hope for the system.

It's time to turn to the recidivism of those accused of being violent felons during that narrow window of opportunity called bail. If we're interested in the damage they do and the risks they impose, we need to turn again to some data about our 2008 group of violent felons. It's important to realize at the outset that there is one group of bailees about whom we can do little but speculate. These are the bailees who become fugitives, understood as those accused of a felony who are offered bail and then disappear for a year at least and sometimes indefinitely. Many evidently change their identities, leave the jurisdiction in which they were charged, and some even leave the country. We know how many fugitives there are but we can only make wild guesses about their recidivism. Table 10 exhibits how the situation looks with our 2008 sample:

Table 10. Bailees and Fugitives, 2008		
Initial crime charged[258]	% of those charged released on bail	% of bailees who become fugitives
Murder	18%	5%
Rape	52%	3%
Robbery	44%	n.a.
Aggravated Assault	63%	2%

Of the 342k persons arrested for violent crimes who were released on bail, 20% failed to appear for their trials. Another 12% were arrested for committing a new felony while on bail.[259] More than 7k of those released on bail had already been convicted of one or more violent crimes.[260] Add to that the approximately 2.3% (8k) who became fugitives, and one begins to see that current bail policies impose non-trivial risks of victimization on the general population. In short, after a supposed vetting to exclude the dangerous among those receiving bail, more than a third of those released on bail for a violent crime violated the conditions of their bail, in many cases by committing new violent crimes. Returning briefly to our example of violent crimes during 2008, Table 11 shows how the data would break down:

Crime[261]	Arrested	Received bail	Became Fugitives	Committed ≥1 felony on bail
Table 11. Bail and Recidivism, 2008				
Murder	13k	2.3k	115	
Rape	22.6k	11.8k	354	
Robbery	129.4k	56.9k	3.4k	
Agg. Assault	430k	270.9k	5.4k	
Total	595k	341.9k	9.3k	27.4k

What conclusions should we draw? This summary reports 27.4k serious felonies *known* to be committed annually by those charged with violent crimes but temporarily free on bail. As usual, I would be inclined to double that recidivism figure to about 55k for reasons explained in chap. 3. But even if we take the number as reported (and ignore all the serious felonies probably committed by these bailees that did not lead to an arrest and by those bailees who became fugitives), we can see that the risk to the average citizen of being the victim of a violent crime committed by someone during his approximately 5-10 months of freedom awaiting trial for a violent crime he is charged with committing is more than twice as great as the risk of that average citizen being falsely convicted of a violent crime! Once again, this kind of data –like our earlier look at the costs of false negatives—drives home the fact that the current fixation with reducing false positives at all costs is mindless and inattentive to the spectrum of risks posed by other errors of the justice system. Ironically, the solution is not difficult to conceive: arguably, those charged with a violent crime should carry the burden of proving that, if released on bail, they would likely not be dangerous. It would also make sense to deny bail routinely to seriously serial felons, since they are much more likely to use their days of freedom in socially destructive ways than first-time offenders are. Such a policy would also drastically reduce the 55k victims annually claimed by current practices.

Some legal authors argue that, however much danger may be posed by bailees, we shouldn't deny them access to bail, since it is a right, derivable from the presumption of innocence. The Supreme Court has scotched that idea on repeated occasions (as Congress also has), insisting that the denial of bail is not a punishment as such but a prudent way of protecting the general population from dangerous felons on the streets. That said, the legal system nonetheless requires that a bail denial demands a proof from the prosecutor by clear and convincing evidence that the applicant for bail would constitute a danger to others. It seems transparently clear that someone under arrest for a violent crime, and with a record of serious offenses and prior bail violations, is a prima facie plausible candidate for being dangerous, as the statistics bear out. Apart from showing the court such a defendant's prior record, no more should be required to establish that, on bail, he constitutes a threat to his fellow citizens. (More than half of those who currently receive bail after being accused of a violent crime are habitual felons.) At least for those convicted of violent crimes, the proof process leading to bail should be reversed, with the applicant having to prove (by citing evidence of his good character and his absence of prior convictions and his prior good behavior while on bail in previous cases if he has earlier arrests) that he probably does not pose a danger if he is released for some 5 to 10 months.[262]

CHRONIC SENTENCING IRREGULARITIES: PROBATION & PAROLE

One hears and reads a great deal about what are widely regarded as excessive sentences and about American prisons bulging with prisoners subjected to inordinately long sentences. Several states have adopted versions of Washington's and California's practice ("three strikes and you're out") of giving prolonged sentences to three-time serial felons, even if their current charge is comparatively minor. Many others claim to have put in place what is called a 'truth-in-sentencing' policy. The federal government encourages states to insist that a convicted felon serve at least 85% of his sentence before he is considered a candidate for parole. (That is not quite 'truth'-in-sentencing, for that would require a convicted felon to serve 100% of his sentence but it is an improvement on what went before.) Sadly, most states fail to satisfy even the demand that convicted felons serve 85% of their sentence. [263] For instance, in 1999, by which time truth-in-sentencing legislation had been adopted by more than half the states, violent offenders nationwide served on average only 55% of their sentences.[264] The *de facto* policy, at least where violent crimes are concerned, might be better dubbed 'deceit-in-sentencing', which involves meting out seemingly tough sentences to violent felons, when the legal system often has no intention whatsoever of enforcing them.

For all the talk about American's humongous prison population, however, the situation —at least where *violent* crimes are concerned—is exactly the opposite of what one might have expected; so much so that there appears to be a case for longer incarcerations (but not necessarily longer sentences) for violent felons. The reason is that, despite political pressure to achieve 'truth-in-sentencing', the vast majority of convicted violent felons spend far less time behind bars than their sentences indicate, and in a significant number of cases, they spend no time whatever in prison and, for a few, no time in jail either.

Consider some pertinent data. In 2012, state prisons were filled with some 1.3m inmates. Of those, slightly more than half (708k) were serving time for violent crimes. Given that there are approximately 360k persons convicted each year of violent crimes, that means that the prison population of violent felons is slightly less than the number of felons convicted of violent crimes in the last two years. Since the median sentence handed down to such felons is about 7.6 years, one has to wonder how it could be possible that there are only about 700k+ violent convicts in our prisons, while the number *convicted* of violent crimes in the last 7.6 years was approximately 2.6m felons.[265] The answer to the conundrum, of course, is that there is a huge discrepancy in most states between time-served and the original sentence handed down. Perhaps most surprising of all is the fact that, as we shall see below, significant numbers of *convicted* violent felons (even murderers and rapists) never even go to prison, receiving no more than a sentence of probation (or a mix of probation and a few months in the local jail). They generally remain free to prowl the streets, if they are so minded.

Table 12. Falsity-in-Sentencing: Sentence Imposed v. Time Served[266]			
Crime	Median Sentence	Median Time Served	Proportion of Sentence Served
Murder	244 mos.	153 mos.	63%
Rape	106 mos.	48 mos.	45%
Robbery	87 mos.	17 mos.	20%
Assault	62 mos.	17 mos.	27%

Table 12 shows the median sentences meted out to convicted defendants in 2006 and compares those to the time actually served by those released from prison in that year. In sum, murderers are generally released after serving less than two-thirds of their sentences; rapists, after serving less than half of their sentences; while armed robbers and those convicted of assault serve on average about a quarter of their sentences in prison. There are obviously huge cost increases in terms of heightened risks of crime if the truly guilty and convicted are freed long before their sentences lapse. Many of these persons will recidivate, committing tens of thousands of crimes every year that would not have occurred had this cohort served their full time. Supposing that the sentencing schedules used in pronouncing the sentences in the first place are punishments that legislators, judges and jurors believe '*fit* the crime' in question, we have to ask ourselves why society should absorb the risks that ensue from the premature release of violent felons, often long before they have repaid their official debt to society. For instance, are the crimes of armed robbery and aggravated assault only deserving of a punishment of less than a year and a half? Has a rapist fully paid his debt after four years behind prison walls?

Table 13. Expected Time in Prison Spent by those Who Commit a Violent Crime[267]	
Crime	Expected Punishment
Rape	8.8 months
Armed Robbery	2.2 months
Aggravated Assault	2.1 months
Murder	62.5 months

There is another way of posing the same conundrum. If one takes probation into account and the policy of early prison releases, it emerges that what is known as the 'expected prison time' associated with a violent crime is generally quite low, despite America's bulging prison population. One calculates the 'expected prison time' by comparing the number of violent crimes committed in a given year with the actual time spent in prison by those convicted of such a crime upon their release in that year. Such quantities are shown in Table (13). A report released by the National Research Council in 2008 claimed that "80% of [convicted] offenders leave prison before the end of their sentence."[268]

The numbers here (except for homicide) are so obscenely low for several reasons: most of those committing violent crimes are never apprehended or, if apprehended, are often falsely acquitted; if convicted, most are given probation, or early parole. Supposing that criminally-minded folks are capable of calculating their rational self-interests, they are likely to be generally unphased by the idea that the likely prison time they will pay for a violent offense is a couple of months (in the case of aggravated assault or robbery). The US problem (leaving drug-related crimes to one side) is not that too many violent felons are in prison for too long but that a). a vast number of violent crimes are committed; b). most of those crimes (except in the case of homicide) go unpunished; and c). it is rare that a person convicted of a violent crime will come anywhere close to serving his full sentence behind bars.

The early release of violent offenders prematurely undercuts both the deterrent and, more importantly, the incapacitative goals of incarceration. While most of these early releases will nominally be under the supervision of a parole or probation officer (leaving the convict free to walk the streets), many of those felons, ostensibly under such supervision, quickly return to a vigorous life of violent crime. As we shall soon see, there can be no doubt but that, if violent felons were imprisoned for the full length of their sentences (especially the serial offenders among them), the victimization of innocent citizens by those convicted of violent crimes (and released early) would be reduced by tens of thousands every year.

More concretely, we saw in chapter 4 that the mean punishment imposed on someone convicted of a violent crime (in 2008) was 7.6 years imprisonment. If one works out the implications of the data in Table 13, we can infer that the average time actually spent in prison or jail by those convicted of violent crimes is roughly 1.8 years. This discrepancy between sentence length and time served is enormously costly. If a violent felon is released from confinement after 1.8 years rather than at the end of the 7.6 years that was his (average) sentence, then we have a gap of 5.8 years when he is at liberty during which time, had his sentence been honored, he would have been incarcerated. Because 350k convicted, violent felons are normally released so soon each year, this gap of almost six years will lead to approximately 0.91 victims of violent crimes perpetrated by the foreseeable average recidivism of *each* of these early releases. (Supposing a modest recidivism rate of 1.2 violent crimes during 7.6 years, which I explained in chapter 4.) That means that the failure to honor the truth-in-sentencing principle enables some 319k violent crimes a year that would not have occurred if the official sentences had been respected.

This unseemly figure–which is close to the 300k victims estimate based on the California study—dwarfs most of our other calculations of violent harm for such errors as false positives (24k victims), false negatives (112k victims), and pre-trial bail (55k victims), not counting whatever violent harms are done by the fugitives from bail and the absconders from parole and probation. Indeed, the harm to innocent victims stemming from premature prison release of violent felons is almost double the harm exacted by *all* the other errors on which we have focused.

While I believe that very short sentences for serious violent felonies are a grievous mistake (in light of plausible recidivism estimates), I am no advocate of very long sentences. Numerous recidivism studies have shown that recidivism rates are closely correlated with the age of serial felons. Between ages 18 and 40, a serial felon on the streets is apt to wreak harm repeatedly. From about 40 onwards, however, the penchant for frequent criminal activity generally declines sharply. Accordingly, imposing a sentence of 20+ years (let alone life) on someone already approaching his 40s, will probably do relatively little to reduce crimes by incapacitation.[269] By contrast, imposing a similar sentence — and insisting on genuine truth-in-sentencing on a known serial offender in his early 20s—is likely to prevent numerous serious crimes during what Blumstein has famously dubbed *'the criminal career'*.[270]

PROBATION

Probation is a very widely used but little understood form of punishment. (In 2008, the US counted 1.33m people in prison or jail and some 4.3m *convicted* persons on probation.[271]) The probation sentence can be simple or complex. In the simplest case, a person serving time on probation will typically be required to engage in various character-reforming acts (often related to drug- or alcohol-addiction), to do some 'community service' and to check-in with authorities from time to time. Occasionally, he will be put under house arrest. In large part, the probationer lives very nearly as a free agent.[272] Sometimes, however, the probation sentence is linked with a certain (usually shortish) period of incarceration, ordinarily in jail rather than prison. The theory behind probation is that those convicted, violent felons receiving probation constitute less of a threat to their community than do those sent to prison. (As we shall see, this may be a wildly optimistic expectation.)

In the 1990s, the Bureau of Justice Statistics did a very ambitious study of recidivism among some 79k felons on probation.[273] According to these findings, some 27% of those convicted of a violent crime received a simple (no jail-time) or mixed (jail/on street) probation sentence. Table 14 gives a brief summary of how probation plays out for various crimes. For some of us, the very thought that 6% of those convicted of murder and 20% of the convicted rapists spend no time in prison is mildly appalling. Such punishments, if we must call them that, serve neither the ends of incapacitation nor of deterrence. But the dismay does not stop there.

If it strikes you as strange that 6% of convicted murderers and 20% of convicted rapists can get off with no prison time whatever and little or no jail time, so it should. More troubling still is the fact that 11% of those on probation vanish from view every year. In recent years, a few states have taken steps to preclude that possibility but as the numbers in this table indicate, probation for violent felons is still a common phenomenon.[274] According to the BJS, 1-in-12 persons on probation in 2008 became an absconder.[275] Of those on parole in the same year, some 11% absconded.[276]

Table 14. Proportion of Convicted Violent Felons Who Receive Probation		
Crime for which Probation Received[277]	% Receiving probation w/no jail time	% Receiving Probation w/partial jail time
Murder	4%	2%
Rape	10%	10%
Armed robbery	12%	8%
Aggravated assault	26%	17%

During their first three years on probation, almost 10% of the probationers simply disappeared.[278] Some 26% of those on probation were arrested and charged with a new felony, committed while on probation.[279] Eighteen percent of violent probationers were arrested for a new violent offense. Perhaps most incredible of all is the fact that, of those probationers who did commit a crime while on probation and were convicted of it, 11% of those newly convicted of murder and 29% of those convicted for rape were give a new sentence *on probation*![280]

Going back to our 2008 case, this means that of the 363k felons convicted for violent crimes, approximately 69k would have received probation.[281] During their first three years on probation, about 7k of these 69k felons simply disappear from view. (See above.) No one knows whether they have adopted a new identity, moved to a different state or what. Neither do we know whether these quasi-fugitives commit new crimes after their disappearance (although it is hard to doubt that—given their prior violent conviction and their later becoming 'absconders'—they are probably wreaking criminal havoc somewhere or other). What we do know, and it is disturbing, is that in 2008 8% of those violent convicts on probation became absconders and vanished.[282]

If we look at the other 92%, about whom we do have statistics, the degree of recidivism is relatively high, even while they are serving their time on probation. A large study of recidivism by the Bureau of Justice Statistics of probationers reported that some 11.2k (18%) of those on probation as a 'punishment' for an earlier violent crime, are rearrested for a violent crime during their first three years on probation. If we double this estimate (on the strength of unsolved crimes and felons' self-reports), we are in the range of 22k victims of the violent, nefarious activities of those on probation for violent crimes. (Recall that this estimate does not include whatever bad acts the probation absconders committed.) Obviously, if these guilty felons had been incapacitated in prison, well over 20k violent victimizations would have been prevented during a three-year period. The solution to this problem is self-evident: eliminate probation as an appropriate 'punishment' for those convicted of violent crimes (especially if, besides their current conviction, they have a record of multiple prior violations of the law). Incapacitating such felons –thereby eliminating probation as a punishment for violent serial felons— would save tens of thousands of innocent citizens from falling prey to the violent instincts of the former. Despite this, American courts have gone on a probation binge. Between 1980 and 1994, the number of those receiving probation in the US increased by 1,565%.[283]

PAROLE

The last of our examples of legal procedures that needlessly impose risks on all of us is that of parole. Essentially, there are five legal ways to get out of prison in the US: mandatory parole, completion of sentence, a pardon, an exoneration and discretionary parole.[284] Statistics specifically on parole and recidivism are hard to come by, in part because most researchers plausibly expect that recidivism rates among those released on parole would be indistinguishable from recidivism rates among those simply released from prisons after serving out their full sentences, about which we do have ample data. Perhaps the most significant fact to note about the costs of parole is that extensive interviews with those now in prison indicate that "24% of persons [currently] in prison were on parole [for another crime] at the time of the offense for which they were [now] serving time in prison."[285] Of the 410,613 felons discharged from State parole in 1999, 42% successfully completed their term of parole supervision, 43% were returned to prison for a new offense, and 10% absconded.[286] It is worth adding that 11% of all violent cases cleared by the police (that is submitted to the prosecutor for trial) in 2009 involved persons then on probation for another felony, and 4% of all new cases (violent and otherwise) involved those on parole for another felony.[287] That's another way of saying that many of those on parole are active recidivists and clearly constitute a significant risk to the general population. Given these values, it seems reasonable to suppose that of the 1.7m violent crimes per year, roughly 187k (11%) were committed by those on probation and another 68k (4%) by those on parole. Seen from this perspective, the annual effect of granting parole and probation to convicted felons is to enable approximately 255k victims of violent crimes that would have been avoided absent these two release mechanisms.

The denial of parole and the insistence that a violent offender serve his full sentence would obviously postpone the recidivist's bad acts for a few years but, after his final release, and especially if his history is that of a young serial offender, it will probably not be long after release before he is back in prison again. Even so, the denial of parole would clearly cut violent crime levels by about 24k per year. To sum up this chapter so far, we can say succinctly that in 2008, there were 185k violent offenders on parole, 430k violent offenders on probation, and 277k accused violent offenders on bail, giving us a grand total of some 892k accused or convicted violent felons at liberty, some 500k of whom were serial felons. It is quite clear that the social contract's guarantee that the state will do whatever is reasonably within its power to protect its citizens from those known to be a danger to others has been abandoned in wholesale fashion by a series of deliberate decisions to ignore the obvious. Figure 11 vividly illustrates how the numbers and proportions of convicted felons has shifted dramatically in the direction of utilizing probation in lieu of incarceration.

ARE WE IMPRISONING TOO MANY VIOLENT FELONS?

It is a familiar cliché (both domestically and in other countries) that the US is imprisoning a disproportionately large part of its population. As an advocate for longer prison times and still more convictions than we now make, my message that the jails should be fuller of violent felons than they currently are will probably fall on skeptical ears and furrowed brows. While it is undoubtedly true that the U.S. already has a higher per capita proportion of its population imprisoned than most civilized countries do, I remain mystified at the thought that we are imprisoning too many violent felons. The one overwhelming reason (rarely mentioned by critics of the prison populations in the U.S. but which offers a wholly natural explanation for our high imprisonment rates) is simple: the U.S. generally has a *much* higher violent crime rate per capita than most of the countries with which we tend to compare ourselves. (Bear in mind, too, that some 65m Americans—one in every four adults—have a 'criminal record'.) Under such circumstances, something would be badly amiss if we did not find that we were imprisoning far more violent felons per capita than most other countries.

Think of it differently. Suppose that someone noted that 8-of-every-10 persons in American prisons are male (which they are), But why are men imprisoned disproportionately? Well, the answer is obvious: victimization studies reveal year-after-year that men are vastly more likely (90%) to commit violent crimes than women are (10%).[288] Suddenly, the mystery about many more men in prison than women vanishes. The same applies to the conundrum about the high rate of incarceration in the US for violent felons. The explanation is fiendishly simple: prisons are bulging because adult Americans—male and female—are more likely to commit violent crimes than their counterparts in most of the rest of the developed world. One may continue to wonder why Americans are more violence-prone than their foreign counterparts just as one may wonder why men are more violent than women. But the explanation of incarceration rates—either for America v. the rest of the world or males v. females—is readily to hand. The former in each case are responsible for more harm than the latter. Men will not stop their violent acts if punishments are made less common or less lengthy any more than Americans will respond to a reduced imprisonment regime by reducing their proclivity to commit violent crimes.

167

Table 15. A Comparative Look at Completed Violent Crimes Reported to the Police In 1999 (per 100k population)[289]					
Crime	US	England/ Wales	Germany	Italy	Spain
Homicide	4.6	1.5	1.2	1.5	1.2
Rape	34	16	9	3.3	15
Aggravated Assault	355	29	139	52	28
Armed Robbery	163	160	75	68	1,332
TOTALS	557	207	224	125	1,376

Table 15 vividly conveys this message. We have roughly three times the homicide rate of England/Wales, Germany, Spain or Italy. We have rape rates twice the size of those in England and France. We have aggravated assault rates more than ten times those of England and some 40 times more than those of Canada. Armed robbery is the only area where we have serious rivals in England and, impressively, Spain. If you put all this information together, it becomes very clear that America *should* have a much higher proportion of its population in prison for violent crimes than most other countries since its overall record of violent crimes puts it in a league of its own (leaving aside Spain's armed robberies), not so much because of long sentencing policies—which, as we have seen, are notoriously foreshortened by actors in the legal system—but because ours is, to be candid, a very violent place in which to live. It is that situation, rather than our prison population of violent felons, that should be the dominant crime-related topic of our time.

Figure 11. Distribution of the Convicted U.S. Population, 1975-2010[290]

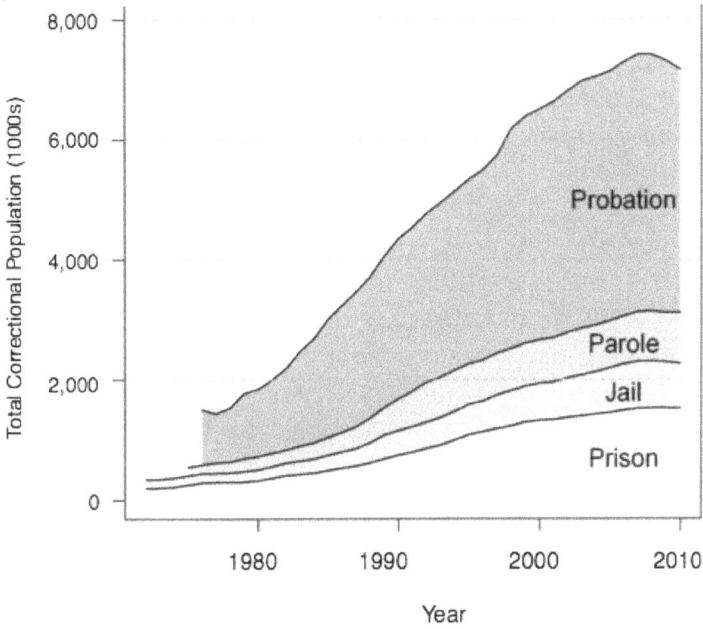

Where prison populations are concerned, the appropriate moral seems to be that, far from our system imprisoning too many people for violent crimes and locking them away for too long a time, it actually errs strongly in the other direction. Very few of those convicted of such crimes serve their full sentences (despite the fact that the latter are supposed to be 'proportional to the severity of the crime' and our spurious commitment to 'truth-in-sentencing'). As we have seen, many of the convicted, even in cases of murder (6%) and rape (20%), *never* set foot in prison. The numbers in the prison population, as far as they concern violent offenders, lead one to conclude that the legal system is seriously remiss in its duties to protect the innocent from potentially violent criminals. Our problem, as I have said, is not that we are imprisoning too many violent felons but, rather, that our country produces far too many violent felons. We convict less than a quarter of those, and often impose paltry sentences (the bulk of which are only partially enforced) on many of the convicted. Bailees sometimes become fugitives; probationers and parolees

169

often become absconders. All of those lucky felons are at liberty to do whatever nasty deeds they can get away with. If we are loathe to build yet more prisons in order to handle the consequences of my proposals for the elimination of probation and parole for violent felons, the problem could be mitigated by decriminalizing many drug-related offenses, which would free up more than 200k places in existing prisons.

The same can be said of many other low-grade misdemeanors (for instance, drinking in public, disorderly conduct, sports betting rings, petty theft and prostitution). If our prisons and jails are currently bulging (as they clearly are), the obvious remedy is not to go easy on punishing violent felons (via a liberal use of probation and parole) but to take whatever steps are necessary to fill up punishment spaces now occupied by those guilty of non-violent crimes with genuinely violent offenders.

THE IMPACT ON MINORITIES OF AN INCREASED RATE OF TRUE CONVICTIONS

It is plausible to conjecture that an increase in the conviction rate of the sort proposed here would have a larger per capita impact on the black and Latino populations than it would have on the white population. Since a larger proportion of blacks and Latinos are arrested and charged with serious crimes than are whites, it is reasonable to believe that a mechanism of the sort proposed here could lead to a disproportionate impact on minority communities. If we re-engineered the system so that there were mildly more true convictions and fewer false acquittals, more Latinos and more Afro-Americans would go to prison than now do. So would more whites, but a smaller proportion of whites would be involved. On the face of it, that disparate impact would be socially undesirable.

But a more careful analysis reveals that the overall harms suffered by minority communities as a result of a decision of the legal system—to convict more of the guilty—would be significantly *reduced* in comparison to the harms produced in those communities by the current system, with its high rate of false acquittals. Here is how the argument should be understood.

Victimization studies reveal, year after year, that an average member of a black or Latino community suffers a much higher risk of being the *victim* of a violent crime than his white counterparts are. A large set of those victimizations are perpetrated by serial felons, many of whom were either falsely acquitted or convicted but released well before completing their sentences. Moreover, a majority of the perpetrators of such crimes against minorities are themselves members of a minority community. There is thus every reason to expect that a higher conviction rate for violent crimes (and an insistence on serving out one's sentence) would significantly reduce minority victimizations, currently enabled by the abundance of false acquittals, fugitives from bail, by parole and probation absconders and by the early release of those convicted of violent crimes. Indeed, the reduction in victims of violent crimes would be proportionally much greater among blacks than whites.

Consider briefly the situation in the most recent year for which data is available, 2014. I will focus on the most grievous of crimes: homicide. In that year the US population was 319m. Whites made up 77% of the population and blacks were 13%. According to figures from the FBI, there were 5.4k white homicide victims and 6.1k black victims. Among the known homicide *offenders*, 4.3k were whites and 5.2k were blacks, meaning that an Afro-American was ~7 times more likely to commit homicide than a white.[291] More troubling still, a black citizen is 12 times more likely to be killed by a black than by a white.[292] If the legal system could incapacitate a larger proportion of violent offenders than it now does, there is strong reason to believe that the frequency of violent crimes (including homicide) would drop dramatically.

Indeed, there is no group in our society that would profit more from a decline in rates of violent crime than the Afro-American community. Not only do they suffer a much higher rate of homicide victimization than other groups, they likewise have a higher victim rate for each of the other violent crimes. The popular recent drive to make the criminal justice system less punitive makes sense only with respect to the incarceration of persons for victim-less or otherwise minor crimes. The idea that we should send fewer *violent* felons to prison (combined with lesser penalties for the convicted perpetrators), even while the rate of violent crimes is as high as it is, is an open invitation to a growth in violent crimes, and no groups would suffer a greater risk of increased victimhood than the poor and the blacks. Since 'black lives do matter', the incarceration of a higher proportion of truly guilty perpetrators of violent crimes—whether black or white—would serve the interests of everyone, save the interests of the perpetrators themselves. Many voices argue that we are sending black males to prison for violent crimes disproportionately to their numbers in the population. We are indeed; but the straightforward explanation for the disparity is that, judging by numerous victimization surveys, they are committing serious felonies out of proportion to their numbers in the population.

Chapter 9 Where Do We Go from Here? How to Turn a Criminal Proceeding into a Genuine, Truth-Seeking and Harm-Reducing Instrument of Inquiry

> The symbol … of a society more concerned with the appearance of justice than with the actual achievement of justice, indeed says much about us. –Daniel Shaviro[293]

> The field of [legal] evidence is no other than the field of knowledge. —Jeremy Bentham (1810)[294]

As we have seen, the handling of violent crime cases in the United States leaves much to be desired in light of the social contract's demand for balancing the principal risks that innocent citizens face (on the one hand, being falsely convicted and, on the other, being violently victimized by a felon whom the state could and should have imprisoned proportionally to the severity of the crime he committed). Sometimes, the failures occur because of the highly demanding standard of proof and the defendant-friendly rules of trial that lead each year to the acquittal of some 94k truly guilty violent felons (who claim some 112k violent crime victims during the period when they should have been incarcerated, since the state had good reason to believe them guilty but just not strong enough reason to believe them guilty beyond a reasonable doubt). Another 11k innocent defendants are falsely convicted, leading to some 24k innocent victims annually.

But, as we have seen repeatedly, falsely acquitted and falsely convicted felons are just one segment of the mess I call 'the law's flaws'. Once arrested, those accused of a violent crime are more likely to be granted bail than denied it, including some accused of murder and others with an active history of recidivism. While on bail awaiting adjudication of their cases, those bailees will add many thousands of innocent citizens to the list of victims (roughly 55k/year). Once the felony defendant has been convicted, he may discover that his punishment is merely probation, usually leaving him free to wander the streets, instead of serving the 7.6-year sentence that is meted out to the average convicted violent felon. Even if he goes to prison with a hefty sentence, he is likely to serve barely half of it (and in most cases—especially robbery and assault—only about a quarter of it). Failures of the mechanisms of probation and parole add another 300k innocent victims to our already depressing list of avoidable errors (136k victims emerging from trial errors).

How did we get in such a mess? The analysis in this book strongly suggests that the American legal system is massively indifferent to the features that give virtually all other forms of empirical inquiry their credentials and thereby give us confidence in the conclusions they reach. I refer, of course, to the following traits, sorely lacking in the criminal law:

a). the necessity to adopt rules of investigation that we have good reasons to believe are *truth-conducive*. With certain exceptions, the criminal law neither knows nor even seems to care whether the rules it imposes on criminal investigations and criminal trials have this crucial trait. Appellate judges will wax enthusiastically about the rights and protections afforded to the defendant. Those are not unimportant issues. But they are not the key issues when it comes to designing a set of rules likely to produce a true verdict;

b). the will and the machinery of an inquiry system to identify its epistemic mistakes, something that the usual legal appeals mechanisms are largely indifferent to; and

c). the ability *to learn from its mistakes* not that only that certain mistakes have occurred but, more importantly, to figure out which procedural rules were responsible for those errors and to modify those error-inducing rules so as to make them less likely to err.

It does not take deep reflection to realize that these flaws constitute a damning indictment of the way in which the criminal law currently works. Indeed, it may give a new connotation to the traditional phrase "trial and error'. We have put in place elaborate and highly ritualized structures of legal inquiry without bothering to put in place the features that would make this system a genuine, legitimate example of searching for the truth. We have relegated both truth-finding and victim-protection to a secondary role and left the shaping of the trial process largely to a series of appellate courts and legislators, who evidently have little comprehension of the rudiments of the epistemology and logic of empirical inquiry.

But the problems that we have been discussing obviously go well beyond the flimsy grasp the judicial system has on what legal inquiry should look like. As Part III argues, the failure to distinguish reliably between the dangerous (on bail, probation and parole) and the non-dangerous leads to hundreds of thousands of additional victims of criminal violence every year. These mistakes, too, violate the social contract's demand whereby the state is obliged to protect its citizens from prima facie dangerous felons.

We can sum up the key conclusions that have emerged here in this way:

There is massive ignorance among the general public (and among law's practitioners) about the frequency and costs of the errors made by the legal system, especially the errors arising from false negatives, bail, and the drastic shortening of sentences;

Our thinking about violent crime and punishment has to be embedded in a coherent theory of the social contract between the state and its citizens, with a special focus on the high risks of recidivism (both among the false negatives and on the part of those persons who escaped justice because of a false positive and including those convicted, violent felons who served only a modest fraction of their sentences);

The set of false acquittals currently generated produces much more harm than the set of false positives, despite the fact that the latter get virtually all of the attention and despite the fact that a single false positive is more harmful than a single false negative. If we are to design a system that reflects the actual value of the relation between the violent harms arising from false negatives and false positives respectively, we should be trying to design a system that produces roughly 2 false acquittals for every false conviction. The 10-for-1 Blackstone proposal that still dominates most thinking on this issue has *never* enjoyed the slightest logical or empirical justification. As the analysis in earlier chapters shows, Blackstone guessed wrong; Voltaire guessed right when he proposed 2-for-1;

In addition, it should be possible both to appeal acquittals and to re-open a case that ended in an acquittal, provided that new, highly inculpatory evidence emerges or that it can be shown that egregious errors occurred in a trial leading to an acquittal;

The existing standard of proof is vague and demonstrably incapable of protecting citizens from becoming victims of crime because it produces a very high frequency of false negatives;

Existing efforts to find a rational way of deciding how demanding the standard of proof should be by invoking the tools of decision theory—attractive as they are in theory—are unworkable because our justice systems is full of procedural rules that dramatically impact the distribution of errors;

There has been too strong an emphasis on protecting the ostensible 'rights of defendants' and too little emphasis on finding out the truth about an alleged crime and protecting prospective victims. Epistemic *and* moral demands must both be acknowledged and given a guiding role in formulating the rules of trial, not least because the epistemic goal of getting a true verdict has a heavy moral implication in terms of the social contract;

The huge discrepancy between the official sentence meted out for a violent felony conviction and the actual sentence served gives rise to much avoidable harm, especially where serial, violent felons are concerned. At a minimum, such felons—especially in the age range from 18 to 40—should be required to serve out their sentences and rarely if ever sentenced to mere probation;

Likewise, bail should usually be denied to serial offenders awaiting trial for a violent crime. It should, however, be possible to override that denial, *provided* the defendant can prove to a preponderance of the evidence that his freedom would not constitute a danger to his fellow citizens;

The power of jurors to draw an adverse inference from the silence of the defendant—when circumstances warrant such an inference—should be reinstated. Failure to do so would mean (as it now does) that more than half of violent offenders on trial will continue to avoid cross examination altogether by refusing to testify;

The number of mistrials of violent offenders arising from a split jury (now approximately 5% of criminal trials and as high as

20% in some jurisdictions) could be drastically reduced if most states (as opposed to the present precious few) went over to a system allowing convictions and acquittals by a super-majority (usually at least 10-to-2);

If appeals are to play—as they should—any *epistemic* (as opposed to a purely procedural) role in weighing the soundness of a verdict, jurors should be directed to submit a brief account of their reason(s) for convicting (or acquitting) the defendant. This would allow appellate courts to evaluate carefully, as they now cannot even begin to, the validity of the inferences that jurors draw from the evidence.

In sum, to meet the demands of the social contract, we need: citizens to report more of the violent crimes that occur; the police to increase the proportion of those suspects who are arrested; prosecutors to convict most of those probably guilty arrestees against whom they are now dropping charges; jurors to be given relevant evidence that is now excluded; and the legal system needs to re-think its current practices of the wholesale use of probation and parole, so as to keep more violent serial felons off the streets.

If we were to implement the changes proposed in this book – revising the rules of legal procedure so that victimhood was minimized by virtue of mistaken verdicts, eliminating the granting of bail to serial felons accused of violent acts, abandoning probation as a legitimate 'punishment' for a violent crime, and requiring violent defendants to serve their full sentences—we could reasonably expect an annual reduction in the number of violent crime victims by some 350,000, including 2,500 fewer homicides. (Preventing thereby a million violent crimes every three years.) That would represent a staggering change in the threats posed by violent crime in the United States. At the same time, it would make trials less error-prone than they are at present, assure that the sentences meted out to convicted violent felons were satisfied, and enable judges to deny bail to potentially dangerous serial felons (without, as now, prosecutors having to prove their dangerousness to a standard of clear and convincing evidence). This book has taken a stab at spelling out some ways in which changes of procedure could drastically reduce criminal victimization. Whether such changes as I have sketched out here have a realistic chance of implementation depends on whether those legislators who shape the law, and those judges who implement and interpret it, are capable of acknowledging the errors of their current ways.

Apart from adopting certain epistemically plausible and harm-controlling policies sketched out in earlier pages, we as a society need to put aside many of the false myths that have become deeply embedded in socio-political discussions of the handling of violent crimes. It is not true that we send too many violent felons to jail; to the contrary, we send too few of them. It is patently false that we are convicting far too many innocent defendants. A false positive rate at or below the present figure of 3% is far from needing to be reduced by pumping up the standard of proof still further than its current high plateau. On the contrary, it only makes sense to lower it if our aim is to minimize harm to innocent citizens. Finally, the persistent notion that in a criminal trial, the cards are mightily stacked against the defendant is preposterous. Current rules give vastly more probative advantages to defendants than they give to prosecutors.

The goddess of justice—whose statue adorns so many courthouses—symbolizes the idea that we must weigh carefully the relevant evidence in her balance scale in a wholly party-neutral fashion (witness her blindfold). American criminal trials are, I have argued here, a far cry from that ideal.

NOTES

¹ See the White House report on imprisonment, *Economic Perspectives on Incarceration* (2016), Figure 7. Barely half (53%) of those in prison in 2014 were violent felons: 19% committed property crimes and 16%, drug crimes (*ibid.*, Fig. 16).

² The famous 18th-century jurist, Lord William Blackstone, insisted that double jeopardy was a "universal maxim of the common law." 4 William Blackstone, *Commentaries*, 335.

³ Larry Laudan, "The Social Contract and the Rules of Trial: Re-Thinking Procedural Rules," in Brian Leiter & Les Green, eds., *Oxford Studies in the Philosophy of Law* 1 (Oxford University Press), (2011), 195-227.

⁴ Sofia Gatowski *et al.*, "Asking the Gatekeepers: A National Survey of Judges," *Law and Human Behavior*, 25 (2001), p.447.

⁵ 509 U.S. 579 (1993).

⁶ The most familiar examples are the many exclusionary rules, which deny admission to certain kinds of evidence, no matter how relevant that evidence may be to the question of defendant's guilt or innocence. But, as I will show in chapter 6, the exclusionary rules are only the tip of a very large iceberg.

⁷ Source: *Convicted by Juries, Exonerated by Science: Case Studies in the Use of DNA Evidence to Establish Innocence After Trial* by Edward Connors, Thomas Lundregan, Neal Miller, Tom McEwen June 1996, p.iii.

⁸ Justice Lewis Powell's dissent in *Bullington v. Missouri*, 451 U.S. 430 (1981).

⁹ *Lindsey v. United States*, 133 F.2d 368, 372, 1942 U.S. App. LEXIS 2507, 16-17, 77 U.S. App. D.C. 1 (D.C. Cir. 1942).

¹⁰ Cited in Harry Kalven & Hans Zeisel, *The American Jury* (Little, Brown & Co: Boston, 1966) p.190.

¹¹ California Department of Corrections and Rehabilitation, 2015.

¹² *Addington v. Texas*, 441 US 418 at 425 (1974).

¹³ *US v. Havens*, 446 US 620 (1980).

¹⁴ Brian Forst, "Managing Miscarriages of Justice from Victimization to Reintegration," 74 *Albany Law Rev.*, p.167 (2010/2011).

¹⁵ Moses Maimonides, *The Commandments* (Charles B. Chavel, trans., 1967), p, 270.

¹⁶ "'Tis much more Prudence to acquit two persons, tho' actually guilty, than to pass Sentence of Condemnation on one that is virtuous and innocent." Voltaire, *Zadig* (London, 1749, ch. 6, 53).

¹⁷ *The Works of Benjamin Franklin*, vol. 2 at 13 (ed. John Bigelow, 1904).

¹⁸ In Alexander Volokh's splendid historical survey of opinions of jurists about the acceptable ratio of false negatives to false positives, he notes that courts in 22 states have ventured opinions about what the ratio should be.

Nine state courts opted for 1:1; four preferred 10:1; five advocated 'many to one'; one proposed 99:1; another, 100:1; and one settled on 5:1. (Alexander Volokh, "*n* Guilty Men," 146 *U. of Penn. Law Rev*, 173 (1997), Table 1.)

[19] *All* the numbers in this summary are derived from sources cited in subsequent chapters. See especially Table 3.

[20] BJS, *Criminal Victimization in the United States, 2008* (2010), Table I.

[21] *Ibid.*, Table 2.

[22] *Ibid.*, Table 3.

[23] BJS, *Homicide Trends in the U.S., 1980-2008* (2011), Table I.

[24] *Ibid.*, Table 6.

[25] *Ibid.*, Table 27.

[26] *Ibid.*, Table 92.

[27] *Ibid.*, Table 11.

[28] *Ibid.*, Figures 32a, 32b.

[29] BJS, *Prisoners in 2013* (2014), Table 17.

[30] The education numbers come from BJS, *Education and Correctional Populations* (2003), Tables 1 and 13.

[31] See the White House Report called *Economic Perspectives on Incarceration* (April 2016), p.33.

[32] *Ibid.*, Table 101.

[33] *Ibid.*, Table 38.

[34] BJS, *Homicide Trends in the United States, 1980-2008* (2011), Table 1.

[35] BJS, *Criminal Victimization in the US 2008*, Table 37.

[36] *Ibid.*, Table 66.

[37] See: "How Many Guns in the U.S.?" http://www.gunpolicy.org/firearms/region/united-states.

[38] BJS, *Alcohol and Crime*, 1998, p. i.

[39] *Drug Use and Dependence, State and Federal Prisoners*, 2004, NCJ 213530.

[40] BJS, *Violent Victimization of College Students*, 1995-2000, NCJ 196143, 2003.

[41] *Op. cit.* note 20, Table 42.

[42] According to the BJS, in 2007 the average annual caseload for *each* prosecuting attorney in state courts was 94 cases. (BJS, *Prosecutors in State Courts, 2007* (2011), p.1.)

[43] Data Source: BJS, *Felony Sentences in State Courts, 2006* (2009), Table 4.1. The rapes numbers reflect only those rapes *reported to the police* that led to conviction. All the other figures are proportions of perpetrators of known victims who were convicted.

[44] Here's what the LexisNexis searches produce:

References to Errors				
Type of error	Legal cases	Law review articles	Legal statutes	Total
'Wrongful conviction'	2,684 cites	2,395 cites	821 cites	5,900 cites
'False conviction'	131 cites	298 cites	3 cites	432 cites
'Wrongful acquittal'	10 cites	77 cites	0 cites	87 cites
'False acquittal'	2 cites	55 cites	0 cites	57 cites

[45] Among the better known recent books on this theme are: B. Garrett, *Convicting the Innocent* (Harvard U Press, 2013), J. Petro, *False Justice: 8 Myths that Convict the Innocent* (Kaplan, 2010), and B. Scheck *et al.*, *When Justice Goes Wrong and How to Make It Right* (Doubleday, 2000).

[46] See especially the discussion in chapter 5.

[47] Between 2011 and 2014, there were, on average, 40 executions per year, according to the Death Penalty Information Center (http://www.deathpenaltyinfo.org/number-executions-state-and-region-1976). In that same time frame, there were approximately 14,000 murders committed annually, leading to approximately 13k persons convicted of murder each year. (FBI, *Crime in the United States, 2012*, Tables 12 and 25) In short, approximately 0.3% of those convicted of homicide are executed. It is also worth bearing in mind that twice as many prison convicts are murdered by fellow inmates in prison each year (85 of them in 2012) than are executed annually on death row. (BJS, *Mortality in Local Jails and State Prisons, 2000-2012,* Table 15 (2014).

[48] See Saul Kassin *et al.,* "The General Acceptance of Psychological Research on Eyewitness Testimony," *American Psychologist* 44 (1989), 1089-1098.

[49] *Ibid.* More recently, a study by the Department of Justice reported that the false positive rate on fingerprint IDs was 4.2% and the false negative rate was 8.7%. (Department of Justice Press Release, "Fingerprint Examiners Found to Have Very Low Error Rates," February 2, 2015.)

[50] BJS, *Violent Felons in Large Urban Counties, 1990-2002* (2006), Table 5.

[51] *Ibid.,* p.1.

[52] BJS, *Recidivism of Prisoners Released in 30 States in 2005* (2014), p. 1 and Table 4.

[53] *Ibid.,* table 7.

[54] See especially the study by Larry Laudan and Ronald Allen, "The Devastating Impact of Prior Crimes Evidence," *Journal of Criminal Law and Criminology*, *101* (2011), 101-135.

[55] Cesare Beccaria, *An Essay on Crime and Punishments* (Philadelphia, 1819), p. 47.

[56] Beccaria, one of the most widely-cited early contract theorists, formulated the attractions of the rule of law over the state of nature thusly: "Weary of living in a continued state of war, and enjoying a liberty, which became of little value, from the uncertainty of its duration, [mankind] sacrificed one part of it[s liberty], to enjoy the rest in peace and security." (*Ibid.*, p.15)

[57] It is sometimes suggested that this potential loss of liberty represents a risk that the citizen runs under the rule of law that he did not run while in a state of nature. That is dubious since it seems plausible to suppose that, even in a stateless society, there would be plenty of surrogate and unofficial forms of vigilante-ism that would mete out a primitive form of justice that would frequently result in persons being punished for actions that they did not commit.

[58] A good, brief account of Beccaria's importance in the development of modern punishment theory can be found in Bernard Harcourt's "Beccaria's 'On Crimes and Punishments': A Mirror on the History of the Foundations of Modern Criminal Law," Coarse Sandor Institute for Law, Working Paper No. 648 (2013).

[59] "The high war death rates among most nonstate societies are obviously the result of several features of primitive warfare: the prevalence of wars, the high proportion of tribesmen who face combat, the cumulative effects of frequent but low-casualty battles, the unmitigated deadliness and very high frequency of raids, the catastrophic mortalities inflicted in general massacres, the customary killing of all adult males, and the often atrocious treatment of women and children. For these reasons, a member of a typical tribal society, especially a male, had a far higher probability of dying "by the sword" than a citizen of an average modern state." (Lawrence Keeley, *War Before Civilization*, Oxford, 1996)

[60] Beccaria put the point this way: "Wearied by living in an unending state of war and by a freedom rendered useless by the uncertainty of retaining it... they sacrifice *a part of that freedom* in order to enjoy what remains in security and calm." C. Beccaria, *On Crimes and Punishments*, R Bellamy (ed.), 1995, p. 9.

[61] There is more use of empirical data here than one usually sees in a "philosophical" essay, so a caveat is in order: many crime-related statistics are distinctly mushy and often presented in a manner that can easily suggest a specious precision. My policy throughout will be to treat the numbers skeptically, while still trying to learn from them what we can about general patterns of theoretical interest. Where they are pertinent to the theses I will be propounding, I will try to err in the direction of construing them conservatively,

so as not to give them more authority in the argument than the vagaries of their collection would justify.

[62] See Herbert Koppel, *Lifetime Likelihood of Victimization*, Bureau of Justice Statistics, NCJ-104274 (1987). See also Michael Rand, James Lynch, and David Cantor, *Criminal Victimization, 1973-1995*. Bureau of Justice Statistics, 1997.

[63] The annual risk that a person aged 12 or older will be the victim of a *successful* violent attack is 0.64%. For the data, see table 28 in *BJS, Criminal Victimization in the US, 2008 Statistical Tables* (2010).

[64] See Michael Rand *et al.*, *Criminal Victimization 1973-1995* (BJS, 1997).

[65] Patricia Tjaden and Nancy Thoennes, *Full Report of the Prevalence, Incidence, and Consequences of Violence against Women*, National Institute of Justice, NCJ-183781, p.17 (2002).

[66] *Ibid.*

[67] David Farrington and Joliffe Darrick, UK section of *Cross-National Studies in Crime and Justice*, US Bureau of Justice Statistics, 2004.

[68] Data from the Rape Crisis Federation, Wales and England (1998).

[69] Anne Morrison Piehl, Bert Useem, and John J. DiIulio, Jr., "Right-Sizing Justice: A Cost-Benefit Analysis of Imprisonment in Three States," *Civic Report,* Manhattan Institute for Policy Research, No. 8, September 1999. (http://www.manhattan-institute.org/html/cr_8.htm)

[70] Adapted from P. Langan & D. Farrington, *Crime and Justice in England and Wales, 1981-1996*. BJS, p. 79.

[71] Data compiled by the US Justice Department's Bureau of Justice Statistics in 1997 suggests that the average American runs a lifetime risk of imprisonment for a serious crime of 5.1%. (See Thomas Bonczar and Allen Beck, *Lifetime Likelihood of Going to State or Federal Prison*, Bureau of Justice Statistics, Washington, 1997.) Supposing that no more than 3% of those sent to prison are wrongfully convicted —see the discussion in chapter 3 for the rationale for this estimate— the lifetime risk of being falsely imprisoned for a serious crime is about 0.1%.

[72] The only significant exception to this generalization, for wholly obvious reasons, is forcible rape, where the average male is nearly as likely to be falsely convicted of the crime as being a victim of it.

[73] The famous legal philosopher Ronald Dworkin has said that if a state were to allow concerns about false acquittals to shape the decisions at trial, it would be a source of "shame and regret." (R. M. Dworkin, *Taking Rights Seriously* (Cambridge, Mass., 1977), p. 12.) For a more detailed treatment of his analysis, see chapter 5 below.

[74] See chapter 6 below for a detailed discussion of such rules in American criminal law.

[75] Pierre Laplace, *Philosophical Essay on Probabilities*, ch. xiii, p. 133. (1812). Adam Smith, a contemporary of Laplace, put the point more succinctly if much less precisely: "mercy to the guilty is cruelty to the innocent". Adam Smith, *The Theory of the Moral Sentiments*, II.II.III.7 (D.D. Raphael & A.L. Macfie, eds.,Oxford Univ. Press 1976) (1790).

[76] Robert Nozick, *Anarchy, State and Utopia*, "(Basic Books, 1977), p.97.

[77] The estimate of the risk of a false conviction derives from the many discussions of false positives over the last 20 years and is founded on the assumption —to be documented in detail further on— that the false positive rate is about 3% for violent crimes.

[78] Of the 1.7m violent crimes in 2008, 79% (1.35m) of the perpetrators escaped punishment.

[79] BJS, *Prisoners in 2012*, Table iii.

[80] *Ibid.* The rest were serving time for property crimes (18.6%), drugs (16.6%), and others (11.3%).

[81] See the White House Report called *Economic Perspectives on Incarceration* (April 2016), Figure 7.

[82] Although its character is obvious, it is probably important to add this caveat explicitly: The claim made throughout this section –that crime rates will fall by raising the proportion of guilty, arrested persons who are subsequently convicted—presupposes that the prevailing standard for arrest (viz., probable cause) remains in place. If it did not (for instance, if police could arrest only those whose guilt was clear beyond a reasonable doubt), then one could foresee a dramatic increase in the proportion of those arrested who are convicted *without* an associated decrease in crime rates.

[83] For instance, the expected punishment for murder would be found by counting up how many years those sentenced to prison for homicide have been incarcerated divided by the number of murders committed in a given year.

[84] There were fewer murders per 100k population in 2014 than in any year in the last half century. According to the FBI's *Uniform Crime Reports*, the homicide rate in 2014 was 4.5/100k, compared with 5.1 (1960), 7.8 (1970), 10.2 (1980), 9.7 (1990), 5.5 (2000) and 4.8 (2010).

[85] Beccaria: "Crimes are more effectually prevented by the *certainty* than the *severity* of punishment." (*op. cit.*, p. 93).

[86] Bureau of Justice Statistics*, Cross-National Studies in Crime and Justice*, p. 185. Bijleveld is currently director of the Netherlands Institute for the Study of Crime and Law Enforcement.

[87] *Ibid.*, p. 105.

[88] See David Pyle and Derek Deadman, "Crime, and the Business Cycle in Post-War Britain," *British Journal of Criminology*, 34 (1994): 339-357. A more recent British study reports the same linkage (D.P. Farrington & D. Jolliffe, "Crime and Justice in England and Wales, 1981-99," in *Crime and Punishment*

in Western Countries. Michael Tonry & David P. Farrington (eds.). University of Chicago Press. (2005), pp. 41-82.

[89] Beccaria himself sometimes doubted whether deterrence works: "Men do not, in general, commit great crimes deliberately, but rather in a sudden gust of passion and they commonly look on the punishment due to a great crime as remote and improbable."*An Essay on Crimes and Punishments (*trans. Edward Ingraham, 2nd American edition, Philadelphia, 1819), p.77.

[90] It is worth adding explicitly that, *if* deterrence plays any role in diminishing crime, then the arguments below about the incapacitative value of incarcerating felons are strengthened by whatever that deterrent effect may turn out to be. Hence, my later arguments —by assuming that deterrence is nil— may be *under*estimating the benefits of incarcerating the guilty.

[91] See Paul Robinson and John Darley, "Does Criminal Law Deter?" *Oxford Journal of Legal Studies,* Vol. 24, No. 2 (2004), pp. 173-205. After analyzing several studies that purport to show deterrence effects, Robinson and Darley conclude that the declines in crime rates noted in such studies almost certainly depend on incapacitation rather than deterrence. They write: "[Such studies] seem undeniably to have found an effect on crime rate, but we suspect that much, if not most, of this is the result of incapacitative rather than deterrent effects." (*ibid.*, at 174-75). See also David Lee and Justin McCrary, "Crime, Punishment, and Myopia," NBER Working Paper No. 11491. National Bureau of Economic Research (Cambridge, MA (2006), who argue that serial felons are largely undeterred from crime by tougher sanctions.

[92] Patrick A. Langan and David J. Levin, "Recidivism of Prisoners Released in 1994" (NCJ-193427). This was the largest-ever study of rates of recidivism in the US.

[93] BJS, *Felony Defendants in Large Urban Counties, 2009*, Table 7 (2013). The numbers in parentheses indicate the percentage of those with prior convictions and come from *ibid.*, Table 9. If you wonder why, in this table, convictions rates are sometimes higher than arrest rates, recall that a single arrest can result in the filing of multiple charges and thereby lead to more convictions than arrests.

[94] The serial character of much criminal activity is perhaps best driven home by noting the following pattern: a significant number of felons, arrested and on bail for a certain violent offense, are arrested for committing other violent offenses *while on bail*. In 2002, for instance, 23% of those charged with murder and released on bail pending trial, were rearrested for a new felony committed after their bail hearing, even though bail normally lasts only about four months! (See Bureau of Justice Statistics, *Felony Defendants in Large Urban Counties, 2002* (February, 2006), p. iv.)

[95] The Halliday Report, *Making Punishments Work*, published by the Home Office, July 2001. Appendix 3.

[96] *Ibid.*, appendix 6, p. 130.

[97] The model is described in R. Tarling, *Analysing Offending Data Models and Interpretation*, HMSO (1994).

[98] A survey of Wisconsin prisoners shows that the median prisoner in that state claims to have committed (apart from drug-related offenses) 12 crimes per year prior to his imprisonment. (See John J. DiIulio Jr. and Anne Morrison Piehl, "Does Prison Pay? The Stormy National Debate over the Cost-effectiveness of Imprisonment." 9 *Brookings Review*, 28 (Fall 1991).

[99] Daniel Nagin, "Deterrence and Incapacitation," in M. Tonry, ed., *The Oxford Handbook of Crime and Punishment* (New York, CUP, 1999), p.351.

[100] F. E. Zimring, and G. Hawkins (1995) *Incapacitation: Penal confinement and restraint of crime* (Oxford: Oxford University Press, 1995), p. 172.

[101] *Congressional Globe*, 39th Cong., 2nd Sess. 101 (1867).

[102] Alan Dershowitz, *The Best Defense* (Warner Books, 1982), 118.

[103] Even the US Supreme Court has avoided this discussion like the plague. In its 1970 ruling (*In re Winship*) that decreed that criminal defendants had a constitutional right to be tried by the standard of proof beyond a reasonable doubt, its chief justification for the reasonable doubt standard (offered by Justice Harlan was that that "it is far worse to convict an innocent man than to let a guilty man go free." It apparently did not occur to the justices that the bare observation that the former is more egregious than the latter leaves the door open to *any* standard of proof greater then the preponderance of the evidence. It does *not* pick out any standard in particular.

[104] I selected the year 2008 because it allows us to follow up on subsequent information about the recidivism patterns of those suspected violent offenders who, for one reason or another, were not convicted. These data on violent crime come principally from Tables 1 and 2 of the Sept. 2009 *Bulletin, Criminal Victimization, 2008,* of the Bureau of Justice Statistics summarizing the 2008 National Crime Victimization Survey and from the more comprehensive BJS publication, *Criminal Victimization in the United States, 2008 Statistical Tables.* (The data derive from random interviews with 67,000 Americans aged 12 and over.) The data on the disposition of cases come from the FBI's *Uniform Crime Reports* of the same year. (I have not included information on simple assaults as opposed to aggravated ones.)

[105] The actual number reported in victimization studies is 1.4m. I have increased by it by 20% to allow for the fact that a). Homicide data are *not* included (because an interview with the victim is clearly impossible) and b). Violent crime victims younger than 12 are not included in victimization data, despite the fact that there is a large cohort of under-12 victims, some of which are reported to the police. Police report that 34% of the known victims of sexual assault are younger than 12. (BJS, *Sexual Assault of Young Children as Reported by Law Enforcement* (2000), Table 1.)

[106] Source: FBI, *Uniform Crime Reports 2008*, Table 29.

[107] This figure slightly overstates the number of convictions since about half of violent crime verdicts are appealed after trial. Among those appeals, some 2% are reversed to an acquittal and 7% lead to a new trial, possibly producing an acquittal. (Based on data reported in a study of 1,750 appeals in California courts by Joy Chapper and Roger Hanson, *Understanding Reversible Error in Criminal Appeals* (National Center for State Courts, 1989).)

[108] Conviction rates (via trial and plea) among those arrested for: murder, 70%; rape, 68%; armed robbery, 66%; and aggravated assault, 56%. *FDLUC 2009*, Table 21.

[109] BJS, *Felony Defendants in Large Urban Counties, 2009*, (2013) Table 7). The numbers in parentheses indicate the percentage of those with prior convictions and come from *ibid.*, Table 9.

[110] See: /www.innocenceproject.org/Content/DNA_Exonerations_Nationwide.php.

[111] See especially Michael Risinger, "Innocents Convicted: An Empirically Justified Factual Wrongful Conviction Rate," 97, *Journal of Criminal Law and Criminology*, 761 (2007).

[112] The formula used by the state of Texas is typical: "the proper test [for an exoneration] is whether applicant has shown 'by clear and convincing evidence that *no reasonable juror would have convicted him in light of the new evidence.*' *Ex parte Elizondo*, 947 S.W.2d 202, 209 (Tex. Crim. App. 1996) (emphasis added).

[113] See the University of Michigan's *National Registry of Exonerations* (available on the web).

[114] According to the same source, there are approximately 5 non-DNA exonerations for every DNA-based one. (In 2014, there were 128 recorded exonerations, 22 of which depended on DNA evidence.)

[115] See the case details on the National Registry of Exonerations: http://www.law.umich.edu/special/exoneration/Pages/detaillist.aspx

[116] Samuel Gross *et al.*, "Exonerations in the United States, 1989 through 2003," 95 *J of Crim Law & Criminology*, 532n21 (2005).

[117] Harry Kalven and Hans Zeisel, *The American Jury* (Little Brown, 1966).

[118] D. Michael Risinger, "Innocents Convicted," 97 J *Crim L & Criminology*, 761 (2007). This is, in my opinion, the single best empirical study of false convictions and I strongly recommend it to all interested in the issue of false positives.

[119] Samuel Gross *et al.*, "Rate of False Conviction of Criminal Defendants Who are Sentenced to Death," http://www.pnas.org/content/111/20/7230.full.pdf.

[120] See Ronald Huff *et al.*, *Convicted but Innocent* (Sage, 1996); John Baldwin and Michael McConvill, *Jury Trials* (Clarendon Press, 1979); and Cline Walter and Keir Starmer, *Miscarriages of Justice* (London, 1999).

[121] Both Risinger and Gross report much lower numbers than 3% where false positives from plea bargains are concerned. (For a detailed discussion of the differences in rates between pleas and trials, see L. Laudan & R. Allen, "Deadly Dilemmas," *Texas Tech Law Review*, 41, No. 1 (2008), 65-92.) Since the vast majority of guilty verdicts now emerge from pleas, there is powerful reason to suppose that the 3% estimate of false positives is almost certainly on the high side. Nonetheless, for reasons of making my estimates as non-controversial as possible, I will work with that number in the rest of this analysis.

[122] Robert Ramsey and James Frank, "Wrongful Conviction," *Crime & Delinquency*, 53 (2007). Table 3.

[123] Samuel Gross and Michael Shaffer, *Exonerations in the United States, 1989-2012* (National Registry of Exonerations, 2012), p.61 Gross – who is editor of the National Registry of Exonerations project— reports that in the 22 years from 1989 to 2011, there were 790 known exonerations (murder, 409; sexual assault, 305; robbery, 47; and assault, 11). During that time, there were some 7.7m convictions (from trials and pleas) for violent crimes. In this study, the seemingly false positive rate for plea bargains was about 0.01%. (*ibid.*, Table 2.)

[124] Oren Gazal-Ayal & Avishalom Tor, "The Innocence Effect," *Duke Law Journal*, 62 (2012), p. 352.

[125] This and other technical difficulties for a Blackstone ratio of 10-to-1 are laid out in my paper, "The Elementary Epistemic Arithmetic of Criminal Justice," *Episteme: A Journal of Social Epistemology*, 5, No. 3 (2008), 282-294.

[126] For a lengthy discussion of the Scottish verdict system, see my "Need Verdicts Come in Pairs?" *International Journal of Evidence and Proof*, vol. 14 (2010), 1-24.

[127] *Scottish Government Statistical Bulletin*, Crim/2006/Part 11. The data come from 2004-2005. (See http://www.scotland.gov.uk/Publications/2006/04/25104019/11.) In a more recent analysis, the Scottish government reported that in rape cases some 35% of acquittals resulted in 'guilt not proven' verdicts. In murder cases, the probably guilty verdict rate was 27% of all acquittals. (See Scottish Government, Criminal Proceedings in Scotland, 2013-14, Table 2B.)

[128] Kalven & Zeisel, *op. cit.*, Table 32.

[129] Given the Scottish estimate of ~70% false negatives at trial and the Kalven-Zeisel estimate of an 85% false negative rate in trials, I shall assume a false negative rate of 75% in acquittals at trial.

[130] Peter Duff and Mark Findlay, "Jury Reform: Of Myths and Moral Panics," 25 *Int. Journal of the Sociology of Law*, 1997, 368 at 370 n14.

[131] Daniel Givelber & Amy Farrell, *Not Guilty: Are the Acquitted Innocent?* (New York: NYU Press, 2012), p.143.

[132] See the data in Table 4 below.

[133] See especially US Dept. of Justice, *United States Attorneys' Annual Statistical Report, 2010.*

[134] *Ibid.*, Table 6.

[135] BJS, *Prosecutors in State Courts, 1994* (1996), p.5.

[136] 5% of those on bail awaiting trial on a murder charge become fugitives. *BJS, Felony Defendants in Large Urban Counties, 2009 –Statistical Tables,* Table 18.

[137] The detailed breakdown of the relevant data can be found in Table 14 of US Dept. of Justice, *United States Attorneys' Annual Statistical Report,* 2010. In that year, the FBI declined to prosecute some 7,252 cases of arrested defendants (794 of these cases were violent crimes) (*ibid.*, Table 3).

[138] The ethics manual of the American Bar Association, the *ABA Standards for Criminal Justice: Prosecution and Defense Function*, insists that prosecutors "should not institute, or cause to be instituted, or permit the continued pendency of criminal charges when the prosecutor knows that the charges are not supported by probable cause." (Standard 3-3.9) It goes on to say that the prosecutor should drop charges against the defendant if there is "reasonable doubt that the accused is in fact guilty." (*ibid.*)

[139] Barbara Boland et al., *The Prosecution of Felony Arrests, 1988.* Bureau of Justice Statistics, 1992.

[140] Here were the data for some of the cities in their study: Denver (46% dropped because of innocence issue); Los Angeles (50%); Manhattan (43%); St. Louis (20%); San Diego (27%); Seattle (25%); and Washington, D.C. (37%). Id., Table 5.

[141] Brian Forst et al., *What Happens after Arrest?* Institute for Law and Social Research (1977), Exhibit 5.1.

[142] Once again, the estimates I have proposed are very conservative. Givelber and Farrell, who are very sympathetic to the idea that there are many innocents to be found among those against whom charges are dropped, argue that –on the strength of BJS data—some 36% of those against whom charges are dropped may be innocent, meaning of course that some 64% of those against whom charges are dropped are probably guilty. (Daniel Givelber & Amy Farrell, *Not Guilty: Are the Acquitted Innocent?* (NYU Press, 2012), p.45. My estimate of a false negative rate of 38% for this group is much more modest than theirs. They also surmise that "9% of all formal criminal charges are dropped because of concerns that the defendants are innocent." (id.) Applying that number to our sample of violence cases for 2008, that would lead to an estimate of about 20k true acquittals whereas I am assuming that there were something like about 82k dropped or dismissed cases involving innocent defendants. If I were to use Givelber and Farrell's estimates, our assessment below of the costs of false negatives would be vastly higher than it is. I resist the temptation to do so in order to produce a number that no one can reasonably object to.

[143] Cesare Beccaria, *On Crimes and Punishments*, (trans. David Young; Hackett Publishing, 1986), p.42.

[144] Beccaria wrote: "It seems that banishment should be imposed on those who have been accused of an atrocious crime, and whose guilt is probable, though not certain." *Ibid.*

[145] A very informative discussion of the use of banishment by the English as a vehicle for ridding themselves of 'undesirables' in the Elizabethan era can be found in Gwenda Morgan and Peter Rushton, *Banishment in the Early Atlantic World* (Bloomsbury Academic, N.Y., 2013).

[146] The National Crime Victimization Survey, which relies on self-reports of victimization, is an ongoing annual survey conducted by the Census Bureau on behalf of the Department of Justice that collects detailed information via interviews from a representative sample of nearly 100,000 adults (age 12 and over) from approximately 50,000-75,000 households. I rely heavily on its data in my analysis.

[147] BJS, *Felony Defendants in Large Urban Counties, 2009 –Statistical Tables*, Table 25. Indeed, the actual jail time served will be much less than that since many violent criminals receive parole long before their full sentence is served. (For details, see below, Part III.)

[148] There is also the impact of a false negative on general crime deterrence. Any acquittal, true or false, arguably lowers the deterrent effect of criminal justice. This is certainly a cost of false negatives but the deterrent effect of such mistakes is virtually impossible to estimate.

[149] See chapter 4 for the pertinent data.

[150] See the appendix to this chapter to understand the basis for this estimate. While the average sentence handed out for conviction of a violent crime is 7.6 years, the actual time-served by convicted violent felons is much less than that, as explained and explored in chapter 7.

[151] BJS, *Recidivism of Prisoners Released in Thirty States (2014)*, Tables 7 & 8.

[152] *Ibid.*, Table 5.

[153] BJS, *Violent Felons in Large Urban Counties, 1990-2002* (2006), Table 5.

[154] BJS, *Felony Defendants in Large Urban Counties, 2009*, Table 9 and BJS, *Violent Felons in Large Urban Counties, 1990-2002*, Table 5.

[155] BJS, *Recidivism of Prisoners Released in 1994*, p.3.

[156] *See* Table 5.

[157] Blumstein, *Criminal Careers*, vol. I, Table B-2 (p.333). The data reflect information reported in a Rand Corporation report written by Petersilia, J., Greenwood, P.W, and Lavin, M *Criminal Careers of Habitual Felons*. Santa Monica, Calif.: Rand Corporation (1977).

[158] The NRC also notes: "The self-report method for measuring this rather sensitive topic—un-detected criminal behavior—appears to be reasonably

valid. The content validity of the recent inventories is acceptable, the construct validity is quite high, and the criterion validity appears to be in the moderate-to-strong range. Putting this all together, it could be concluded that for most analytical purposes, self-reported measures are acceptably accurate and valid." (John V. Pepper and Carol V. Petrie, eds., *Measurement Problems in Criminal Justice Research: Workshop Summary*, National Research Council (2003), p.63.)

[159] Blumstein offers a dramatic graphic illustrating how the severity of crimes committed by recidivists increases as their 'criminal careers' evolve. (*Ibid.*, vol. I, Table B-3)

[160] In 2008, 20% (325k) of the violent crimes identified by victims involved more than one perpetrator. See BJS, *Criminal Victimization in the United States, 2008* (2010), Statistical Tables 40 and 44. Some 4.4% (75k) of violent crimes had multiple victims. (*Ibid.*, Tables 36 and 44).

[161] The breakdown of average sentences for violent crimes in 2009 looks this:

murder	31 years
rape	12 years
armed robbery	7.5 years
aggravated assault	5.2 years

Source: BJS, *Felony Defendants in Large Urban Counties, 2009*, Table 25. As we shall see in chapter 7, only a tiny proportion of convicted violent offenders serve their full sentences. Most of them spend less than half their sentence in prison; a sizeable minority, despite being convicted, never spend a day in prison.

[162] BJS, *Criminal Victimization in the United States, 2008* (2010), Table 2.

[163] According to the BJS, some 24% of defendants convicted of a violent crime appeal their cases. BJS, *Federal Criminal Appeals* (1999), p.2.

[164] BJS, *Statistical Tables, 2008,*Tables 4.,2 & 6.2.

[165] In 2009, 8% of those convicted of rape received probation without incarceration; armed robbery, 10%; assault, 18%. The mean length of the probation sentences for this group was 35 months. BJS, *Felony Defendants in Large Urban Counties, 2009 Statistical Tables,* Tables 24, 26 and 27.

[166] BJS, *Probation and Parole in the United States, 2012,* Appendix Table 3.

[167] Although this statement is widely quoted on the internet, I have been able to find no one who gives its original source.

[168] It is worthy of mention that if a false conviction of a person who genuinely acted in self-defense is actually less costly than other forms of false conviction, it would follow that those states that require in cases of alleged self-defense a lower standard of proof from the prosecutor than in other cases are (perhaps inadvertently) behaving in accordance with the idea that a false

conviction in a self-defense case is less harmful/costly than a false conviction in the usual case of a violent crime.

[169] "Annual Determination of Average Cost of Incarceration," *Federal Register*, 3/18/2013, p. 1.

[170] Michael Tanner, *The American Welfare State*, Cato Policy Analysis, No. 694, April 11, 2012, p. 1.

[171] Prosecutors dealing with more than 7,000 cases brought by FBI agents in 2010, indicate that they dropped the charges when they concluded that no crime had occurred (7% of dismissals), or when they concluded a lack of criminal intent (20.5%) or when the evidence was 'weak or insufficient' (25%). (US Dept. of Justice, *United States Attorneys' Annual Statistical Report, 2010.*) The figure entered in this table represents the remaining 47.4% of dismissals and acquittals, whom I shall identify as probably guilty felons since the reasons for dropping charges in their cases apparently had nothing to do with innocence or guilt. (Recall that each of them was judged by the police as likely to be guilty and was not culled out for reasons of the evidential weakness of the case against them.) Data on the frequency of false acquittals arising from trials are discussed in chapter 3.

[172] In many cases, an arrest by the police counts as a double error: a) the arrest of an innocent person for crime x and b). the failure to arrest the person truly guilty of x.

[173] This extrapolation from annual to lifetime rates is based on the method of calculation developed by Herbert Koppel (of the BJS) in BJS, *Lifetime Likelihood of Victimization* (1987).

[174] See the discussion of the work of Blumstein and Farrington above.

[175] The two studies are BJS, *Recidivism of Prisoners Released in 1994* (2002) and BJS, *Recidivism of Prisoners Released in 30 states in 2005: Patterns from 2005 to 2010* (2014).

[176] *Ibid.*, Table 10.

[177] Table 10 of the 2005 study cited in note 51.@

[178] Known as the Halliday Report (*Making Punishments Work: A Review of the Sentencing Framework for England & Wales*) and published by the British Home Office in 2000, Appendix 6, p.130).

[179] Emily Owens, "More Time, Less Crime? Estimating the Incapacitative Effect of Sentence Enhancements," 52 *J. Law & Econ.*, 2009, p.565. An 'index crime' includes our four paradigm violent cases (murder, rape, aggravated assault, and armed robbery) along with burglary, car theft and larceny). Even so, my assumption of only 0.16 violent crimes per year for released prisoners is vastly lower than almost all reported recidivism levels. That is not an accident on my part. By adopting a very modest figure for the violent recidivism rate, I want to make a case for taking false acquittals seriously that is not open to the charge that I have exaggerated their importance.

[180] Justice Powell's dissent in *Bullington v. Missouri*, 451 US 430 (1981).

[181] *Victor v. Nebraska*, 511 US 1 at 38 (1994).

[182] *Ibid.* at 24.

[183] *Dunbar v. U.S.*, 156 at 189 US 39.

[184] *Ibid.*

[185] *Young v. Oklahoma*, 1962 OK CR 70 (1962).

[186] *U.S. v. Lawson*, 507 F.2d 422, at 433 (7th Cir. 1974).

[187] *In re Winship*, 397 U.S. 358, at 364 (1970).

[188] *Ibid.*

[189] Justice Antonin Scalia, concurring in *Kansas v. Marsh*, June 26, 2006.

[190] Lawrence Tribe, "A Further Critique of Mathematical Proof," 84 *Harvard Law Review* 1810 at 1818 (1971).

[191] R. M. Dworkin, *Taking Rights Seriously* (Cambridge, Mass., 1977), 12.

[192] *Ibid.*, 13.

[193] R. M. Dworkin, *A Matter of Principle* (Cambridge, Mass., 1985), 197.

[194] *Ibid.*, 89. For Dworkin's most detailed formulation of his arguments about the right to be tried according to the BARD standard, see *ibid.* 80ff.

[195] R. Kitai, "Protecting the Guilty," *Buff. Crim Law Rev,* 2003, p 1175. This is a bizarre sense of 'duty'. While we arguably have a duty not to convict the innocent if it can be avoided, we have equally have a duty to convict the guilty. Saying that we are duty bound to acquit the guilty unless their guilt 'has been proven with the greatest certainty possible" profoundly confuses what duties we have. The rationale for a very high standard is to protect the innocent against false conviction not to shield the guilty from getting their just deserts.

[196] Tim Bakken, "Truth and Innocence Procedures to Free Innocent Persons," 41 *U Mich J. L. Reform* 547 (2008), p. 549. Quite what a standard that was similar to 'absolute certainty' would look like is rather unclear.

[197] John Kaplan, "Decision Theory and the Factfinding Process," in 20 *Stanford L Rev.* 1065 (1967-68).

[198] Tribe proposes the decision-theoretic formula, $SoP = 1/[1 + (u(\text{true positive}) - u(\text{false negative}))/(u(\text{true negative}) - u(\text{false positive})]$, where the crucial ratio in question is a ratio of two utility differences. Plugging in plausible values for the utilities of the four outcomes yields results more convincing than those in Kaplan's theorem. Tribe proposed this idea in his classic "Trial by Mathematics," 84 *Harvard L. Rev.*, 1329, at 1383 (1970-71).

[199] Harry Saunders and I discuss this issue at length in "Re-Thinking the Criminal Standard of Proof: Seeking Consensus about the Utilities of Trial Outcomes," *International Commentary on Evidence*, Vol. 7 : Iss. 2, Article 1 (http://www.bepress.com/ice/vol7/iss2/art1/)

[200] Since the ratio of truly guilty to truly innocent defendants will shift upwards as the standard of proof is raised and downwards as it is lowered, the figures here assume: a). that a mild increase in the standard would put us in the region where the ratio of the truly guilty to the truly innocent is ~(40-to-1) and b). that a mild lowering of the standard would find us in a region ratio of the guilty to the innocent is ~(25-to-1).

[201] This is the annual risk imposed on a citizen of a). being falsely convicted of a violent crime, b). being victimized by someone who was falsely acquitted, or c) being victimized by the true perpetrator of a crime that led to a false positive.

[202] Katherine Goldwasser, "Vindicating the Right to Trial by Jury and the Requirement of Proof beyond a Reasonable Doubt," 86 *Georgetown Law Journal* 621 at 635 (1998).

[203] As Justice Blackmun pointed out in dissent, the Constitution provides for trial by jury but nowhere in that document is there any statement that a conviction requires proof of guilt beyond a reasonable doubt. (*In re Winship*, 397 US 358, at 383 (1970).

[204] Writing for the majority in *Patterson v. New York*, 432 US 197, 208 (1977).

[205] One intriguing study in this direction is by Harry Saunders, "Quantifying Reasonable Doubt: A Proposed Solution to an Equal Protection Problem," bepress Legal Series, 2005, paper 881.

[206] *U.S. v. Garsson*, 291 F.646 at 649.

[207] I owe the terminology to my friend and frequent co-author, Ronald Allen. His best-known treatment of the issue can be found in his "Structuring Jury Decisionmaking in Criminal Cases: A Unified Constitutional Approach to Evidentiary Devices," 94 *Harv. L. Rev.* 321 (1980).

[208] See especially Jeanne C. Marsh et al., *Rape and the Limits of Law Reform*, (Auburn House Publishing, 1982), pp. 21-25 and 44-45. The impact of the rape shield laws on both the frequency of rape convictions and on the fall in rape victimizations also shows up in Figure 3 in Chapter 3.

[209] *Mapp v. Ohio*, 367 U.S., 643 (1961).

[210] In 1984, the Supreme Court acknowledged that: "The Fourth Amendment contains no provision expressly precluding the use of evidence obtained in violations of its commands... the use of fruits of a past unlawful search and seizure 'works no new Fourth Amendment wrong'." (Majority opinion by Justice White in *U.S. v. Leon,* 468 U.S. 897, 104)

[211] German law has an ingenious solution to this problem. If evidence has been seized without a warrant, it is generally excluded. However, if the case involves a serious crime and if the seized evidence is crucial to the prosecution's case, it will usually be admitted. In general, where exclusions of relevant evidence are concerned, the German Supreme Court insists that judges must weigh the importance of convicting a guilty defendant against the cost of

violating that defendant's rights. In the US, by contrast, the court-created rights of a defendant almost invariably trump the interests of finding the truth and convicting the guilty. (See Stephen Thaman, *Comparative Criminal Procedure*, 2nd ed. (Carolina Academic Press, 2008), pp. 109-110.)

[212] *Silverthorne Lumber Co., Inc. v. United States*, 251 U.S. 385 (1920).

[213] For data on and a detailed discussion of this issue, see R. Allen and L. Laudan, "The Devastating Impact of Prior Crimes Evidence," *Journal of Criminal Law & Criminology*, 101, pp. 493-528.

[214] There has been precious little empirical work on how to weigh the relevance of a piece of evidence against its potential 'unfair prejudice'. Accordingly, every judge is left almost entirely to his own devices in making this decision.

[215] In the case of testimony from clergy, most states allow the defendant alone to decide whether the clergy can testify; eight other states allow both the defendant and the clergy to decide whether the clergy testifies; in four states, clergy is flatly forbidden from testifying about communication between the two; and in two states, the clergy is the unique holder of the privilege. Despite these variations, it is fair to say that in every state, the clerical privilege acts as a burden-enhancer by allowing the exclusion of relevant, inculpatory evidence.

[216] See also *Sanabria v. U. S.*, 437 U.S. 54, 69 (1978).

[217] As pointed out in Table 6, some 2% of appealed convictions are transformed into acquittals and another 7% are sent for retrial. This gives a distinct asymmetric advantage to convicted defendants not enjoyed by prosecutors in cases where the defendant is acquitted.

[218] See also *Brooks v. Tennessee*, 406 U.S. 605 (1972).

[219] *Ashe v. Swenson*, 397 US. 436 (1970).

[220] For a fascinating discussion of the debates about what sort of lineup is desirable, see Steven Clark, "Blackstone and the Balance of Eyewitness Identifications," *Albany Law Review*, 74 (2010-11). See also the discussion of lineup procedures later in this chapter.

[221] Kalven & Zeisel, *The American Jury*, 460-63. For more recent data, see Paula Agor et al., *Are Hung Juries a Problem?* National Center for State Courts and National Institute of Justice, 2002.

[222] See Agor, *ibid., p.3.* The study found that in Washington, D.C. Superior Courts some 22.4% of jury trials ended in a hung jury; In Los Angeles Superior Courts, the hung jury rate was 19.5%.

[223] It is worth adding that in the case of an indigent defendant, the state is generally obliged to cover expenses for hiring private investigators and expert witnesses.

[224] ABA, *Criminal Justice in Crisis*, 1988.

[225] The report can be found at http://www.druglibrary.org/special/king/cjic.htm.

[226] Approximately 5% of convictions are successfully appealed. There is no intrinsic reason to expect that a trial leading to an acquittal is any less likely to commit serious errors than a trial leading to conviction is. (A large study of appeals in the intermediate court of appeal in California found that 4.8% of appeals by criminal defendants resulted in complete reversals, Thomas Y. Davies, "Affirmed: A Study of Criminal Appeals and Decision-Making Norms in a California Court of Appeal," 7 *AM. BAR FOUND. RES. J.* 543, at 551 (1982).)

[227] Kalven and Zeisel, p. 146. For a detailed discussion of the impact of the *Carter* rule on testimony, see Ron Allen & Larry Laudan, "The Devastating Impact of Prior Crimes Evidence," *Journal of Criminal Law & Criminology*, 101 (2011), pp. 493-528.

[228] The National Center for State Courts, *Are Hung Juries a Problem* (2002), p. 43.

[229] Article I, sec. 13 of the California state constitution stated: "[Defendant's] failure to explain or to deny by his testimony any evidence or facts in the case against him may be commented upon by the court and by counsel, and may be considered by the court or the jury."

[230] Instruction 5-21, 1-5 Modern Federal Jury Instructions-Criminal § 5.07.

[231] *Carter v. Kentucky*, 450 U.S. 288, 306 (1981) (Stewart, J., concurring).

[232] *Griffin v. California*, 380 U.S. 609, at 618 (1965). (Italics added.)

[233] *Adamson v. California*, 332 U.S. 46, at 56 (1947).

[234] H. Kalven & H. Zeisel, *The American Jury*, 146 (1966).

[235] T. Eisenberg and V. Hans, *Taking a Stand on Taking the Stand*, 94 CORNELL L. REV. 1353, 1357 (2009). These figures come from their summary of the NCSC results. The actual figures that appear in their Table I suggest that defendants with no priors testify 62% of the time (*id.* at 1371).

[236] These calculations can be found in Steven Clark's "Costs and Benefits of Eyewitness Identification Reform," *Perspectives on Psychological Science*, 7, 2012. See my discussion of Clark's research in the same issue. ("Eyewitness Identifications: One More Lesson on the Costs of Excluding Relevant Evidence," *Perspectives on Psychological Science*, 7 (May), 2012, pp.272-275.)

[237] Corey Ayling, "Corroborating Confessions," *Wis. L. Rev.*, 1121, at 1199 (1984).

[238] Katherine Goldwasser, "Vindicating the Right to Trial by Jury and the Requirement of Proof beyond a Reasonable Doubt," 86 *Georgetown Law J.* 621, at 635 (1998).

[239] See Richard Friedman, "Review of Damaska," 107 *Yale Law J.* 1921 (1998).

[240] Ayling, *op. cit.*

[241] Goldwasser, *op. cit.*

[242] Daniel Seidmann and Alex Stein, "The Right to Silence Helps the Innocent," 114 *Harvard L. Rev.*. 430, at 494 (2000).

[243] See Larry Laudan & Harry Saunders, "Re-Thinking the Criminal Standard of Proof: Seeking Consensus about the Utilities of Trial Outcomes," *International Commentary on Evidence*, Vol. 7 : Iss. 2, Article 1.

[244] The Supreme Court: "The central purpose of a criminal trial is to decide the factual question of the defendant's guilt or innocence." (*Rose v. Clark*, 478 U.S.570 at 577 (1986).) Another key assertion: "There is no gainsaying that arriving at the truth is a fundamental goal of our legal system." Justice White, *U.S. v. Havens*, 446 US 620 (1980).

[245] The *German Code of Criminal Procedure* [StPO], section 244(2).

[246] 479 US 157, at 166 (1986).

[247] Paul Cassell, "*Miranda*'s Social Costs: An Empirical Reassessment," 90 *NW. U. L. Rev.*, 387 (1996).

[248] *Rodrigues v. Hawaii*, 469 U.S. 1078, 1079 (1984).

[249]The Connecticut Supreme Court, more than a century ago, got it right when they insisted: "The principle of finality is essential; but not more essential than the principle of justice. A final settlement is not more vital than a right settlement." *State v. Lee*, 65 Conn. 265, 272 (Conn., 1894).

[250] Martin Friedland, *Double Jeopardy*, 4 (1969).

[251] Akhil Amar, "Double Jeopardy Law Made Simple," 106 *Yale L. J.*. 1807, 1844(1997).

[252] http://www.healthycal.org/archives/10888. See also *The Impact of Probation and Parole Populations on Arrests in Four California Cities*: A report prepared by the Council of State Governments Justice Center (2013). In Sacramento, active parolees and probationers represented more than 1-in-4 of those arrested for violent crimes (p.41).

[253] *Ibid.*, p. 2.

[254] A much fuller account of the costs of bail-granting for violent criminals can be found in R. J. Allen & Larry Laudan, "Deadly Dilemmas II: Bail and Crime," *Chicago-Kent Law Review*, 85, 23ff. (2010).

[255] The official figures on the size of the gap between arrest and trial for those on bail vary enormously, depending on the source and the nature of the crime. According to a study published by the BJS in 2009, the estimated time between arrest and sentencing for those accused of violent crimes is 295 days. BJS, *Felony Sentences in State Courts, 2006* (2009), Table 4.5. A slightly later study, published in 2013, claims that those on bail, charged with a violent crime, wait, on average, 163 days before their trials. (BJS, *Felony Defendants in Large Urban Counties, 2009* (2013), p. 22.) Fortunately, differences about the length of the wait do not impinge on the recidivism figures cited here.

[256] BJS, *Pretrial Release of Felony Defendants in State Courts* (2007), Table 4. Many of the non-released arrestees are granted bail by a judge but lack

the resources to find the cash or a bondsman. Very similar data can be found in BJS, *Felony Defendants in Large Urban Counties, 2009*, Table 18.

[257] BJS, *Pretrial Release of Felony Defendants*, 1992, p.1.

[258] These data come from BJS, *Felony Defendants in Large Urban Counties, 2009*. Tables, 12 and 18. Very similar figures are available in BJS, *Pretrial Release of Felony Defendants in State Courts* (2007), Table 4.

[259] *Ibid.*, p. 18.

[260] BJS, *Felony Defendants in Large Urban Counties, 2009*, Table 13.

[261] Most of these data came from BJS, *Criminal Victimization, 2008*. The numbers on robbery-fugitives came from BJS, *Pretrial Release, 2007*, table 7 and the numbers on re-arrests are from BJS, *Pretrial Release, 1992*, Table 15.

[262] BJS, *ibid.*, p. 22.

[263] "The lack of impacts of 'Three Strikes' nationally can be attributed in large part to the fact that the law is very rarely used in the majority of states that have a law by that name. By August 1998, "two-thirds of states with Three Strikes laws had only used it a dozen or fewer times." (Elsa Chen, "Impacts of Three Strikes and Truth in Sentencing on The Volume and Composition of Correctional Populations," a report from the National Institute of Justice (2000), pp. i-ii. Washington was the first state to implement the three strikes rule. Within three years of its implementation, the total number of serial felons imprisoned under the rule was 83. Given that the Washington prison/jail population then was about 27k, this is clearly a miniscule proportion (0.3%). (R. David LaCourse, Jr. *Three Strikes, You're Out: A Review*, 1997, https://www.washingtonpolicy.org/publications/brief/three-strikes-youre-out-review.)

[264] University of Albany, *Sourcebook of Criminal Justice Statistics*, 2003, Table 6.43.

[265] For up-to-date figures on US prison populations, see BJS, *Prisoners in 2013* (2014).

[266] The figures on sentences handed down come from BJS, *Felony Sentences in State Courts, 2006* (2009), Tables 1.3 & 2.4. The figures on the actual time served come from BJS, *Truth in Sentencing in State Prisons* (1999), Table I and from BJS, *Prisoners in 2013*, Table 17 (2014). It should be added that these figures do not include those sentenced to probation.

[267] These figures were calculated drawing on a variety of sources: BJS, *Criminal Victimization*, 2008, Table I; FBI, *Uniform Crime Reports 2008*, Figure 1 and the 'offenses cleared table'; BJS, *Felony Defendants in Large Urban Counties*, 2009 (2013).

[268] National Research Council, *Parole, Desistance from Crime, and Community Integration* (2008), p. 8.

[269] As the National Research Council recently pointed out in a lengthy meta-study of recidivism: "Because recidivism rates decline markedly with age, lengthy prison sentences, unless they specifically target very high-rate or

198

extremely dangerous offenders, are an inefficient approach to preventing crime by incapacitation." NRC, *The Growth of Incarceration in the United States: Exploring Causes and Consequences* (2014), p. 5.

[270] Alfred Blumstein *et al., Criminal Careers and "Career Criminals"*, 2 vols., National Academy Press (1986).

[271] BJS, *Probation and Parole in the United States, 2008* (2009). Table1. Of these probationers, some 430k were on probation for a violent offense. *Ibid.*, appendix Table 10. A year later, there were 426k violent, convicted felons on probation. (BJS, *Probation and Parole in the United States, 2009* (2010), Table l0.)

[272] For many years in Texas (a state not generally thought of as high on the clemency scale and with a high record of capital executions to its discredit), a person convicted of murder –provided he had no prior felony convictions—could be recommended by the jury for probation or a fine as low as $1. If the murderer served his probation on 'good behavior', he could have the murder conviction scrubbed from his record. (http://www.deathpenaltyinfo.org/node/2217) Of those convicted of murder in Dallas, Texas between 2000 and 2013, 9% were sentenced to probation.

[273] BJS, *Recidivism of Felons on Probation, 1986-89* (1992). A more recent figure is 11% absconders. (BJS, *Probation and Parole in the United States, 2008* (2009), Table 5.)

[274] In 2007, the Texas Legislature passed a probation reform bill (House Bill 1678) saying that juries no longer have the power (as they once did) to recommend probation for those convicted of murder.

[275] BJS, *Probation and Parole, 2008* (2009), p. 6.

[276] *Ibid.*, Table 5.

[277] *Ibid.*, p. 3.

[278] *Ibid.,* note 15, p. 6.

[279] *Ibid.*, p. 8.

[280] *Ibid.*, Appendix Table 5.

[281] According to a BJS study of violent crimes between 1990 and 2002, 19% of violent felons "received a probation term without incarceration." (p.1)

[282] BJS, *Probation and Parole in the United States, 2008* (2009), p. 6.

[283] Doris MacKenzie, "Reducing the Criminal Activities of Known Offenders and Delinquents," in L. Sherman *et al., Evidence-Based Crime Prevention* (Routledge, N.Y., 2006), p. 332.

[284] According to BJS statistics, only 18% of those sent to prison serve their full sentence. BJS, *Trends in State Parole, 1990-2000* (2001), Table 3. The typical violent offender serves only 55% of his sentence (*ibid.*, table 5). Five states in the US do not allow a parole system. (M. Tonry, *Sentencing and Corrections*, National Institute of Justice, 1999), p. 3.

[285] BJS, *Trends in State Parole, 1990-2000*, p. 13.

[286] *Ibid.*, p.10.

[287] BJS, *Felony Defendants in Large Urban Counties, 2009* (2013), Table 6. Remember, too, as I have argued before, that actual recidivism is generally twice as great as known recidivism.

[288] See BJS, Bureau of Justice Statistics, *Correctional Population in the United States, 2010*, (2012), Appendix Table 3.

[289] UN Office on Drugs and Crime, *Seventh UN Survey of Crime Trends, 1995-2000*. (http://www.unodc.org/unodc/en/data-and-analysis/Seventh United-Nations-Survey-on-Crime-Trends-and-the-Operations-of-Criminal-Justice-Systems.html)

[290] Source: National Research Council, *The Growth of Incarceration in the United States*, 2014, Figure 2-4.

[291] FBI, *Crime in the United States, 2014: Expanded Homicide Data*. Table 1.

[292] *Ibid.*, Table 6.

[293] Daniel Shaviro, " Statistical Probability Evidence and the Appearance of Justice," 103 *Harvard Law Review* 554 (1989).

[294] Jeremy Bentham, "An Introductory View of the Rationale of the Law of Evidence for Use by Non-lawyers as well as Lawyers" (vi *Works* 1-187 (Bowring edition, 1837-43), p. 2.

INDEX OF NAMES & CASES